Lecture Notes in Computer Science 12419

More information about this series at http://www.springer.com/series/7410

Harley Eades III · Olga Gadyatskaya (Eds.)

Graphical Models for Security

7th International Workshop, GraMSec 2020
Boston, MA, USA, June 22, 2020
Revised Selected Papers

Springer

Editors
Harley Eades III 🄳
Augusta University
Augusta, GA, USA

Olga Gadyatskaya 🄳
Leiden University
Leiden, The Netherlands

ISSN 0302-9743 ISSN 1611-3349 (electronic)
Lecture Notes in Computer Science
ISBN 978-3-030-62229-9 ISBN 978-3-030-62230-5 (eBook)
https://doi.org/10.1007/978-3-030-62230-5

LNCS Sublibrary: SL4 – Security and Cryptology

This Springer imprint is published by the registered company Springer Nature Switzerland AG
The registered company address is: Gewerbestrasse 11, 6330 Cham, Switzerland

Preface

The 7th International Workshop on Graphical Models for Security (GraMSec 2020) was held virtually on June 22, 2020, colocated with the Computer Security Foundations Symposium (CSF 2020).

Since its establishment in 2014, GraMSec seeks to bring together academic researchers and practitioners from industry and government to discuss the latest challenges and insights in graphical models applied in the security domain. It enjoys a large community of security professionals passionate about designing and applying graphical models and visualizations for capturing security of systems. Such graphical models and visualizations are often very versatile, being able to represent a multitude of security facets and to support security experts in tasks like formal socio-technical security modeling or automated security assessment.

These post-proceedings contain revised versions of the 7 full technical papers and 3 short papers, which were selected from 14 submissions. In addition to the presentations of these papers, Mariëlle Stoelinga from University of Twente and Radboud University, The Netherlands, gave a keynote talk titled "Safety Versus Security: Why Have They Not Married Yet?" This talk, which focused on similarities and discrepancies between security and safety models and approaches, showed the GraMSec audience several inspiring research directions.

The organization of GraMSec 2020 was affected by the COVID-19 global health crisis. The workshop was held online and authors and the Program Committee members were touched by this global emergency. We thank all authors for submitting their research results to GraMSec 2020. We thank all Program Committee members and the external reviewers for their time and effort toward a balanced and exciting workshop program. We are grateful to the invited speaker and the presenters for delivering their engaging talks online. Finally, we would also like to thank the Steering Committee of GraMSec, and especially Barbara Fila, for their support in organizing the workshop.

September 2020

Harley Eades III
Olga Gadyatskaya

Organization

Program Chairs

Harley Eades III   Augusta University, USA
Olga Gadyatskaya   Leiden University, The Netherlands

Program Committee

Ludovic Apvrille	Télécom Paris, France
Marco Angelini	Sapienza University of Rome, Italy
Paul Attie	Augusta University, USA
Stefano Bistarelli	University of Perugia, Italy
Carlos E. Budde	University of Twente, The Netherlands
Bram Cappers	TU Eindhoven, The Netherlands
Daniele Codetta-Raiteri	Università del Piemonte Orientale, Italy
Julia Eisentraut	TU Munich, Germany
Mathias Ekstedt	KTH Royal Institute of Technology, Sweden
Barbara Fila	INSA Rennes, IRISA, France
Holger Hermanns	Saarland University, Germany
Ross Horne	University of Luxembourg, Luxembourg
Dong Seong Kim	University of Canterbury, New Zealand
Rajesh Kumar	Birla Institute of Technology and Science, Pilani, India
Kate Labunets	TU Delft, The Netherlands
Tong Li	Beijing University of Technology, China
Sjouke Mauw	University of Luxembourg, Luxembourg
Per Håkon Meland	SINTEF, Norway
Federica Paci	University of Verona, Italy
Stéphane Paul	Thales Research and Technology, France
Sophie Pinchinat	University of Rennes, CNRS, IRISA, France
Saša Radomirovic	Heriot-Watt University, UK
Riccardo Scandariato	University of Gothenburg and Chalmers University of Technology, Sweden
Ketil Stølen	SINTEF Digital, University of Oslo, Norway
Axel Tanner	IBM Research, Switzerland
Rolando Trujillo-Rasua	Deakin University, Australia
Katja Tuma	University of Gothenburg and Chalmers University of Technology, Sweden
Luca Viganò	King's College London, UK
Lingyu Wang	Concordia University, Canada
Wojcieh Widel	KTH Royal Institute of Technology, Sweden
Jan Willemson	Cybernetica, Estonia

Steering Committee

Sushil Jajodia	George Mason University, USA
Barbara Fila	INSA Rennes, IRISA, France
Sjouke Mauw	University of Luxembourg, Luxembourg
Christian W. Probst	Unitec, New Zealand
Ketil Stølen	SINTEF Digital, University of Oslo, Norway

Publicity Chair

Barbara Fila	INSA Rennes, IRISA, France

Web Chair

Reynaldo Gil Pons	University of Luxembourg, Luxembourg

Additional Reviewers

Ivan Merkanti
Raúl E. Monti
Matthias Ramparison
Carlo Taticchi

Safety Versus Security: Why Have They Not Married Yet? (Abstract of Invited Talk)

Mariëlle Stoelinga[1,2]

[1] University of Twente, The Netherlands
[2] Radboud University, The Netherlands
m.i.a.stoelinga@utwente.nl

Abstract. Safety and security are two historically separated fields that have many aspects in common. Safety is the absence of disruptions due to unintended failures; security is the absence of disruptions due to malicious attacks. While both safety and security aim at mitigating system risks with cost-effective counter measures, they take opposing views when in comes to modelling, measuring, and mitigating. In this talk, I will present the main differences and similarities between safety and security risk analyses, as well as directions to reconcile these important fields, through mathematical game theory, uncertainty reasoning, and stochastic analysis. The research is funded by an ERC consolidator grant CAESAR: integrating safety and cybersecurity through stochastic model checking.

Contents

Attack Trees

Causal Model Extraction from Attack Trees to Attribute Malicious Insider Attacks

Amjad Ibrahim[1](✉), Simon Rehwald[1], Antoine Scemama[2], Florian Andres[1],
and Alexander Pretschner[1]

[1] Department of Informatics, Technical University (TUM) of Munich,
Garching b. Munich, Germany
{ibrahim,rehwald,andres,pretschn}@cs.tum.edu
[2] Brainloop AG, Munich, Germany

Abstract. In the context of insiders, preventive security measures have a high likelihood of failing because insiders ought to have sufficient privileges to perform their jobs. Instead, in this paper, we propose to treat the insider threat by a detective measure that holds an insider accountable in case of violations. However, to enable accountability, we need to create causal models that support reasoning about the causality of a violation. Current security models (e.g., attack trees) do not allow that. Still, they are a useful source for creating causal models. In this paper, we discuss the value added by causal models in the security context. Then, we capture the interaction between attack trees and causal models by proposing an automated approach to extract the latter from the former. Our approach considers insider-specific attack classes such as collusion attacks and causal-model-specific properties like preemption relations. We present an evaluation of the resulting causal models' validity and effectiveness, in addition to the efficiency of the extraction process.

1 Introduction

Security is crucial in systems that deal with *sensitive customer assets*. Adversaries are constantly trying to compromise the integrity, confidentiality, or availability of such assets. These attempts are carried out by *insiders* or *outsiders* of the system. In this paper, we are chiefly interested in *insiders*, specifically *malicious insiders* such as a rogue employee. For instance, according to the Cyber Security Intelligence Index by IBM X-Force Research [29], insiders carried out 60% of all attacks in 2015. Insiders can, tamper with records in the database, leak or delete documents, which leads to *reputation damage, legal costs, and reimbursements* [13]. Reports show that *insiders* carry out the most significant, and costly attacks [13, 29]. Such attacks are likely to succeed, and their impact is

TUM partners were in part funded by the Deutsche Forschungsgemeinschaft (DFG, German Research Foundation) under grant no. PR1266/4-1, Conflict resolution and causal inference with integrated socio-technical models.

ⓒ Springer Nature Switzerland AG 2020
H. Eades III and O. Gadyatskaya (Eds.): GraMSec 2020, LNCS 12419, pp. 3–23, 2020.
https://doi.org/10.1007/978-3-030-62230-5_1

significant [31]. In this context, preventive measures have a high likelihood of failing because insiders ought to have sufficient privileges for their jobs. They may abuse their privileges. The term "abuse" makes this problem especially hard due to the unpredictable nature of insiders and the necessity of their privileges. That said, insiders are mostly not malicious. Typically, there is a trust base between a company and its employees, not to mention the contracts an employee signs upon starting a job.

We propose addressing the insider threat using a detective approach that helps a company to attribute malicious acts [36]. Detective approaches, such as *accountability*, provide a mechanism to answer questions about security incidents (e.g., "why was the document leaked?") and attribute responsible parties a posteriori. Attack attribution is the process of identifying the perpetrator of a cyber-attack [22]. This mechanism increases forensic readiness, and establishes the basis for taking legal action against an attacker [9,30,34]. As such, attribution can be considered in many cases as a deterrent measure [9,33].

Insider attack attribution does not inherit the challenges facing attribution such as tools prepositioning [37], and the Internet anonymity [9]. Still, there are no robust approaches to attribute insider attacks. Surveys show that the attribution literature focused on the IP level in network attacks [9,33,37]. Instead, we tackle insider attacks attribution through an automated reasoning capability.

Accountability, fundamentally, means preserving evidence and supporting reasoning about the causal relationships within the collected evidence [11]. Actual causality, as an essential ingredient for accountability, is studied in different fields of computer science [7]; however, it was not utilized for attributing insiders. For that, we adopt the definition of Halpern and Pearl (HP) [6,7] to infer *actual causality*. HP is a formal foundation to answer causal queries in a way that matches the human way of thinking. This enables us to explain insider attacks. However, the first challenge towards this adoption is constructing *causal models* which are required by HP. We propose to solve this problem by relating causal models to security models.

Security models [17] such as ATs [32] are appealing to scientists for their formalism [21,28], to managers for their visual nature, and to engineers for their systematic categorization of threats. ATs are used for risk estimation, cost approximation, and defense planning. We aim to add forensics analysts to the list of AT beneficiaries, and supporting causality reasoning to its purposes. However, ATs are not readily sufficient to be used for after-the-fact forensic analysis.

Our goal is to create models that attribute blame to a human, i.e., an insider. However, ATs do not usually include potential attackers (suspects). This is what differentiates ATs from causal models. Thus, we analyze the implications of adding suspects to ATs. Then, we detail a complete approach to extract causal models from AT and show their utilization to infer causality automatically [12]. We focus on models for insiders because we think that accountability is a deterrent measure against insiders. Further, while creating those models, we exploit the unique property of insider threats, i.e., the ability to identify *suspects* beforehand. Our contributions are: **a)** a proposal of utilizing actual causality theories in insider threat attribution and forensics. We discuss the usefulness of this proposal throughout the paper. **b)** an automated extraction approach of causal models from ATs. This transformation enables *attributing suspects, creating exogenous variables*, and *recommending preemption relations*. **c)** an open-source tool (**ATCM**) that implements the approach with an evaluation of the efficiency, the validity of the approach, and the effectiveness of the model.

2 Preliminaries

We review the formalism of attack trees in Sect. 2.1, we elaborate on the foundations of *causality* in Sect. 2.2, with an example in Sect. 2.3.

2.1 Foundations of Attack Trees

ATs model potential security threats within a system and the steps necessary to perform an attack [32]. The root node contains the ultimate goal of an attack tree while the sub-nodes describe activities that are necessary to conduct the respective parent activity/goal. The relationship between a node and its children can be either *OR* or *AND* (represented by a circular line below the node).

Depending on the required purpose, attack trees have been defined using different semantics such as multi-set semantics [21], linear-logic semantics [8], timed automata [18], Markov decision process [2], and propositional logic [28]. In this paper, we aim to reason about the actual causality relations among binary events, i.e., whether the occurrence or absence of a specific event was the cause of another event. Hence, we use the equation-propositional semantics similar to [28]. Such formalism is simple, expressive, and general. The main difference between our definition and the definition in [28] is that we create a propositional formula for each node in the tree (excluding the leaves), while the whole tree is represented with a minimized formula of the root in [28].

For the formal definition, we follow Mauw and Oostdijk's [21] way of defining an attack tree. However, we adapt it to use propositional logic semantics. Formally, Definition 1, adapted from [21], expresses attack trees.

Definition 1. *Attack Tree [21] is a 4-tuple* $AT = (\mathcal{N}, \rightarrow, n_0, [[n]])$ *where*

- $\mathcal{N}$ *is a finite set of attack nodes*
- $n_0 \in \mathcal{N}$ *is the root node*
- $\rightarrow \subseteq \mathcal{N} \times \mathcal{N}$ *is a finite set of acyclic relations.*
- $[[n]]$ *is a function that returns a propositional formula for each* $n \in \mathcal{N}$, *the formula represents the semantical dependency of a node on its children nodes.*

2.2   Actual Causality

HP is the influential formal framework proposed by Joseph Halpern and Judea Pearl [7] to define actual causality. It is based on *counter-factual reasoning* (CF), in which we think of alternative worlds where if the cause is removed, the effect does not occur. Essentially it is a simple but-for test, i.e., but for the existence of some event X, would Y have occurred? The naive CF reasoning fails to deal with many situations in the literature [20]. Thus, HP is introduced on the basis of structural equations causal models (SEMs). The utilization of structural equations in this context allows for *interventions*, which enables CF. Intervention is the act of changing a value in the model and checking the effects that it has on other values; this allows us to answer the metaphysical counter-factual queries.

Causal Model. A causal model, which is the focus of this paper, is formally defined by Halpern and Pearl in Definition 2 [6]. It uses variables to describe properties of the world, and their values present states of these properties. The influence of the variables on each other is modeled by the equations [6]. An *equation* represents a mechanism, F_Y, in the modeled world, which describes how variable Y is set depending on the values of the other variables. Variables are classified into *exogenous* ($\mathcal{U}$) and *endogenous* ($\mathcal{V}$) variables. *Exogenous* variables are determined outside the model; they represent the factors that the modeler does not consider as causes, but rather given. *Endogenous* variables represent the factors deemed causal; their values are determined by the equations.

Definition 2. *Causal Model [6] M is 4-tuple $M = (\mathcal{U}, \mathcal{V}, \mathcal{R}, \mathcal{F})$, where*

- $\mathcal{U}$ *is a set of exogenous variables,*
- $\mathcal{V}$ *is a set of endogenous variables,*
- $\mathcal{R}$ *associates with every $Y \in \mathcal{U} \cup \mathcal{V}$ a set $\mathcal{R}(Y)$ of possible values for Y,*
- $\mathcal{F}$ *associates with $X \in \mathcal{V}$ $F_X : (\times_{U \in \mathcal{U}} \mathcal{R}(U)) \times (\times_{Y \in \mathcal{V} \setminus \{X\}} \mathcal{R}(Y)) \to \mathcal{R}(X)$.*

We focus on binary acyclic models in which all the variables are boolean and there is always a unique solution to the equations, given a *context*. A specific set of values for the exogenous variables is called a *context*. Models are visualized in causal graphs with variables $\mathcal{U} \cup \mathcal{V}$ as nodes. There is an edge from a node X to a node Y, if the equation of Y, denoted as F_Y, depends on X in the model.

Reasoning About Causality. We present the notations used by HP [6], before defining actual causes in Definition 3. A sequence of variables $X_1, \ldots, X_n$ is abbreviated as a vector $\overrightarrow{X}$, values of the variables are denoted by small letters $x_1, \ldots, x_n$. Analogously, $X_1 = x_1, \ldots, X_n = x_n$ is abbreviated $\overrightarrow{X} = \overrightarrow{x}$. Values of all exogenous variables $\mathcal{U}$, also called (actual) *context*, is written as $\overrightarrow{u}$. A variable Y is set to value y writing $Y \leftarrow y$, i.e., we substitute the equation of Y (F_Y) with a constant. For a causal model $M = (\mathcal{U}, \mathcal{V}, \mathcal{R}, \mathcal{F})$ and a vector $\overrightarrow{X}$ of variables in $\mathcal{V}$, a *submodel* $M_{\overrightarrow{X} \leftarrow \overrightarrow{x}}$ can be obtained by setting $\overrightarrow{X}$ to $\overrightarrow{x}$ in all functions $\mathcal{F}$ and removing $\overrightarrow{X}$ from $\mathcal{V}$ in the model M. A *primitive event*, given a model M, is a formula of the form $X = x$ for $X \in \mathcal{V}$ and $x \in \mathcal{R}(X)$. A *basic causal formula* is of the form $[Y_1 \leftarrow y_1, \ldots, Y_k \leftarrow y_k]\varphi$, where φ is a

Boolean combination of primitive events. $Y_1, \ldots, Y_k$ (abbreviated $\vec{Y}$) are distinct variables in $\mathcal{V}$, and $y_i \in \mathcal{R}(Y_i)$, that are intervened on, i.e., their functions are substituted with constants. A causal formula ψ can be evaluated in M given a context $\vec{u}$. We write $(M, \vec{u}) \models \psi$ if ψ evaluates to true in the causal model M given context $\vec{u}$. The statement $(M, \vec{u}) \models [\vec{Y} \leftarrow \vec{y}](X = x)$ implies that solving the equations in the submodel $M_{\vec{Y} \leftarrow \vec{y}}$ with context $\vec{u}$ yields the value x for variable X. Definition 3 shows the three conditions of an actual cause.

Definition 3. Actual Cause [6] $\vec{X} = \vec{x}$ *is an actual cause of φ in $(M, \vec{u})$ if the following three conditions hold:*

AC1. $(M, \vec{u}) \models (\vec{X} = \vec{x})$ and $(M, \vec{u}) \models \varphi$.

AC2.   *There is a set $\vec{W}$ of variables in $\mathcal{V}$ and a setting $\vec{x}'$ of the variables in $\vec{X}$ such that if $(M, \vec{u}) \models \vec{W} = \vec{w}$, then $(M, \vec{u}) \models [\vec{X} \leftarrow \vec{x}', \vec{W} \leftarrow \vec{w}]\neg\varphi$.*

AC3. $\vec{X}$ *is minimal in satisfying the first two conditions.*

Given a causal model, we use Definition 3 to answer causal queries by checking the conditions. AC1 sets a trivial condition: $\vec{X} = \vec{x}$ can only be a cause of φ, if $\vec{X} = \vec{x}$ and φ are true under $(M, \vec{u})$. AC2 checks the counter-factual relation between the cause and the effect, i.e., changing the cause $\vec{X} = \vec{x}$ leads to the non-occurrence of φ. AC2 allows us to fix a set of variables $\vec{W}$ at their actual value $\vec{w}$. AC3 is a minimality condition to ensure only essential events are part of the cause. In this paper, we aim to enable this kind of reasoning, in the context of insider attacks, by proposing an automated method for constructing causal models. We discuss, in the following, why we believe *instantiating* the HP framework in the security domain is a beneficial capability.

Distinguishing between exogenous and endogenous variables as suggested in HP, at first sight, does not appear to be revolutionary. However, this distinction enables the choice of what to count as a possible cause (*endogenous*) and what not to (*exogenous*), hence, it treats cases of **irrelevance**. As such, in security we can limit our attribution based on the goal. If we are looking for legal evidence, then we can include possible human actors as endogenous variables. If we are looking for an intrusion explanation, then we can include the running services as endogenous variables. Furthermore, HP correctly classifies the **non-occurrence** of events as causes. For example, an administrator "forgetting" to install the latest update of the firmware on a server can be a cause of an exploit.

A typical problem of causality definitions, which HP deals with, is *preemption*. It resembles the confusing cases where several potential causes exist and coincide, but one cause preempts the others. The problem for simple CF definitions is that if the earlier cause A had not been there, cause B would have triggered the effect anyway (just a bit later). Thus, A is not classified as a cause. HP deals with this by using $\vec{W}$ from Definition 2 and auxiliary variables. Accounting for preemption, in insiders attacks, is beneficial. Specifically, in attacks with different strategies of attacking. For example, an administrator copying a DB backup file, although this is a policy violation, is not the actual cause of the data breach that happened. The copy act was preempted by a privilege abuse of another employee. Further, differentiating actual causes in cases of preemption is crucial when preventive measures such as an intrusion detection system (IDS) are deployed. For example, an IDS may preempt an attack from succeeding although the basic steps of the attack were carried out.

Conjunction and Disjunction. HP can consider a combination of events as a cause. There are attacks that are carried out by multiple steps, and hence are modeled using an *AND* gate. For example, to read a service's memory, an attacker accesses the machine, then attaches a debugger to the running process. On the other hand, there are attacks that can be carried out using different techniques or by exploiting different vulnerabilities. For example, to steal the master key from a system, the attacker can either obtain it decrypted from memory *or* encrypted from the database (the attacker then has to decrypt it). A more interesting scenario would be if two insiders cooperated in performing an attack, i.e., a collusion attack. Such attacks are a major threat class of insiders [15]. We will see in Sect. 3 that our approach exploits this ability in HP.

2.3   Malicious Insider Example

In this section, we consider a simplified real-world example, inspired by an industrial partner, to illustrate the previous definitions; we also use it as a running example throughout the paper. The example introduces a model of insider behavior leading to sealing a master encryption-key in production. It is simple enough to be explained yet expressive to illustrate HP, especially with *preemption*.

An excerpt of the causal graph is shown in Fig. 1. Although it is similar to an AT, it visualizes a causal model according to Definition 2; as a result of this paper, we aspire to construct such models using ATs. The model represents one strategy to steal the key (MKS) by obtaining its encrypted version and decrypting it (as opposed to stealing it decrypted, which is omitted for readability). The attack can be executed by one of two administrators (assuming no collusion), Suzy (S) or Billy (B). They both have sufficient privileges in the system; however, S has more expertise in the system. The event of S or B decrypting the key is denoted by the variables $S.DK, B.DK$ respectively. For that, each of them needs to read the pass-phrase from a script ($Get(P)$) *and* read the key from the database ($Get(K)$). For now, we assume an arbitrary causal connection between $S.DK$ and $B.DK$ which is meant to represent a *preemption relation*, i.e., a bias to represent S's stronger abilities; such relations are crucial in causality [11]. In this paper, we model them using dashed arrows because we think they can be dynamically altered by a modeler to express different concepts, e.g., *S has higher privileges, B has a better history in the company, S came earlier in the morning when the incident was reported, or a combination of these factors.* We have four exogenous variables (omitted from the model) that set the values for $Get(P)/Get(K)$ for both S and B, i.e., $\mathcal{U}$ is $\{S.Get(P)_{exo}, S.Get(K)_{exo}, B.Get(P)_{exo}, B.Get(K)_{exo}\}$. The equations of the model follow; the dashed part of the equations shows the *preemption* relation.

– $S.DK = S.Get(P) \wedge S.Get(K)$

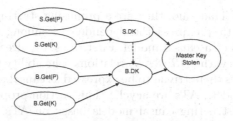

Fig. 1. An excerpt of steal master key causal model

- $B.DK = B.Get(P) \wedge B.Get(K) \wedge \boxed{\neg S.DK}$
- $MKS = S.DK \vee B.DK$

The model is not sufficient for causality inference, we still need to set the *context* (exogenous variables). This is done through logging, and auditing. Assume we have the following context $(1, 1, 1, 1)$ (S and B both got the pass-phrase and the key) when considering the ordering of the variables as provided. We use the *context* and the *model* to answer causal queries such as: *Q1: is Suzy the cause of stealing the key?*, or *Q2: what is the actual cause of exposing the key?*. Let us answer *Q1* by checking if $S.Get(K)$ is a cause of MKS with $W = \{B.DK\}$ using the conditions from Definition 3. Equation 1 shows the crucial steps (of checking AC2) to conclude that $S.Get(K)$ is the cause. Note that with an empty set W, AC2 does not hold (case of preemption), but with $W = \{B.DK\}$ (Step 3 Eq. 1), the effect does not happen (Step 4) and hence $S.Get(K)$ is a cause.

$$
\begin{array}{lll}
Step\ 1 & S.Get(K) = 0 & \text{Intervening on x} \\
Step\ 2 & S.DK = 1 \wedge 0 = 0 & \text{Other variables state} \\
Step\ 3 & B.DK = 0 & \text{Cannot change this variable} \\
Step\ 4 & MKS = 0 \vee 0 = 0 & \text{Effect is not happening}
\end{array}
\tag{1}
$$

Additionally, we can answer *Q2* by checking *if $B.Get(K)$ is a cause?* Following similar steps, the answer is no, because no matter how W is set, MKS will still be True. These questions cannot be answered using an attack tree only. Even if we have attributed the attack tree with the potential suspects, we still cannot infer actual causality directly in cases of preemption or missing events. In this paper, we contribute a method that uses attack trees to construct causal models with suspects and preemption relations; thus, establishing the ability to use causal reasoning to answer queries in the context of insider attacks.

3   Attack Trees to Causal Models

Causality is model-relative; thus, the creation of a model is a crucial requirement for causality and blame attribution. Although attack trees are widely used to model attacks on a system, they are not readily *sufficient* to attribute blame. Mainly because they normally do not include the attacker; rather, they represent the attack strategies. That said, they are a promising starting point to creating causal models since they express the dependencies among attacker acts, and match the properties of a causal model. First, ATs are already a propositional combination of events with *(OR, AND)* relations. The ability to formalize ATs in boolean algebra makes them trivial to be expressed as causal models. Second, HP focuses on acyclic models; ATs are acyclic. This section proposes an automated methodology for constructing causal models based on ATs. Our methodology refers to the following activities that are discussed throughout this section.

1. *Suspect Attribution.* Refers to representing potential suspects in the model. In Sect. 3.1, we transform the original AT $\mathcal{T}$ to an *attributed* AT $\mathcal{T}'$.
2. *Tree to Model transformation* (Sect. 3.2). It includes a.) *variable selection*: listing the different factors that are considered in the model. They represent the causes, effects, and the environment. Each factor is expressed as a variable in the model. b.)*variable classification*: classifying what can be considered as a cause (or effect) (endogenous) and what not (exogenous). c.) *semantics expression*: representing how the variables affect each other using propositional logic operators like *and, or and negation.*
3. *Preemption Relations Addition* (Sect. 3.3). Refers to incorporating useful knowledge about the variables to create preemption relations.

3.1   Suspect Attribution

To bring it closer to causal models, we add *suspects* to ATs. As shown in this section, the way suspects are added is crucial in determining the scope of the causal queries that can be answered using the resulting model. To the best of our knowledge, no prior work has tried to explore approaches to restructure ATs to include *roles* in an automated manner. *Instances* of roles (e.g., data-center admin Suzy) are the potential attackers (suspects) that have privileges to perform an attack. We refer to the process of adding suspects to AT as *suspect attribution.*

Suspect attribution is an automated *unfolding* (duplicating) task of parts of the tree followed by *allotting* the new parts to a suspect. To create a new branch for each suspect, we keep the parent node of the gate, and introduce an intermediate level of new nodes (attribution nodes) that correspond to insiders. The allotment is represented by renaming the nodes to include the suspect identifier, e.g., *Billy.Read_Pass_Phrase.* Regardless of its location, a subtree containing a node and all its descendants is attributed according to Definition 4.

Definition 4. *A subtree $\mathcal{B} = (\mathcal{N}, \rightarrow, n_0, [[n]])$ is attributed with suspects $\{s_1, s_2, \ldots s_l\}$ by: 1) Creating a set (size l) of $\mathcal{B}$ duplicates, denoted $\{\mathcal{B}_1, \mathcal{B}_2 \ldots \mathcal{B}_l\}$. A duplicate $\mathcal{B}_i$ contains the nodes of $\mathcal{B}$ with every node renamed with i suffix.*
2) Constructing a new tree $\mathcal{AB}$ with root n_0 from $\mathcal{B}$, then adding the disconnected $\{\mathcal{B}_1, \mathcal{B}_2 \ldots \mathcal{B}_l\}$, and connecting their root nodes using an OR function with n_0.

Unfolding a tree can be done at different levels. However, depending on the internal structure, this may produce trees that model different attack vectors.

Consequently, the range of the causal-queries that can be analyzed using the resulting models depends on the unfolding level. For example, in Fig. 2, we present the complete AT of the example in Sect. 2.3, including stealing the key decrypted. Figure 2 is modeled using ADTool [5,16], which denotes an AND relation by the presence of a horizontal edge touching the input arcs of a node. Let us consider attributing the left subtree of Fig. 2 with *two* instances of an *admin* role, i.e., Billy and Suzy. We can do that at *level two* (root level is one). The resulting tree is represented in Fig. 3. It clearly models the possible ways to steal the master key by *either* Billy or Suzy. The complete attack paths in the tree allow expressing the behavior of *one* suspect performing an attack.

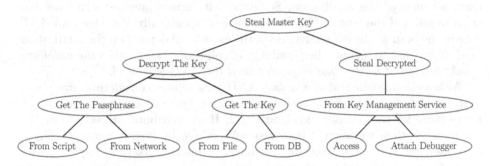

Fig. 2. Steal key attack tree (drawn using ADTool [5,16])

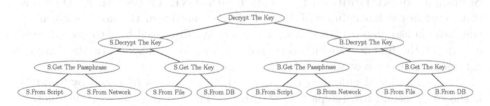

Fig. 3. L-2 unfolding (drawn using ADTool [16])

Alternatively, we can attribute the suspects at the *third* level (*L-3*). Interestingly, the resulting attack tree, as seen in Fig. 4, models more possibilities than the previous case; now, we can model attack paths with a possibility of *collusion* between insiders [15]. As a result, attacks that involve *both* Suzy and Billy cooperating to steal the master key are now covered in this tree, and hence, causal-queries to blame them are possible on the resulting model.

Since collusion attacks are plausible among insiders [15], we use the second attribution *(L-3)*, especially since it also includes the attacks within *(L-2)* attribution. This comparison is an instance of the specialization concept proposed by Horne et al. [8].

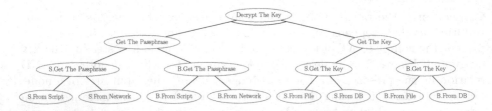

Fig. 4. L-3 unfolding (drawn using ADTool [16])

Actually, the *attribution level* is not the crucial factor in determining the expressiveness of the attribution. Somewhat, it depends on the structure and the semantics of the branch (first-level subtree). Specifically, if we have an *AND* gate in the branch, the expressiveness of the model will depend on the attribution level. If we want to include the possibility of collusion attacks, *then the unfolding should happen at a level that is greater than the AND gate level.*

Although, unfolding after the last AND gate allows considering any possibility of colluding attacks, in some cases it may be unnecessary. For example, let us consider the second branch in Fig. 2. If we attribute suspects after the fourth level, then we assume that suspects collude by having one accessing a container *and* the other attaching a debugger; this is unlikely to happen. Still, it produces a model that can be used for single-agent queries. We propose to generate causal models from *attributed ATs* based on different *attribution levels.* The branch structure automatically determines the level (based on the above), or the modeler can explicitly specify the attribution level.

Semantics of Attribution. Let us start with **AND Gates**. An AND gate is visualized in the left column of Table 1. The semantics of the node is given by the formula associated with it, i.e., $a = b \wedge c$. We discussed how to unfold such a gate, at the first level which does not account for collusion attacks (middle column), or at the second level (right column).

The semantics of unfolding the (L_1) with two suspects (denoted by $'$ and $''$) is shown in second row (steps 1–3) of Table 1. The last step shows a disjunctive normal form (DNF) of the formula. Similarly, the right column shows the formulas and simplification of unfolding at (L_2). Comparing the forms shows that the possible attack scenarios of (L_1) unfolding are included in the (L_2) unfolding (this can be seen as a specialization [8] of attack trees). In other words, the formula (L_1) *implies* (L_2), i.e., $L_1 \implies L_2$ is a *tautology.* Thus, causal queries of the single blame can also be answered when unfolding on the second level.

Unfolding allows us to attribute possible suspects of an attack to the best of the modeler's knowledge. Simplifying the unfolded gates into their DNF proves the *preservation* of the original gate semantics, i.e., $a = b \wedge c$. Essentially the occurrence of the two concrete actions (b, c) combined causes an event (a). This is expressed in each clause of the DNFs. Informally, a clause is one instance of the original formula. We have to keep in mind, that this transformation is built on the assumption that the list of suspects is the universe of all the possible

Table 1. Unfolding AND

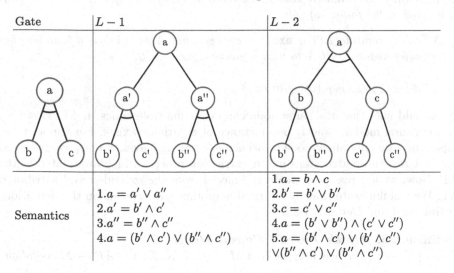

Gate	$L-1$	$L-2$
Semantics	$1.a = a' \vee a''$ $2.a' = b' \wedge c'$ $3.a'' = b'' \wedge c''$ $4.a = (b' \wedge c') \vee (b'' \wedge c'')$	$1.a = b \wedge c$ $2.b' = b' \vee b''$ $3.c = c' \vee c''$ $4.a = (b' \vee b'') \wedge (c' \vee c'')$ $5.a = (b' \wedge c') \vee (b'' \wedge c'')$ $\vee (b'' \wedge c') \vee (b'' \wedge c'')$

agents that can perform this attack. This assumption allows us to say that the semantics of the transformed tree (or branch) is now refined to enumerate all the possible scenarios, each presented as a clause that combines single or multi-suspects. Lastly, the case of unfolding OR gates is similar and simpler because the complication of the unfolding level is eliminated. Regardless of the level, an original formula like $a = b \vee c$, will be unfolded to $a = b' \vee c' \vee b'' \vee c''$.

3.2 Attributed Attack Tree Transformation

Since we are reusing the existing knowledge in the attributed attack trees, the three activities *variable selection, semantics expression, and variable classification* are trivial. Basically, we consider each node as an *endogenous* variable that defines whether or not an attack step has been conducted. Since the nodes are connected with different operators, we use them to construct the equations and therefore express the semantic relationships between the variables. Before we do the transformation, we need to extend the tree, i.e., duplicate its leaves.

In attack trees, a leaf node represents an atomic step that is not further refined [32]. When transferring leaves into *endogenous* variables of a causal model, they lack corresponding formulas. Alternatively, we can consider them as *exogenous* variables that represent the environment (context), but then they cannot be regarded as potential causes in our reasoning. Thus, we extend the tree with a duplicate set of leaves. In other words, each leaf on the tree gets an inbound edge from a new node that has the same name with an _exo suffix. Tree extension aids us in *classifying the variables*, and it also maintains the possibility that any node in the original tree can be considered as a cause. Definition 5 is a tree extension function, where $E(T)$ copies the set of leaves of a tree T.

Definition 5 *Extension Rule. The relation* $T(\mathcal{N}, \rightarrow, n_0) \rightrightarrows T''(\mathcal{N}'', \rightarrow'', n_0)$ *is defined by the following rule.*

- $\mathcal{N}'' : \mathcal{N} \bigcup rename(E(T), \_\mathtt{exo})$; *where* $rename(\ A, \mathtt{suffix})$ *is a function that renames nodes in set* A *to with a given suffix.*

- $\rightarrow'' : \{\rightarrow\} \bigcup \forall_{m \in E(T)} (m \rightarrow m\_exo)$.

We should note that the same node can occur multiple times in AT. However, in our causal model, exactly one instance of a variable exists. For the scope of this paper, we only allow node re-occurrence among leaves. So far, we discussed the first *two* automated steps in our extraction process which are related to the AT. Now, we are ready to create the model from the extended and attributed AT. We will illustrate that by a formal mapping that depends on the definitions Definition 1 and Definition 2.

Definition 6. *Attack Tree To Causal Model*
$AT = (\mathcal{N}, \rightarrow, n_0, [[n]])$ *is mapped to a* $M = (\mathcal{U}, \mathcal{V}, \mathcal{R}, \mathcal{F})$ *i.e.* $AT \rightarrowtail M$ *as follows*

- $\mathcal{U} = E(AT)$, *where* $E(AT)$ *returns the leaf nodes of a tree* AT
- $\mathcal{V} = \mathcal{N} \backslash E(AT)$, *where* $\backslash$ *is the difference between two sets.*
- $\mathcal{R} = \{0, 1\}$.
- $\mathcal{F}$ *associates with each* $X \in \mathcal{V}$ *a propositional formula* $F_X = [[X]]$, *which corresponds to the semantical formula from the AT.*

3.3 Adding Preemption Relations

So far, we discussed how to map the structure (variable and dependencies), the semantics (formulas), and their causal importance (endogenous or exogenous). Now, we augment the model with suspect-related information that is useful to create *preemption relations*. HP introduces a treatment of preemption cases by relating the involved variables "somehow." As we mentioned in Sect. 2.3, *preemption relations* represent auxiliary connections among variables that express the same event conducted by a different suspect (e.g., *Billy. Get Key/Suzy. Get Key*). They are decisive in models that have potential identical causal relations, especially, with the symmetrical nature of our models brought by our attribution approach [7,11]. Since preemption relations can stem from different facts, it can be hard to model them. For example, they represent the level of Suzy's privileges in a system, Billy's criminal record, or a combination of such factors. To automate their modeling in the context of insiders, we propose to base the creation of preemption relations on metrics of insiders' risk assessment. Specifically, we introduce the *suspiciousness metric* (SM), which provides an order relation over the set of suspects conducting a particular type of attack. In other words, it is a value given to each suspect that aggregates their ability to perform an event or willingness to commit an attack. The precise way of calculating SM depends on the context of an incident; hence, we do not provide one; it can be a simple reflection of privileges in the system; it can be a sum of weighted factors (privileges and record). Since *SM* values reflect disparity among suspects, they can be *global* (a value of the attacker ability for all possible attacks) or *local* (a value of attacker ability for a specific attack). This flexibility in deciding how to calculate SM, and whether it is global or local, give the modeler some freedom to decide how to model preemption. Yet, the whole concept can be automated.

We introduce preemption relations among attribution variables *one level* after the attribution level. At that level the tree contains variables representing the same event allotted for different suspects. We connect every two variables with an edge *from* the *more suspicious* suspect (higher SM) *to* the *less suspicious* suspect (in case of equal values the edge is not added). Assume we have three suspects: X_1, X_2, X_3, each performing event Z, and the order of their ability is $X_1 > X_2 > X_3$. Then, the following acyclic preemption relations are added $X_1.Z \dashrightarrow X_2.Z$, $X_1.Z \dashrightarrow X_3.Z$, $X_2.Z \dashrightarrow X_3.Z$ to the graph. The semantics of this arrow is represented by a *negation* clause added to the *less suspicious* suspect about the *more suspicious* one, i.e., $X_3.Z = \ldots \wedge \neg X_1.Z \wedge \neg X_2.Z$.

Definition 7. *Given a model resulting from Definition 6, a preemption relation ($\dashrightarrow$) is a added between two attribution variables ($S_1.e$, $S_2.e$) of the same event (e) for different suspects, denoted $S_1.e \dashrightarrow S_2.e$, if $SM(S_1.e) > SM(S_2.e)$.*

3.4 Tool Support

Having introduced our approach, we present a tool **ATCM** (Attack Tree to Causal Model). *ATCM* is a command line tool that automates suspect attribution, tree to model transformation, and preemption relation addition.[1] As the name suggests, *ATCM* takes an attack tree and suspects' specification as an input and generates a causal model. Attack trees are created using a variety of tools. To get access to the information stored in such a AT, it needs to be exportable to a format that can be accessed and used by us. An example of tools fulfilling this requirement is *ADTool* [5,16], which provides XML-representation of its trees. Consequently, we are able to use those as input for *ATCM*.

In general, *ATCM* incorporates a three-step approach: parsing, transformation, and extraction. First of all, we need to create a machine-readable object, i.e., binary, representation out of a given XML-File that defines an attack tree (Parsing). For this purpose, we have developed our own parsing components. However, since this object representation is specifically tailored to each of the supported file formats, we want to transform the latter into a uniform tree representation, which comprises both attack and other similar models such as fault trees, while ensuring that no semantic information is lost (Transformation). For this representation, we are using the *Model Exchange Format (MEF)* (https://open-psa.github.io/mef/) in a slightly simplified form.

The advantage of abstracting the specific format such as ADT format is that the most essential functionality of this tool, i.e., the extraction of the causal model, needs to be developed only once. This reduces its error-proneness and

---

[1] *ATCM* is available at: https://github.com/amjadKhalifah/ATCM.

increases maintainability. Once an attack has been transferred into this uniform representation, the described generation of the causal model can begin (Extraction). We export the results in a human-readable report and generate a causal graph in the *DOT* format, which is a commonly used for describing graphs in a textual format and can be rendered into a visualization by multiple tools.

4 Evaluation

In our evaluation, we analyze the following qualities: *the efficiency* of the model extraction, *the validity*, and *the effectiveness* of the resulting models. For the first, we discuss (in Sect. 4.1) the performance cost and the size expansion of the tree in relation to different variables. In Sect. 4.2, we focus on the quality of the model. Clearly, we do not aim to discuss the expressiveness of AT since their refinement and granularity are decided by the modeler. However, we discuss the validity of our models in relation to the input AT. Lastly, we discuss how to use the causal model in a technical setting to infer causality.

Table 2. Use cases of our evaluation

Class	Use case	Nodes	# Potential attackers
HP	HP_1	3	2
	HP_2	2	2
Insider (industry)	Steal master key	12	$\{2,8\}$
Insider (literature)	$BecomeRootUser_1$	8	$\{2,8\}$
	$BecomeRootUser_2$	11	$\{2,8\}$
Artificially generated	$Artificial_1$	255	$\{2,8\}$
	$Artificial_2$	1017	$\{2,8\}$
	$Artificial_3$	3057	$\{2,8\}$

We use *four* classes of use-cases in our experiments. Table 2 shows the particular attack trees of each class, along with the number of nodes in the tree. Each class contains one or more trees that cover different sources as follows: **1)** HP examples: We use two famous examples from the causality domain [6]. This class is mainly used for the discussion of the validity. **2)** Insiders from industry: This class includes a real-world attack tree which comes from an industrial partner. It represents insider's strategies to *steal a master key* from a deployment of an enterprise solution. **3)** Insiders from Literature: This class includes two attack trees borrowed from [35]. They represent privilege escalation. The first uses windows command line and scheduler, and the other uses Metasploit and Internet Explorer. **4)** Artificially generated trees: This class contains three trees that we generated automatically. They do not hold any semantic value. The aim of using them is to analyze the efficiency of extraction. In our experiments, we will vary the number of suspects and test our model extraction for *2, and 8* suspects.

4.1 The Efficiency of the Extraction

Depending on the size, the structure of the AT, the *attribution level l* of each branch, and the number of suspects s, the size of the resulting model will vary. Since we are attributing branches at different levels, the size of the resulting model is the sum of attributed branch-sizes plus one. This is expressed as $((\sum_{i=1}^{n} |b_{li}(s)|) + 1)$, where n is the number of branches, and $|b_{li}|(s)$ is the size (number of nodes) of branch i attributed at level l with s suspects. We express the attributed branch size $|b_{li}|(s)$ as a function of suspects and its original size.

Definition 8. *Attributed Branch Size* $|b_{li}|(s)$

$$|b_{li}(s)| = (s \cdot (|b_i| - |b_i|_{l>L>1} + |b_i|_{Leafs}) + |b_i|_{l \geqslant L>1})$$

- $|b_i|, |b_i|_{Leafs}$ *are the sizes of the original branch b_i and the number of its leaves,*
- $|b_i|_{l>L>1}, |b_i|_{l \geqslant L>1}$ *are the size of the exclusive and inclusive subtree between the branch root and attribution level. Inclusion refers to counting the root and the leaves or excluding them.*

We clearly see that our approach increases the tree size. Especially with very large trees, forensic analysts are not supposed to inspect their models manually. Rather, as we point in Sect. 4.3, there exist automated tools to analyze causal models. Thus, analysts focus on managing their ATs and formulating their causal queries. Next, we evaluate the efficiency of the extraction process.

Table 3. Evaluation of the efficiency

AT	n	l	b	2 suspects						8 suspects					
				Top		Middle		Leafs		Top		Middle		Leafs	
				n	exec(s)	n	exec(s)	n	exec(s)	n	exec(s)	n	exec(s)	n	exec(s)
SMK	12	5	2	37	0.0002	36	0.0002	36	0.0003	139	0.0004	126	0.0004	108	0.0004
Be.Root1	8	4	1	24	0.0002	25	0.0002	23	0.0002	90	0.0004	91	0.0004	71	0.0004
Be.Root2	11	4	1	32	0.0002	35	0.0002	32	0.0003	122	0.0006	125	0.0006	98	0.0006
T_1	255	8	2	767	0.0069	767	0.0117	767	0.0512	3059	0.0283	2879	0.0460	2303	0.1925
T_2	1017	8	8	3065	0.0354	3065	0.1133	3065	0.7473	12233	0.1380	11513	0.4610	9209	2.99
T_3	3057	8	16	6129	0.0939	6129	0.4084	6129	2.94	24465	0.3700	23025	1.65	18417	11.97

Table 3 shows the execution time *exec(s)* in seconds and the model size n of six ATs. Their properties are shown as n: number of nodes, l: depth of the tree, and b: number of branches. We have attributed the trees with 2 and 8 suspects. We attributed each tree at *root-level, middle-level, and leaf-level*. We created benchmarks, based on *Java Microbenchmark Harness* to measure the execution time. The benchmarks measure the time from parsing an AT until the creation of the corresponding causal model. The values shown in Table 3 have been obtained by running 10 warm-up and 20 measurement iterations on a Windows 10 machine equipped with 8 GB of RAM and a quad-core Intel® i7 processor.

For the small use cases (SMK, Be.Root1, and Be.Root2) the execution time is small (below 0.7 ms). The interesting part is with the artificial trees, where we see a clear proportional increase of execution time with the *deeper* attribution levels. This is due to our recursive algorithm. Model size, on the other hand, is of less importance in that context, we can see that a 23025 node model took 1.7 s to be extracted (L-4), while a 9209 node model took 2.9 s (L-8). Nevertheless, these values do not exhibit a bottleneck. Hence, based on this empirical evaluation, our approach should be efficient enough for any reasonable-sized AT.

4.2   The Validity of the Approach

There are no properties that discuss the validity of a causal model. Rather, scientists have dealt with modeling by example. We use a similar approach. We apply our approach to problematic examples in the literature [7] and compare the results. Our goal is to check if we were able to automate the method of creating models by splitting the general knowledge represented as trees from the suspects. Although those examples are not security attacks, we model them as such.[2] To that end, we followed the following process. *First*, represent the abstract causal knowledge as a tree (Table 4 middle column). *Second,* configure the actors in the scenarios, e.g., Billy and Suzy. *Third,* generate the model (Table 4 right column). *Lastly,* compare the generated model with the model presented in the papers.

For space limit, we only present two examples (**Arsonists, Rock Throwing**). Arsonists (example 3.2 in [7]): Suppose that *two* arsonists drop lit matches in different parts of dry forest, and both cause trees to start burning. Either match by itself suffices to burn down the whole forest. HP describes the essential structure with 3 endogenous variables ML_1 and ML_2, where $ML_i = 0$ if arsonist i does not drop the lit match and 1 otherwise, and similarly, a variable FB for forest burning down. Rock Throwing (example 3.2 in [6]: "Suzy and Billy both pick up rocks and throw them at a bottle denoted in the model as (ST and BT). Suzy's rock gets there first, shattering the bottle denoted in the model as (BS). Since both are perfectly accurate, Billy would have shattered the bottle, if Suzy's throw did not preempt his throw." Table 4 shows that the models vary a bit. This variation is negligible because it does not affect the semantics from a causal perspective. Our model can be proved easily to be a conservative extension [7] of the model from HP. Lastly, the fact that these examples are not limited to insiders suggests that our approach generalizes to a broader class of attacks. However, as we argued in the introduction, the potential deterrence brought by our solution (accountability) is only apparent in the context of insider attacks.

---

[2] Arsonists and Rock-Throwing are typical examples in the causality literature. We may consider setting a forest on fire as an attack on the forest, with lighting matches being a possible step of an attack. We may also consider shattering a bottle an attack on the bottle, with throwing a stone being a possible step of an attack. The point here is to show that our mechanism produces valid results also for well-known examples.

Table 4. Models from HP examples

Example	HP Model	Attack Tree	Our Model
Arsonists			
Rock-Throwing			

4.3 The Effectiveness of the Model

To evaluate the effectiveness of our models, we briefly show how they are used in a real-world production environment. We experimented with a technical setting of the example from Sect. 2.3. First, we created the corresponding *model* using ATCM. Second, we set the *context* for two concrete scenarios: *Sce-1*, in which Suzy stole the key with the existence of preemption, and *Sce-2*, in which Billy did. Third, using formal proof systems from [11,12], we reason about the causality. We tested the models in an environment that contains a set of micro-services and third-party software that are deployed as docker containers. To set the *context*, we utilized monitoring tools namely, auditD to monitor file accesses, and Couchbase audit to monitor queries. These tools generate logs that we used to set the exogenous variables. For our experiment, we set the context manually. For example, this sentence from auditD ... *"MESSAGE": "PATH name=..../ **script.txt** "..auid= **1001** uid= 1001..* is translated into $S.From\_Script\_exo = 1$ (Suzy's id=1001). $\mathcal{U} = \{S\_Script_{exo}, S\_DB_{exo}, S\_File_{exo}, S\_NW_{exo} \ldots\}$.

Accordingly, we have two contexts, namely *Sce-1* $\{1,1,1,1,1,1,1,1\}$ and *Sce-2* $\{0,0,0,0,1,1,1,1\}$ when we consider the ordering of the variables.

Due to our recent solver of actual causality queries [12], we analyzed the two contexts using the *steal master key* 8-suspects model with 91 endogenous and 48 exogenous variables. We used the two questions from Sect. 2.3: *Q1: is Suzy the cause of stealing the key?*, *Q2: Is Billy's decryption of the key or Suzy's the actual cause of stealing it?*. *Sce-1* represented the situation of having multiple tentative suspects. The results matched our ground truth, i.e., Suzy was concluded to be responsible for the incident. Although this may seem intuitive, it was only enabled by the fact that we made our knowledge explicit using a causal model. The analysis of *Q1* took 3.07 ms and consumed 3.2 MB of memory. For *Sce-2*, it was easier to conclude that Billy is the reason for stealing the key since the context was clearer (Suzy and other suspects did not log into the system). The analysis of the model for *Q2* took 2.78 ms and consumed 3.2 MB of memory.

5   Related Work

Security. To the best of our knowledge, no previous work has tried to generate HP models for malicious insiders. However, the thorough work on attack and defense modeling is interesting. Kordy et al. classified DAG-based models into two classes: tree or Bayesian network (BN) based models. Although a BN is similar to a causal model, there are two differences in utilizing them in security. First, BNs are used for the probabilistic inference of an attack likelihood and prediction. However, we aim to use the causal models for inferring *actual* causality. Second, a causal model contains a semantic perspective represented by the SEM, while BN only contains a dependency relation supported by conditional probability table. In this direction, we see the work by Qin et al. [26] which indeed converts attack trees to BN to correlate alerts to predict attacks. Similarly, Althebyan and Panda [1] present a BN model to evaluate and analyze a system after an insider attack. Their evaluation and analysis do not include attributing the attacker. Poolsapassit and Ray [25,27] use AT in a similar way. They do not convert it to other models but rather combine it with insider's intent to predict malicious activity. In [25] they use AT to investigate logs. The two papers are related to our goal but different in the approach of converting AT to causal models annotated with possible suspects. Most of the work reporting on insiders aims to detect the attacks at run-time [15,24,31]. Although our work can be combined with such approaches, it is different since we consider post-mortem attribution. Chinchani et al. [4] proposed a specific modeling language for insiders; however, we used AT for reasons of industry utilization and tool support [16].

For attack attribution, researchers [9,33] have identified three techniques: digital forensics, malware based analysis, and indirect attribution techniques that use statistical models to identify attackers. Most of these techniques target outsider attackers. Unlike our approach, digital forensics tools mainly face the challenge of scalability with the size of logs [33], whereas we can elicit requirements of logging from our modes. That is, we only monitor the properties that set our context. Malware based analysis targets a different attack vector than us. Indirect attribution techniques are interesting since they use statistical models; however, they require massive amounts of data. In contrast, we make use of explicit knowledge represented in attack trees.

Causality is a cross-domain concept. An overview of different application fields of causality is presented by Halpern in [7]. An example of research based on the HP definition is the work by Kuntz et al. [19], who are using counterexample traces of model checking tools to construct fault trees. This is similar to our target in general but different in two key aspects. First, it does not leverage security threat models to construct causal models that are used to infer causality in the postmortem. Second, our approach is to model only unwanted behavior while they utilize behavioral models of the systems. Some of the authors of this paper also discussed the idea of creating holistic causal models for Cyber-Physical Systems from different technical models in [10] and human models in [14]. The approach focused on combining those models without targeting one attack vector like insiders. Further literature examining model discovery is listed in a paper by Chen and Pearl [3,23]. These approaches are data-driven methods that differ from our approach of creating causal models from other models.

6   Conclusions and Future Work

To handle the insider threat, we proposed enabling accountability through supporting causal reasoning. To that end, we presented a methodology that introduces HP causal models into the security domain. We showed that such models are beneficial in the context of insiders, and we considered AT as a source for creating them. However, we identified suspect attribution as a crucial step in the conversion. Thus, we introduced a method to add suspects to AT considering the possibility of them colluding. Also, we focused on creating models that include preemption relations. This work can then be combined with causality reasoners to enable forensics analysis of insider accidents. Although it is hard to evaluate models reasonably, we showed that our approach is *efficient* to extract *valid and useful* models. For future work, we plan to study other notions of threat models such as attack-defense trees or ATs with sequential conjunction and analyze how do they relate ton automated causal modeling and contextualization.

References

1. Althebyan, Q., Panda, B.: A knowledge-based Bayesian model for analyzing a system after an insider attack. In: Jajodia, S., Samarati, P., Cimato, S. (eds.) SEC 2008. ITIFIP, vol. 278, pp. 557–571. Springer, Boston, MA (2008). https://doi.org/10.1007/978-0-387-09699-5_36
2. Aslanyan, Z., Nielson, F.: Model checking exact cost for attack scenarios. In: Maffei, M., Ryan, M. (eds.) POST 2017. LNCS, vol. 10204, pp. 210–231. Springer, Heidelberg (2017). https://doi.org/10.1007/978-3-662-54455-6_10
3. Chen, B., Pearl, J.: Graphical tools for linear structural equation modeling. Tech. rep., DTIC Document (2014)

4. Chinchani, R., Iyer, A., Ngo, H.Q., Upadhyaya, S.: Towards a theory of insider threat assessment. In: Proceedings of International Conference on Dependable Systems and Networks, 2005, DSN 2005, pp. 108–117. IEEE (2005)
5. Gadyatskaya, O., Jhawar, R., Kordy, P., Lounis, K., Mauw, S., Trujillo-Rasua, R.: Attack trees for practical security assessment: ranking of attack scenarios with ADTool 2.0. In: Agha, G., Van Houdt, B. (eds.) QEST 2016. LNCS, vol. 9826, pp. 159–162. Springer, Cham (2016). https://doi.org/10.1007/978-3-319-43425-4_10
6. Halpern, J.Y.: A modification of the Halpern-pearl definition of causality. In: Proceedings of the Twenty-Fourth International Joint Conference on Artificial Intelligence, IJCAI 2015 (2015)
7. Halpern, J.Y.: Actual Causality. MIT Press, Cambridge (2016)
8. Horne, R., Mauw, S., Tiu, A.: Semantics for specialising attack trees based on linear logic. Fundamenta Informaticae **153**(1–2), 57–86 (2017)
9. Hunker, J., Hutchinson, B., Margulies, J.: Role and challenges for sufficient cyber-attack attribution. Institute for Information Infrastructure Protection (2008)
10. Ibrahim, A., Kacianka, S., Pretschner, A., Hartsell, C., Karsai, G.: Practical causal models for cyber-physical systems. In: Badger, J.M., Rozier, K.Y. (eds.) NFM 2019. LNCS, vol. 11460, pp. 211–227. Springer, Cham (2019). https://doi.org/10.1007/978-3-030-20652-9_14
11. Ibrahim, A., Klesel, T., Zibaei, E., Kacianka, S., Pretschner, A.: Actual causality canvas: a general framework for explanation-based socio-technical constructs. In: ECAI 2020, the 24th European Conference on Artificial Intelligence. Frontiers in Artificial Intelligence and Applications. IOS Press (2020)
12. Ibrahim, A., Rehwald, S., Pretschner, A.: Efficient checking of actual causality with sat solving. Eng. Secur. Dependable Softw. Syst. **53**, 241 (2019)
13. Institute, P.: 2015 cost of cyber crime study: global (2015)
14. Kacianka, S., Ibrahim, A., Pretschner, A., Trende, A., Lüdtke, A.: Extending causal models from machines into humans. Electron. Proc. Theor. Comput. Sci. **308**, 17–31 (2019)
15. Ko, L.L., Divakaran, D.M., Liau, Y.S., Thing, V.L.: Insider threat detection and its future directions. Int. J. Secur. Netw. **12**(3), 168–187 (2017)
16. Kordy, B., Kordy, P., Mauw, S., Schweitzer, P.: ADTool: security analysis with attack-defense trees. In: Quantitative Evaluation of Systems - 10th International Conference, QEST, pp. 173–176 (2013)
17. Kordy, B., Piètre-Cambacédès, L., Schweitzer, P.: Dag-based attack and defense modeling: don't miss the forest for the attack trees. Comput. Sci. Rev. **13**, 1–38 (2014)
18. Kumar, R., Ruijters, E., Stoelinga, M.: Quantitative attack tree analysis via priced timed automata. In: Sankaranarayanan, S., Vicario, E. (eds.) FORMATS 2015. LNCS, vol. 9268, pp. 156–171. Springer, Cham (2015). https://doi.org/10.1007/978-3-319-22975-1_11
19. Kuntz, M., Leitner-Fischer, F., Leue, S.: From Probabilistic Counterexamples via Causality to Fault Trees. Springer, Heidelberg (2011). https://doi.org/10.1007/978-3-642-24270-0_6
20. Lewis, D.: Counterfactuals and comparative possibility. J. Philos. Logic **2**(4), 418–446 (1973). https://doi.org/10.1007/BF00262950
21. Mauw, S., Oostdijk, M.: Foundations of attack trees. In: Won, D.H., Kim, S. (eds.) ICISC 2005. LNCS, vol. 3935, pp. 186–198. Springer, Heidelberg (2006). https://doi.org/10.1007/11734727_17
22. Nicholson, A., Janicke, H., Watson, T.: An initial investigation into attribution in SCADA systems. In: ICS-CSR (2013)

23. Pearl, J.: Causality. Cambridge University Press, Cambridge (2009)
24. Phyo, A., Furnell, S.: A detection-oriented classification of insider it misuse. In: Third Security Conference (2004)
25. Poolsapassit, N., Ray, I.: Investigating computer attacks using attack trees. In: Craiger, P., Shenoi, S. (eds.) DigitalForensics 2007. ITIFIP, vol. 242, pp. 331–343. Springer, New York (2007). https://doi.org/10.1007/978-0-387-73742-3_23
26. Qin, X., Lee, W.: Attack plan recognition and prediction using causal networks. In: 20th Annual Computer Security Applications Conference. IEEE (2004)
27. Ray, I., Poolsapassit, N.: Using attack trees to identify malicious attacks from authorized insiders. In: di Vimercati, S.C., Syverson, P., Gollmann, D. (eds.) ESORICS 2005. LNCS, vol. 3679, pp. 231–246. Springer, Heidelberg (2005). https://doi.org/10.1007/11555827_14
28. Rehák, M., et al.: Runtime monitoring and dynamic reconfiguration for intrusion detection systems. In: Kirda, E., Jha, S., Balzarotti, D. (eds.) RAID 2009. LNCS, vol. 5758, pp. 61–80. Springer, Heidelberg (2009). https://doi.org/10.1007/978-3-642-04342-0_4
29. Research, I.X.F.: 2016 cyber security intelligence index (2016)
30. Rowlingson, R.: A ten step process for forensic readiness. Int. J. Digit. Evid. 2(3), 1–28 (2004)
31. Salem, M.B., Hershkop, S., Stolfo, S.J.: A survey of insider attack detection research. In: Stolfo, S.J., Bellovin, S.M., Keromytis, A.D., Hershkop, S., Smith, S.W., Sinclair, S. (eds.) Insider Attack and Cyber Security. Advances in Information Security, vol. 39. Springer, Boston (2008). https://doi.org/10.1007/978-0-387-77322-3_5
32. Schneier, B.: Attack trees. Dr. Dobb's J. 24(12), 21–29 (1999)
33. Shamsi, J.A., Zeadally, S., Sheikh, F., Flowers, A.: Attribution in cyberspace: techniques and legal implications. Secur. Commun. Netw. 9(15), 2886–2900 (2016)
34. Tan, J.: Forensic readiness. Cambridge, MA:@ Stake, pp. 1–23 (2001)
35. Tu, M., Xu, D., Butler, E., Schwartz, A.: Forensic evidence identification and modeling for attacks against a simulated online business information system. J. Digit. Forensic Secur. Law 7(4), 4 (2012)
36. Weitzner, D.J., Abelson, H., Berners-Lee, T., Feigenbaum, J., Hendler, J., Sussman, G.J.: Information accountability. Commun. ACM 51(6), 82–87 (2008)
37. Wheeler, D.A., Larsen, G.N.: Techniques for cyber attack attribution. Tech. rep., Institute for Defense Analyses Alexandria VA (2003)

Library-Based Attack Tree Synthesis

Sophie Pinchinat$^{(\boxtimes)}$, François Schwarzentruber, and Sébastien Lê Cong

Univ Rennes/IRISA/CNRS, Rennes, France
sophie.pinchinat@irisa.fr

Abstract. We consider attack trees that can contain OR-, AND- and SAND-nodes. Relying on a formal notion of library inspired from context-free grammars, we introduce a generic attack tree synthesis problem that takes such a library and a trace as inputs. We show that this synthesis problem is NP-complete. The NP membership relies on an involved adaptation of the so-called CYK parsing algorithm. The NP hardness is established via a reduction from a recent covering problem. Finally, we show that the addressed synthesis problem collapses down to P for bounded-AND-arity libraries.

1 Introduction

In security analysis, *attack trees* [23] offer a representation to describe many attacks with brevity. They offer a reading of high-level *explanations* of attacks using different levels of abstractions. Also, they are convenient to perform quantitative analysis on attacks in order to select efficient counter-measures, as well as to identify attacker profiles in *e.g.,* forensic [21]. As general objects, they are useful in various situations in the industry: they are used for assessing the security of physical infrastructures [17], cyber security platforms such as voting systems [8] or specific machines like an ATM [9], and also to conduct quantitative analyses of a system that uses radio-frequency identification (RFID) technology [6].

We here informally introduce the attack tree model on a toy running example in physical security.

Example 1. A museum has two possible entries, both monitored by the same two cameras. The two cameras have a mutual protection system (distinct from the visual surveillance) so that they monitor each other: if a camera gets frozen while being monitored by the other, then an alarm is triggered. In order to neutralize a camera, the attacker can launch a virus on any camera: this virus immediately disables its ability to monitor the other camera, then, possibly after some time, it freezes the camera. Additionally, the freezing is temporary so that a frozen camera may recover from freezing.

Assume at least one camera has been infected by a virus. The attack tree of Fig. 1 describes ways of attacking the museum to steal the painting: each node of the tree matches a task, and the children of a node match the subtasks. This tree displays three types of inner nodes, that specify how the subtasks should be accomplished. In OR-nodes, one subtask has to be achieved. In SAND-nodes,

H. Eades III and O. Gadyatskaya (Eds.): GraMSec 2020, LNCS 12419, pp. 24–44, 2020.
https://doi.org/10.1007/978-3-030-62230-5_2

subtasks should be realized sequentially (from left to right). In AND-nodes, all subtasks have to be executed in parallel. According to this tree, stealing the painting can be achieved for example by (1) turning the security off, then (2) entering the museum, and finally (3) taking the painting.

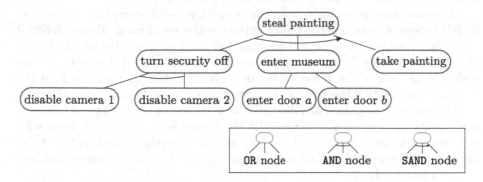

Fig. 1. An attack tree for stealing a painting in a museum with two doors, protected by two security cameras.

The design of attack trees can be a tedious and error-prone process if done manually: indeed, security experts may run into trouble as soon as the material they work on gets fairly big (lengthy log files, for example). In this context, gathering information becomes a complex task, and the resulting trees can get quite large. Hence, automated attack tree synthesis, even partial, is useful.

As shown in the Sect. 2, many algorithms have been proposed for several variants of attack tree synthesis. In particular, some previous works rely on models for representing the accumulated expert knowledge about existing attack patterns, in order to synthesize attack trees [10,14]. Regrettably, the quality of the deployed algorithms can hardly be evaluated because of a lack of results on the intrinsic complexity of the tree synthesis problem.

It is therefore desirable to have a clear understanding of the attack tree synthesis problem(s) at a theoretical level in order to justify any algorithm. This requires a sleek definition of the attack tree synthesis problem, generic and simple enough to capture the core difficulty of the issue.

The present paper is about such a study. Our mathematical setting is the one of attack trees with a trace semantics, in the spirit of [2,3]. The main reason for it comes from the generic notion of trace. Indeed, traces can be found in most domains: as abstractions of system executions in verification, as sequences of events in monitoring, as log files in security, as plans in AI, as sequences of letters in formal languages and in bioinformatics, etc.

We define the notion of *library* as an abstract model for some expert knowledge, inspired from context-free grammars [12], and generic enough to resemble proposals from the literature on attack tree generation, and in particular the ones of [14] and [10].

Importantly, our approach is *model-free*, which makes it relevant for situations where the system model is unknown; only a trace, reminiscent of some system observation, matters. The synthesis decision problem, that we simply call the *attack tree synthesis problem* is defined as: given an input a *library* and an input *trace*, answers whether there exists an attack tree based on the given library whose trace semantics contains the input trace.

We prove that the attack tree synthesis problem is NP-complete. Noticeably, its NP-hardness is obtained by reducing the recently considered "Packed Interval Covering Problem" [22]. The NP-membership relies on a non-trivial adaptation of the classic Cocke–Younger–Kasami parsing algorithm [15]. Interestingly, we highlight the role of the AND-operator by showing a drop to the class P in the problem complexity if the arity of this operator is bounded in the input libraries.

The paper is organized as follows: in Sect. 2, we consider related works and their limits. In Sects. 3 and 4, we settle the formal setting of attack trees with their trace semantics and with the library model, respectively. Section 5 contains the full synthesis problem study. The paper ends with a concluding section and research perspectives.

2   Related Work

We focus on the attack tree synthesis literature of the last two decades, in a chronological order; the reader interested in a survey on attack tree literature can refer to [26] (notice that the assumptions are quite diverse, but that there is an agreement that attack trees should help experts reasoning about ways of attacking a system). In some contributions, the formal semantics of attack trees is omitted, which makes hard stating properties of the generated trees, and in particular about what they describe. Also some works do not define the synthesis problem as a formal problem, making hard to evaluate the efficiency of the proposed approach with regards to the intrinsic complexity of the problem.

In Hong et al. [11], the semantics of the considered attack trees is not provided. The tree generation does not rely on any notion of library. The input is a set of attacks (that can be given or inferred as paths from some attack graph). Their procedure considers as the first step the naive tree obtained as the complete disjunction of all input attacks, where each attack is represented by the mere sequential conjunction of all its actions. In a second step, (although not told this way in the paper) the procedure resorts to controlled regular expression manipulations to make the former huge tree hopefully smaller. The purpose of this technique is mostly used to achieve quantitative analysis in an attack graph, and does not target readability of the tree. No meaning of the subtasks that inhabit the internal sub-nodes can be inferred by this procedure that artificially creates internal nodes from algebraic laws on regular expressions. Also, the approach lacks the use of AND operator that can provide more succinct trees and indeed, as explained by the authors, the synthesized trees have exponential size in the size of the input.

Vigo et al. [25] do not use a library and do not consider the sequential conjunction of subtasks (SAND operator). The input are a "program" representing the system and a point to reach in the former. The programs are described in so-called "value-passing quality calculus", a calculus which derives from the π-calculus. The system program with its point to reach is translated into a propositional formula that is interpreted as an attack tree (with intended meaning of disjunction and conjunction operators). However, since the internal nodes of the synthesized trees are abstract, the resulting trees are used more for quantitative analysis than for explaining ways of attacking.

Pinchinat et al. [18,19] present a tool for synthesizing attack trees. The method is very close to our approach, since it is based on a library, and on a bottom-up construction of the tree inspired by context-free grammar syntactic analysis. The used library is defined aside the synthesis functionality; it can be defined manually in the tool, but may also be imported from previous projects. However, the procedure does not support operator AND.

In the setting of Ivanova et al. [13], the authors suggest a high-level language intended to turn a graph, a so-called "graphical system model", into an attack tree with the intention to make the graph more readable. Those graphical models specify an initial state of some system – vertices represent elements (such as doors, agents, information, and so on), and the attacker has to reach some final configuration. The translation from one setting to another does not rely on a precise semantic framework. The translation from the graph to an attack tree is generic, not taking advantage of any specific expert knowledge. The library is implicitly based on ad-hoc patterns (with first-order logic features) correlated with fixed ontologies (locations, actors, processes, items). As a result, the obtained trees are unbalanced, and not readable. Also, only disjunction and sequential conjunction are considered.

Gadyatskaya et al. [10] define a library-based generic synthesis problem parameterized by the semantics of attack trees. The library is called a refinement specification. However, the paper focuses on the particular series-parallel graph (SP) semantics, where the AND operator has a truly concurrent meaning. Surprisingly, the authors restrict to SP graphs without any AND operator, that is as a set of traces. This prevents to address the synthesis problem for arbitrary refinement rules. Also, the paper does not provide the complexity analysis of the addressed synthesis problem. The tree models we consider here are not based on actions (at the leaves), but it can be established that our semantics coincides with the SP semantics if the AND operator is discarded. Our synthesis problem can therefore be seen as a restriction of their work to a singleton set of single traces, but also as an extension of it as we allow AND operators.

Jhawar et al. [14] consider the issue of automating the completion of an attack tree rather than synthesizing one, by an iterated top-down approach. A criterion based on annotations of nodes with preconditions and postconditions, makes it possible to attach subtrees from some library at some leaves. The logical setting to describe the annotations lacks dynamic features (such as temporal modalities) amenable to the use of sequential conjunction.

In [5], Audinot et al. study the non-emptiness of an attack tree, in a framework similar to what we consider here: given an attack tree, they query the existence of an attack described by the input tree. Our problem can be read as the dual of this problem since the trace is known but a tree has to be found.

3   Attack Trees and Their Trace Semantics

We consider the setting of [3], where attack tree leaves are labeled by atomic goals, but due to our concern, we equip them with a trace semantics instead of a path semantics, in natural manner. Indeed, traces are mere abstraction of finite paths (in some transition system), by replacing each state along the path by its set of true facts; thus a trace is a finite sequence of facts. In formal approaches facts are modeled by abstract *propositions* in a set $Prop = \{p, q, r, \dots\}$.

Intuitively, an atomic goal at a leaf of an attack tree describes the achievements of some primitive task by providing two Boolean formulas that we call the *precondition* and the *postcondition*. An achievement is a finite sequence of facts called a *trace*, formalized as a finite sequence of *valuations* over a set of some propositions. Now, a trace *achieves an atomic goal* if the precondition of that goal holds at the beginning of the sequence and the postcondition of that goal holds at its end. The *trace semantics* of a non-leaf attack tree is given in a compositional manner by means of operations on (sets of) traces, such as concatenation.

We now get into the formal definitions.

3.1   Attack Trees

Formally, an attack tree is a tree whose leaves are *atomic goals* of the form $\langle \iota \text{ to } \gamma \rangle$, where ι and γ are Boolean formulas over a set of atomic propositions $Prop$, called the *precondition* and the *postcondition* respectively. Each inner node of an attack tree is labelled by some operator OP ranging over OR (disjunction), SAND (sequential conjunction) or AND (conjunction), and is called an *OP-node*.

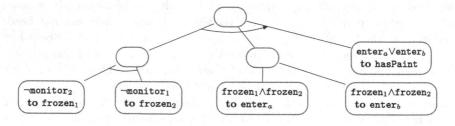

Fig. 2. The formal attack tree for the museum example.

Example 2. Figure 2 shows a formalization of the informal attack tree from Fig. 1, with 3 inner nodes and 5 leaves. Propositions occurring in the atomic goals of the leaves are interpreted as follows: $monitor_i$ means "camera i is being monitored (by the other camera)", $\mathtt{frozen}_i$ means "camera i is frozen", $\mathtt{enter}_j$ means "entered in museum via door j", and $\mathtt{hasPaint}$ means "the painting was stolen". Therefore, the atomic goal $\langle\neg\mathtt{monitor}_2 \text{ to } \mathtt{frozen}_1\rangle$ models the task of hacking camera 1: launching the virus immediately stops camera 1 from monitoring camera 2 and eventually freezes camera 1. Symmetrically, goal $\langle\neg\mathtt{monitor}_1 \text{ to } \mathtt{frozen}_2\rangle$ regards the hacking of camera 2. We will elaborate on the camera-hacking phase later, in Subsect. 3.4. Also, goal $\langle\mathtt{frozen}_1 \wedge \mathtt{frozen}_2 \text{ to } \mathtt{enter}_a\rangle$ models the task of entering the museum via door a without surveillance.

Definition 1 (Attack tree). *An attack tree τ over Prop is:*

- *either a leaf of the form $\langle\iota \text{ to } \gamma\rangle$ where ι, γ are Boolean formulae over Prop;*
- *or an expression $OP(\tau_1, \ldots, \tau_m)$ where OP is the operator OR, AND or $SAND$, $m \geq 1$ is the arity, and $\tau_1, \ldots, \tau_m$ are attack trees.*

In Definition 1 we confuse a node and the subtree rooted at that node. This is standard when trees are defined inductively.

Example 3. The attack tree given in Fig. 2 is

$\mathtt{SAND}(\ \mathtt{AND}(\langle\neg\mathtt{monitor}_2 \text{ to } \mathtt{frozen}_1\rangle, \langle\neg\mathtt{monitor}_1 \text{ to } \mathtt{frozen}_2\rangle),$
  $\mathtt{OR}(\langle\mathtt{frozen}_1 \wedge \mathtt{frozen}_2 \text{ to } \mathtt{enter}_a\rangle, \langle\mathtt{frozen}_1 \wedge \mathtt{frozen}_2 \text{ to } \mathtt{enter}_b\rangle),$
  $\langle\mathtt{enter}_a \vee \mathtt{enter}_b \text{ to } \mathtt{hasPaint}\rangle)$

The second central objects of concern are *traces*.

3.2 Traces and Operations on Sets of Traces

Executions of systems are alternating sequences consisting of states and actions. In our setting for attack trees, the focus is put on states. In fact, the states themselves are not "observable" along an execution, but only the truth values of facts/propositions about them. A truth value of propositions is formally captured by the standard notion of *valuation* in propositional logic. Thus an observation of a (finite) execution, usually called a *trace* [7], is a finite sequence of valuations; two successive valuations in a trace correspond to a state transition in the observed system.

We now formally define *traces*, sets of traces, and particular operations over languages that provide the semantics of operators $\mathtt{OR}$, $\mathtt{SAND}$ and $\mathtt{AND}$ in attack trees. For the rest of this section, we fix a set *Prop* of propositions.

A *valuation* is a subset of *Prop* with the meaning that propositions in this set are true while the others are false; for the empty valuation $\varnothing$, all propositions are thus false. We therefore write 2^{Prop} for the set of valuations on the set *Prop*, with typical element $\nu \in 2^{Prop}$. Given a Boolean formula φ over *Prop*, we write $\nu \models \varphi$ to denote that ν satisfies φ.

Traces are finite sequences of valuations, and we denote by ε the empty sequence. Given a trace $t \in (2^{Prop})^*$, the *length* $|t|$ of t is defined as its number of valuations. For $1 \leq i \leq |t|$, the ith valuation of t is denoted by $t(i)$. We set $t.first = t(1)$ and $t.last = t(|t|)$ and we denote by $t[i,j]$ the subsequence of t starting at position i and ending at position j. For instance, if $t = \nu_1\nu_2\nu_3\nu_4\nu_5$, then $t.first = \nu_1$, $t.last = \nu_5$ and $t[2,4] = \nu_2\nu_3\nu_4$.

Example 4. Consider the trace $\{\text{monitor}_1\}$ $\{\text{monitor}_1\}$ $\varnothing$ $\{\text{frozen}_1\}$ $\{\text{frozen}_1, \text{frozen}_2\}$ $\{\text{enter}_b, \text{frozen}_1, \text{frozen}_2\}$ $\{\text{hasPaint}, \text{frozen}_1, \text{frozen}_2\}$ of length 7 from the museum example. It reflects the scenario where, during the first two timesteps, both cameras work, camera 1 is monitored and camera 2 is not. At the third step, camera 1 is not any more monitored. Then, camera 1 is frozen, before camera 2. Next, the intruder enters the building via door b while both cameras are frozen, and finally steals the painting while the cameras are still frozen.

In the following, we may write traces with arrows between their valuations in order to emphasize the underlying state transitions that take place: $t = \nu_1 \rightarrow \nu_2 \rightarrow \nu_3 \rightarrow \nu_4 \rightarrow \nu_5$.

Regarding the trace semantics of attack trees that will be given in Definition 4, the OR operator will be understood as the union operation over sets of traces, whereas the two other operators SAND and AND will be given less classic interpretations that we present now.

3.3 Synchronized Concatenation

The *synchronized concatenation* $\odot$ slightly differs from the usual concatenation in formal languages and conveys the notion of sequential executions of scenarios; it will provide the semantics of the SAND operator in attack trees.

Definition 2 (Synchronized concatenation). *The synchronized concatenation of two traces is defined only if the last valuation of the former is equal to the first valuation of the latter, and simply concatenates the two traces by merging this common element. Formally,*

$$\nu_1 \ldots \nu_n \nu \odot \nu \nu_1' \nu_2' \ldots \nu_m' = \nu_1 \ldots \nu_n \nu \nu_1' \ldots \nu_m'.$$

Example 5. $\{\text{frozen}_1, \text{frozen}_2\}$ $\{\text{enter}_b, \text{frozen}_1, \text{frozen}_2\}$ $\odot$ $\{\text{enter}_b, \text{frozen}_1, \text{frozen}_2\}$ $\{\text{hasPaint}, \text{frozen}_1, \text{frozen}_2\}$ $=$ $\{\text{frozen}_1, \text{frozen}_2\}$ $\{\text{enter}_b, \text{frozen}_1, \text{frozen}_2\}$ $\{\text{hasPaint}, \text{frozen}_1, \text{frozen}_2\}$; the synchronized concatenation is possible thanks to the common matching valuation $\{\text{enter}_b, \text{frozen}_1, \text{frozen}_2\}$.

The synchronized concatenation $\odot$ is associative, so that binary $\odot$ suffices. We lift the synchronized concatenation to sets L, L' of traces by letting

$$L \odot L' = \{t \odot t' \mid t \in L, t' \in L' \text{ and } t \odot t' \text{ is defined}\}.$$

3.4   Parallel Composition

The *parallel composition* written ⋏ is adapted from [3] to traces. This operation reflects the meaning of achieving subgoals in a concurrent manner, and aims at capturing what the AND operator expresses in attack trees. We motivate its definition on an example with the concurrent achievement of two atomic goals: consider the AND-node from Fig. 2 and the following trace (a prefix of the trace in Example 4) realizing a successful hacking of both cameras, namely goal $\langle\neg\texttt{monitor}_2 \text{ to frozen}_1\rangle$ and goal $\langle\neg\texttt{monitor}_1 \text{ to frozen}_2\rangle$.

$$\underbrace{\{\texttt{monitor}_1\} \rightarrow \{\texttt{monitor}_1\} \rightarrow \varnothing \rightarrow \overbrace{\{\texttt{frozen}_1\} \rightarrow \{\texttt{frozen}_1,\texttt{frozen}_2\}}^{\langle\neg\texttt{monitor}_1 \text{ to frozen}_2\rangle}}_{\langle\neg\texttt{monitor}_2 \text{ to frozen}_1\rangle} \quad (1)$$

Right from the start, camera 1 gets a virus and cannot monitor camera 2 ($\texttt{monitor}_2$ is false). The observation does not change for one step, and then, camera 2 gets infected too ($\texttt{monitor}_1$ turns false). Then, camera 1 gets frozen first ($\texttt{frozen}_1$), and next camera 2 does too ($\texttt{frozen}_2$). Realizing the conjunction of the hacking subgoals means that they are executed concurrently: any transition of the global hacking task falls under one of the hacking subgoals, and the global task is embedded in the achievement of both subgoals. On the contrary, the following trace does not reflect a conjunction of the two hacking subgoals because the second transition does not serve any of the hacking subgoals.

$$\underbrace{\{\texttt{monitor}_1\} \rightarrow \{\texttt{monitor}_1,\texttt{frozen}_1\}}_{\langle\neg\texttt{monitor}_2 \text{ to frozen}_1\rangle} \rightarrow \underbrace{\{\texttt{monitor}_2\} \rightarrow \{\texttt{monitor}_2,\texttt{frozen}_2\}}_{\langle\neg\texttt{monitor}_1 \text{ to frozen}_2\rangle}$$

In concrete terms, a virus is launched on camera 1, then camera 1 gets frozen, then a virus is launched on camera 2 while camera 1 gets back to normal operation, then finally, camera 2 gets frozen. In this scenario, the second hacking task starts too late and the alarm is triggered (camera 1 is able to notice the discrepancy in camera 2's behaviour). The AND-node of the tree expresses that it is necessary for the two hacking subgoals to take place with some overlapping of their transitions to be successful. This is formalized in Definition 3 as *parallel composition* of traces which can be interpreted as follows: if one sees a trace, of length n, as displaying some "activity", every transition (*i.e.*, action) along this trace corresponds to a 1-length subinterval $[k, k+1] \subseteq [1, n]$, while subgoals correspond to arbitrary subintervals. In the example, the camera 1 hacking subgoal of the 5-length trace of Expression (1) corresponds to subinterval $[1, 4]$ and the camera 2 hacking subgoal corresponds to subinterval $[3, 5]$. Therefore each transition along this trace serves at least one of the two camera hacking subgoals.

More formally, let us say that the intervals $I_1, \ldots, I_m$ *cover* an interval I whenever

$$\bigcup_{\ell=1}^{m} I_\ell = I \text{ and each } [k, k+1] \subseteq I \text{ is contained in some } I_\ell.$$

We can now proceed to the formal definition of the parallel composition.

Definition 3 (Parallel composition). *A trace t is a* parallel composition *of traces $t_1, \ldots, t_m$ if there are m intervals $I_1, \ldots, I_m$ that cover $[1, n]$ for some positive integer n and such that $t[I_\ell] = t_\ell$, for every $1 \leq \ell \leq m$. We also simply say that traces $t_1, \ldots, t_m$* cover *trace t.*

Example 6. Figure 3 shows that the trace $t = \nu_1 \ldots \nu_7$ is a parallel composition of traces t_1, t_2 and t_3 with respective intervals $[1, 2]$, $[4, 7]$, $[2, 5]$. Indeed, all transitions $\nu_1 \to \nu_2$, $\nu_2 \to \nu_3$, $\ldots$, $\nu_6 \to \nu_7$ are covered. On the contrary, t is not a parallel composition of t_1, t_2 and t'_3 since the only interval candidates are respectively $[1, 2]$, $[4, 7]$, $[3, 5]$, but none of them fully includes the subinterval $[2, 3]$. In other words, the transition $\nu_2 \to \nu_3$ is not covered.

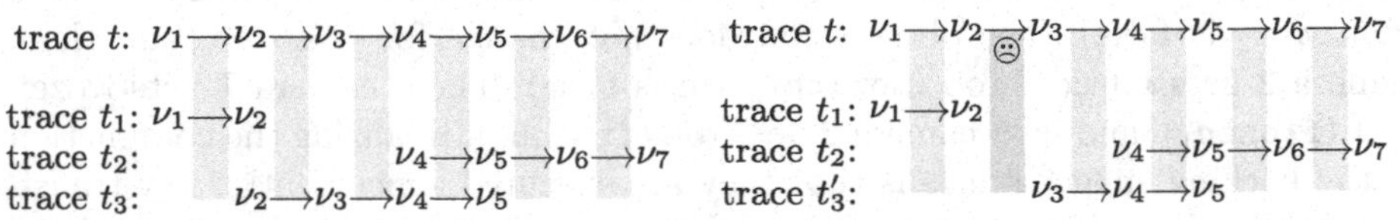

trace t: $\nu_1 \to \nu_2 \to \nu_3 \to \nu_4 \to \nu_5 \to \nu_6 \to \nu_7$ trace t: $\nu_1 \to \nu_2 \to \nu_3 \to \nu_4 \to \nu_5 \to \nu_6 \to \nu_7$

trace t_1: $\nu_1 \to \nu_2$ trace t_1: $\nu_1 \to \nu_2$

trace t_2: $\nu_4 \to \nu_5 \to \nu_6 \to \nu_7$ trace t_2: $\nu_4 \to \nu_5 \to \nu_6 \to \nu_7$

trace t_3: $\nu_2 \to \nu_3 \to \nu_4 \to \nu_5$ trace t'_3: $\nu_3 \to \nu_4 \to \nu_5$

Fig. 3. The trace t is a parallel composition of t_1, t_2, t_3 but not of t_1, t_2, t'_3.

The parallel composition reflects the conjunctive execution of activities and not the conjunction of the effects of these activities, which is a legitimate interpretation of the AND operator in attack trees (see the series-parallel graph semantics considered in [10]). Typically, requiring to open and to close a door does mean to attain a situation where the door is both open and closed.

Traces $t_1, \ldots, t_m$ may cover several traces, i.e. may have several parallel compositions. We let $\mathbb{M}(t_1, \ldots, t_m)$ be the set of parallel compositions of $t_1, \ldots, t_m$. For instance, $\mathbb{M}(\nu'\nu\nu, \nu\nu\nu'') = \{\nu'\nu\nu\nu'', \nu'\nu\nu\nu\nu''\}$. We lift the parallel composition to sets $L_1, \ldots, L_m$ of traces by letting

$$\mathbb{M}(L_1, \ldots, L_m) = \bigcup_{t_1 \in L_1, \ldots, t_m \in L_m} \mathbb{M}(t_1, \ldots, t_m).$$

It should be remarked that the synchronized concatenation $\odot$ is associative, so that binary $\odot$ suffices, while this is not the case for $\mathbb{M}$ in general: for example, $\nu_1\nu_2\nu_3\nu_4 \in \mathbb{M}(\nu_1\nu_2, \nu_3\nu_4, \nu_2\nu_3)$, but $\mathbb{M}(\mathbb{M}(\nu_1\nu_2, \nu_3\nu_4), \nu_2\nu_3) = \varnothing$ because $\nu_1\nu_2$ and $\nu_3\nu_4$ do not share any valuation.

3.5   Trace Semantics of Attack Trees

Now, we define the *trace semantics* of attack trees. Operators in attack trees are interpreted as operations on trace sets: OR means union $\cup$, SAND means synchronized concatenation $\odot$, and AND means parallel composition $\mathbb{M}$.

Definition 4 (Trace semantics of attack tree). *The* trace semantics *of an attack tree τ is a set of traces $L(\tau) \subseteq (2^{Prop})^*$, inductively defined on τ:*

$$
\begin{aligned}
L(\langle \iota \text{ to } \gamma \rangle) \quad &= \{t \in (2^{Prop})^* \mid t.first \models \iota \text{ and } t.last \models \gamma\}; \\
L(OR(\tau_1, \ldots, \tau_m)) \quad &= L(\tau_1) \cup \ldots \cup L(\tau_m); \\
L(SAND(\tau_1, \ldots, \tau_m)) &= L(\tau_1) \odot \ldots \odot L(\tau_m); \\
L(AND(\tau_1, \ldots, \tau_m)) \quad &= \mathbb{M}(L(\tau_1), \ldots, L(\tau_m)).
\end{aligned}
$$

Since the SAND operator relies on the associative operation $\odot$, we may sometimes assume for convenience and w.l.o.g. that the degree of the SAND-nodes is 2. In contrast, such an assumption would not hold for operator AND since $\mathbb{M}$ is not associative.

Example 7. Revisiting the attack tree τ from Example 3, the following trace from Example 4 is a possible trace of the museum example that can be explained by the tree τ, *i.e.*, that is in $L(\tau)$:

$$\{\text{monitor}_1\}\{\text{monitor}_1\} \varnothing \{\text{frozen}_1\}\{\text{frozen}_1, \text{frozen}_2\}$$
$$\{\text{enter}_b, \text{frozen}_1, \text{frozen}_2\}\{\text{hasPaint}, \text{frozen}_1, \text{frozen}_2\}.$$

Indeed, first its prefix $\{\text{monitor}_1\}\{\text{monitor}_1\} \varnothing \{\text{frozen}_1\} \{\text{frozen}_1, \text{frozen}_2\}$ belongs to $L(AND(\langle \neg\text{monitor}_2 \text{ to frozen}_1\rangle, \langle \neg\text{monitor}_1 \text{ to frozen}_2\rangle))$, as a parallel composition of $\{\text{monitor}_1\}\{\text{monitor}_1\} \varnothing \{\text{frozen}_1\} \in L(\langle \neg\text{monitor}_2 \text{ to }\rangle)$ $L(\langle \text{frozen}_1 \text{ to }\rangle)$ and $\varnothing\{\text{frozen}_1\}\{\text{frozen}_1, \text{frozen}_2\} \in L(\langle \neg\text{monitor}_1 \text{ to }\rangle)$ $L(\langle \text{frozen}_2 \quad \text{to} \quad \rangle)$. Second, its factor $\{\text{enter}_b, \text{frozen}_1, \text{frozen}_2\} \in$ $L(\langle \text{frozen}_1 \wedge \text{frozen}_2 \text{ to } \text{enter}_a\rangle)$, thus its belongs to the trace semantics of the subtree of τ rooted at the OR-node. Third, its suffix $\{\text{enter}_b, \text{frozen}_1, \text{frozen}_2\}\{\text{hasPaint}, \text{frozen}_1, \text{frozen}_2\}$ belongs to the trace semantics of the last child of the SAND-node.

4   Libraries

The attack tree synthesis problem seems trivial: the single-node tree $\langle \top \text{ to } \top \rangle$, where formula $\top$ means tautologically true, explains any trace! In order to synthesize interesting attack trees, we consider a *library*, that is a set of *refinement rules*, alike a context-free grammar rules. We will as much as possible keep close to notations introduced in [10]: for instance, we use ρ to denote a refinement rule.

In a context-free grammar style, we consider $\mathcal{G}$ a finite set of *non-terminal goals*, with typical elements g, g_1, g_2, and *terminal goals* that are atomic goals $\langle \iota \text{ to } \gamma \rangle$ (where ι, γ are Boolean formulas).

Definition 5 (Refinement rules and library). *A refinement rule (over $\mathcal{G}$) ρ is either a so-called* elementary rule $g \lhd \langle \iota \text{ to } \gamma \rangle$ *where ι, γ are Boolean formulas; or a rule $g \lhd OP(g_1, \ldots, g_m)$ where OP is an operator, $m \geq 1$, and $g_1, \ldots, g_m \in \mathcal{G}$. A refinement rule $g \lhd OP(g_1, \ldots, g_m)$* refines g. *The* arity *of a refinement rule is 0 if it is elementary, and the arity of the operator OP appearing in the rule otherwise.*

A library $\mathcal{L}$ over $\mathcal{G}$ is a finite set of refinement rules (over $\mathcal{G}$). The size of $\mathcal{L}$ is the total number of non-terminal goal occurrences that appear in all its rules, both in left-hand and right-hand sides of rules.

Example 8. Let us continue with the museum example where we add the proposition `incenter` read as "the intruder is in the control center". The following set of rules $\mathcal{L}_{\text{museum}}$ is library (and relies on the vocabulary of Example 2), where non-terminal goals are sentences written in italic to emphasize their role in our model of a library.

$$
\begin{cases}
\textit{go to center} & \lhd \; \langle \top \; \textbf{to incenter} \rangle \\
\textit{blow up a bomb} & \lhd \; \langle \textbf{incenter to frozen}_1 \wedge \textbf{frozen}_2 \rangle \\
\textit{enter via door a} & \lhd \; \langle \textbf{frozen}_1 \wedge \textbf{frozen}_2 \; \textbf{to enter}_a \rangle \\
\textit{enter via door b} & \lhd \; \langle \textbf{frozen}_1 \wedge \textbf{frozen}_2 \; \textbf{to enter}_b \rangle \\
\textit{take} & \lhd \; \langle \textbf{enter}_a \vee \textbf{enter}_b \; \textbf{to hasPaint} \rangle \\
\textit{disable camera 1} & \lhd \; \langle \neg \textbf{monitor}_2 \; \textbf{to frozen}_1 \rangle \\
\textit{disable camera 2} & \lhd \; \langle \neg \textbf{monitor}_1 \; \textbf{to frozen}_2 \rangle \\
\textit{steal} & \lhd \; \textsf{SAND}(\textit{disable cameras}, \textit{enter}, \textit{take}) \\
\textit{disable cameras} & \lhd \; \textsf{AND}(\textit{disable camera 1}, \textit{disable camera 2}) \\
\textit{disable cameras} & \lhd \; \textsf{SAND}(\textit{go to center}, \textit{blow up a bomb}) \\
\textit{enter} & \lhd \; \textsf{OR}(\textit{enter via door a}, \textit{enter via door b})
\end{cases}
$$

Goal *go to center* represents reaching the control center (without any precondition, which is written $\top$), while goal *blow up a bomb* represents setting up a bomb that will disable both cameras while being in the control center. The other goals are clear. Note that there are two rules that refine goal *disable cameras* which reflects different ways of disabling both cameras. Allowing for different refinement rules for an abstract goal is of utter importance because libraries are filled by experts analysing different systems: for example, the rule to hack a USB key may drastically vary depending on the underlying OS. Encapsulating alternatives into a single OR means that they may occur in the same system. Having a different rule for each alternative means that they correspond to different systems.

We now fix a library $\mathcal{L}$ over some set of non-terminal goals $\mathcal{G}$. We define $\mathcal{L}$-attack trees, in the spirit of what was called a "correct tree" in [10]: intuitively, they are attack trees obtained by iteratively applying refinement rules of the library on leaf-nodes until the leaves correspond to atomic goals.

Definition 6 ($\mathcal{L}$-attack tree). *An $\mathcal{L}$-attack tree is an attack tree τ (in the sense of Definition 1) equipped with a mapping ℓ that maps every node of τ onto a non-terminal goal of $\mathcal{G}$ in such a way that:*

– *if x is a leaf $\langle \iota \; \textbf{to} \; \gamma \rangle$, then the rule $\ell(x) \lhd \langle \iota \; \textbf{to} \; \gamma \rangle$ is in $\mathcal{L}$;*
– *if x is a node $\textsf{OP}(x_1, \ldots, x_k)$ then the rule $\ell(x) \lhd \textsf{OP}(\ell(x_1), \ldots, \ell(x_k))$ is in $\mathcal{L}$.*

The label $\ell(x)$ of a node in Definition 6 is a non-terminal goal. This non-terminal goal arising from the library carries information, such as text – as done in Example 8, or a CVE identifier[1]. It is this information that makes $\mathcal{L}$-attack trees readable to experts.

Example 9. Figure 4 shows two $\mathcal{L}_{\text{museum}}$-attack trees for $\mathcal{L}_{\text{museum}}$ defined in Example 8.

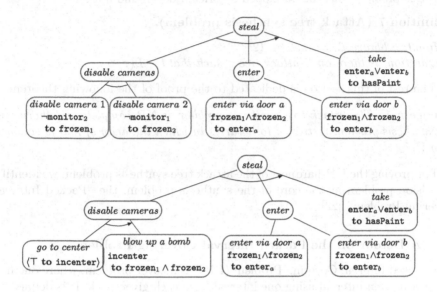

Fig. 4. Two $\mathcal{L}_{\text{museum}}$-attack trees.

We say that the non-terminal goal g *derives* the trace t if there exists an $\mathcal{L}$-attack tree τ whose root's label is g and such that t is in $L(\tau)$.

Given a library $\mathcal{L}$, we can always manage to find an equivalent library $\mathcal{L}'$ where all SANDs are binary, in the sense that the trace semantics of an $\mathcal{L}'$-attack tree is equal to trace semantics of some $\mathcal{L}$-attack trees, and vice versa. Note that $\mathcal{L}'$ can be computed in polynomial time in the size of $\mathcal{L}$.

In the rest of this paper, we assume that every refinement rule based on SAND operator has arity 2. Table 1 sums up the formal notions defined so far.

Table 1. Important formal notions defined in the paper.

Formal notions	Intuitive meanings
A trace	An observed attack (e.g. a log file)
An attack tree (Definition 1)	An explanation of an observed attack
A non-terminal goal	A high-level attack objective
A refinement rule	A known attack tree pattern
A library (Definition 5)	A set of known attack tree patterns
An $\mathcal{L}$-attack tree (Definition 6)	An explanation of an observed attack constructed with the known attack-tree patterns in $\mathcal{L}$

---

[1] CVE is a dictionary of publicly disclosed cybersecurity vulnerabilities and exposures https://cve.mitre.org/cve/.

5   Attack Tree Synthesis

The attack tree synthesis problem consists in building a tree (if any) that *explains* an observed trace t (e.g. a log file) in terms of a given library $\mathcal{L}$. Formally, we address the underlying decision problem for analyzing the complexity for this synthesis problem, but the developed algorithm does build a tree.

Definition 7 (Attack tree synthesis problem).

– *Input: a library $\mathcal{L}$, a trace $t \in (2^{Prop})^*$.*
– *Question: is there an $\mathcal{L}$-attack tree τ such that $t \in L(\tau)$?*

The rest of this section is dedicated to the proof of the following theorem.

Theorem 1. *The attack tree synthesis problem is NP-complete. Furthermore, the synthesis problem restricted to libraries in which the arity of* **AND** *is bounded is in* P.

For proving the NP-hardness of the attack tree synthesis problem, we identify a decision problem at the core of the synthesis problem: the "Packed Interval Covering Problem" [22].

5.1   A Detour on the Packed Interval Covering Problem

The Packed Interval Covering Problem (PIC) is a cover problem, where one has to cover a given interval using one interval from each given pack. It is defined as follows.

– Input: a non-empty interval I of integers and a family of finite sets $P_1, \ldots, P_m$ (*packs*) of subintervals of I.
– Question: are there subintervals $I_1 \in P_1, \ldots, I_m \in P_m$ such that $I = \displaystyle\bigcup_{k=1..m} I_k$?

Example 10. We borrow the example in [22]: for interval $[1, 9]$, there are three packs $\{[1, 6], [5, 9]\}$, $\{[1, 3], [4, 6], [7, 7]\}$, $\{[4, 4]\}$. Interval $[1, 9]$ can be covered by selecting $[5, 9]$, $[1, 3]$ and $[4, 4]$ in the respective packs, as shown in Fig. 5.

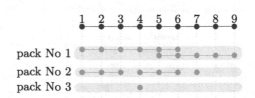

Fig. 5. Example of an instance of the Packed Interval Covering Problem.

Theorem 2 [22]. *PIC is NP-complete.*

5.2 NP-Hardness of the Synthesis Problem

We establish a reduction from PIC to the attack tree synthesis problem.

Consider an arbitrary instance of PIC with target interval $I = [1, N]$ and packs $(P_k)_{1 \leq k \leq m}$, each of the form $P_k = \{[m_j^k, n_j^k] \mid 1 \leq j \leq |P_k|\}$.

We now describe an instance $\langle \mathcal{L}, t \rangle$ of the attack tree synthesis problem as follows. Take N distinct propositions $p_0, \ldots, p_N$.

First, define trace $t = \{p_0\} \ldots \{p_N\}$ to encode the target interval $[1, N]$: each subtrace $\{p_{i-1}\}\{p_i\}$ of t of length 2 is intended to match integer $i \in [1, N]$.

Second, the library $\mathcal{L}$ contains exactly the following rules.

- Rule $g_{\text{select}(k,j)} \lhd \langle p_{m_j^k - 1} \text{ to } p_{n_j^k} \rangle$ for every $k \in \{1, \ldots, m\}$ and every $j \in \{1, \ldots, |P_k|\}$ that amounts to requiring that if the j-th interval $[m_j^k, n_j^k]$ of pack P_k is selected, then it is covered;
- Rule $g_{\text{pack}(k)} \lhd \text{OR}(g_{\text{select}(k,1)}, \ldots, g_{\text{select}(k,|P_k|)})$, for every $k \in \{1, \ldots, m\}$ requiring to select one of the $|P_k|$ intervals in the pack P_k;
- Rule $g_{\text{union}} \lhd \text{AND}(g_{\text{pack}(1)}, \ldots, g_{\text{pack}(m)})$ expressing that one must select an interval in each pack P_k;

Example 11. For the PIC instance of Example 10, we get trace

$$t = \{p_0\}\{p_1\}\{p_2\}\{p_3\}\{p_4\}\{p_5\}\{p_6\}\{p_7\}\{p_8\}\{p_9\}$$

and the following library:

$$
\left\{
\begin{array}{ll}
& g_{\text{select}(1,1)} \lhd \langle p_0 \text{ to } p_6 \rangle \\
g_{\text{union}} \lhd \text{AND}(g_{\text{pack}(1)}, g_{\text{pack}(2)}, g_{\text{pack}(3)}) & g_{\text{select}(1,2)} \lhd \langle p_4 \text{ to } p_9 \rangle \\
g_{\text{pack}(1)} \lhd \text{OR}(g_{\text{select}(1,1)}, g_{\text{select}(1,2)}) & g_{\text{select}(2,1)} \lhd \langle p_0 \text{ to } p_3 \rangle \\
g_{\text{pack}(2)} \lhd \text{OR}(g_{\text{select}(2,1)}, g_{\text{select}(2,2)}, g_{\text{select}(2,3)}) & g_{\text{select}(2,2)} \lhd \langle p_3 \text{ to } p_6 \rangle \\
g_{\text{pack}(3)} \lhd \text{OR}(g_{\text{select}(3,1)}) & g_{\text{select}(2,3)} \lhd \langle p_6 \text{ to } p_7 \rangle \\
& g_{\text{select}(3,1)} \lhd \langle p_3 \text{ to } p_4 \rangle
\end{array}
\right.
$$

The obtained instance $\langle \mathcal{L}, t \rangle$ is computed in polynomial time from the PIC instance $\langle I, P_1, \ldots, P_m \rangle$. Clearly, the instance $\langle \mathcal{L}, t \rangle$ of the attack tree synthesis problem is positive if, and only if, the original PIC instance $\langle I, P_1, \ldots, P_m \rangle$ is positive. Indeed, there is a correspondence between the choice of intervals in packs, and the children of nodes labelled by $g_{\text{pack}(1)}, \ldots, g_{\text{pack}(m)}$ whose respective semantics exhibits m subtraces that cover the full trace t.

5.3 NP-Membership of the Synthesis Problem

The following table shows the correspondence between some refinement rules and context-free grammars (CFG) rules in formal languages. Notice that there is no grammar rules counterpart for refinement rules with an AND operator.

Refinement rule	CFG production rule
$g \lhd \langle \iota \text{ to } \gamma \rangle$	$X \to a$
$g \lhd \text{OR}(g_1, g_2)$	$X \to Y \mid Z$
$g \lhd \text{SAND}(g_1, g_2)$	$X \to YZ$

Still, we are able to design an algorithm based on a variant of the classic bottom-up parsing algorithm "Cocke–Younger–Kasami algorithm" (CYK) [15,24,27]. The original algorithm answers whether some input context-free grammar can generate some input word. It relies on a *dynamic programming* solution that computes, for each subword by increasing length, the set of non-terminals that generate it.

Algorithm Design. As in CYK, we handle sets $\text{Goals}[i,j]$ that collect goals of $\mathcal{G}$ that derive the subtrace $t[i,j]$. Nevertheless, we cannot rely on the mere dynamic programming anymore since the three operators do not necessarily make use of decreasing intervals. The following example illustrates the phenomenon with an artificial example of library.

Example 12. For $Prop = \{p_1, p_2, p_3, p_4\}$, take trace $t = \{p_1\}\{p_2\}\{p_3\}\{p_4\}$ and the following library $\mathcal{L}$:

$$\begin{cases} \rho_1 : g \lhd \text{OR}(g') & \rho_4 : g \lhd \text{SAND}(g', g'') \\ \rho_2 : g' \lhd \text{SAND}(g, g) & \rho_5 : g \lhd \langle p_2 \text{ to } p_3 \rangle \\ \rho_3 : g \lhd \text{SAND}(g', g) & \rho_6 : g' \lhd \langle p_1 \text{ to } p_1 \rangle \end{cases} \quad \begin{aligned} \rho_7 &: g' \lhd \langle p_1 \text{ to } p_2 \rangle \\ \rho_8 &: g'' \lhd \langle p_3 \text{ to } p_4 \rangle \end{aligned}$$

Figure 6 shows an $\mathcal{L}$-attack tree for the trace t. Although the nodes marked * and the node marked ** are at different levels in the tree, we will see that both arise when computing $\text{Goals}[1,3]$ to parse subtrace $t[1,3] = \{p_1\}\{p_2\}\{p_3\}$.

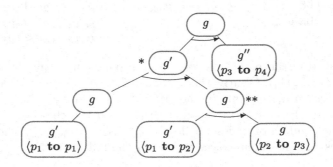

Fig. 6. An $\mathcal{L}$-attack tree for t.

Let us zoom on a bottom-up parsing of the trace t, by successively increasing the length of the subintervals $[i,j]$ to compute $\text{Goals}[i,j]$ that derives $t[i,j]$.

During the treatment of the 1-length interval $[1, 1]$, g' is put in $\texttt{Goals}[1, 1]$ thanks to Rule ρ_6, which allows next to add g by Rule ρ_1; $\texttt{Goals}[2, 2]$, $\texttt{Goals}[3, 3]$ and $\texttt{Goals}[4, 4]$ are empty.

We skip the computation for intervals of length 2, and focus on the treatment of interval $[1, 3]$: in order to obtain the subtree of Fig. 6 rooted at node marked * for subtrace $t[1, 3]$, the parsing procedure should have added goal g in $\texttt{Goals}[1, 3]$ according to Rule ρ_3 (corresponding to the marked ** node) before adding g' (node *) thanks to Rule ρ_2. But because of the mutual recursivity of the rules, it seems difficult to know *a priori* which of Rule ρ_2 and Rule ρ_3 should be considered first.

In order to face the potential inability to exhibit a hierarchy of the rules for an arbitrary input library, we propose an algorithm that iterates over rules until stabilization for each interval of the input trace.

Importantly, the ability to solve the synthesis problem even for libraries with mutual recursivity between rules is not a mere technical achievement but a true need: indeed, libraries may be fed incrementally by uncoordinated experts, which prevents us from requiring any sort of (in)dependencies between rules. Thus restricting to non recursive libraries (as for the museum Example 8) would be a very limited solution.

Regarding the technical aspects of our algorithm, the parsing of $\texttt{SAND}$-rules is handled with a minor adaptation of the CYK algorithm because of the tiny difference between classic concatenation and synchronized concatenation. On the contrary, since $\texttt{AND}$-rules of libraries do not have any counterpart in CF grammars, we resort to a novel method based on non-deterministically guessing one interval per subgoal, hence a non-deterministic algorithm.

Algorithm Pseudo-Code. Algorithm 1 presents the pseudo-code of our non-deterministic algorithm that decides the attack tree synthesis in polynomial-time. As in CYK, we consider each interval $[i, j]$ of $[1, n]$ by increasing length (line 1), and we compute $\texttt{Goals}[i, j]$ (in the **repeat-until** loop, lines 2–18) that is a set of goals that derive $t[i, j]$ (possibly the set of exactly all such goals when the *right* non-deterministic choices are taken). The **repeat-until** loop stops when $\texttt{Goals}[i, j]$ *stabilizes*, that is when nothing has been added to $\texttt{Goals}[i, j]$ in the last iteration.

We iterate over all the rules of the library and update $\texttt{Goals}[i, j]$ according to the semantics given in Definition 4. For a rule $g \lhd \langle \iota \textbf{ to } \gamma \rangle$, we add the goal g to $\texttt{Goals}[i, j]$ if ι holds at time i and γ holds at time j. For a rule $g \lhd \texttt{OR}(g_1, \ldots, g_m)$, as long as there is a goal g_k in $\texttt{Goals}[i, j]$, we add g to $\texttt{Goals}[i, j]$. For a rule $g \lhd \texttt{SAND}(g_1, g_2)$, if there is a mid-position t between time i and j such that g_1 is in $\texttt{Goals}[i, t]$ and g_2 is in $\texttt{Goals}[t, j]$, we add g to $\texttt{Goals}[i, j]$. For a rule $g \lhd \texttt{AND}(g_1, \ldots, g_m)$, we first non-deterministically choose intervals $I_1, \ldots, I_m$ included in $[i, j]$. In the case $I_1, \ldots, I_m$ is a covering of $[i, j]$ and goals $g_1, \ldots, g_m$ are respectively in $\texttt{Goals}[I_1], \ldots, \texttt{Goals}[I_m]$, we add g in $\texttt{Goals}[i, j]$. Note that if g is added in $\texttt{Goals}[i, j]$ then the rule $g \lhd \texttt{AND}(g_1, \ldots, g_m)$ can be applied to construct an attack tree. The reverse is false: it might be the case that the

---

Algorithm 1. attackTreeSynthesis($\mathcal{L}, t$): it has an accepting execution iff there is an $\mathcal{L}$-attack tree whose semantics contains t.

```
 1: for all intervals [i, j] of [1, n] by increasing length do
 2:   repeat
 3:     for all rules ρ in L do
 4:       match ρ do
 5:         case g ◁ ⟨ι to γ⟩:
 6:           if t(i) ⊨ ι and t(j) ⊨ γ then
 7:             Goals[i, j] := Goals[i, j] ∪ {g}
 8:         case g ◁ OR(g₁, ..., gₘ):
 9:           if there is 1 ≤ k ≤ m and gₖ ∈ Goals[i, j] then
10:             Goals[i, j] := Goals[i, j] ∪ {g}
11:         case g ◁ SAND(g₁, g₂):
12:           if there is i ≤ t ≤ j such that g₁∈Goals[i, t] and g₂∈Goals[t, j] then
13:             Goals[i, j] := Goals[i, j] ∪ {g}
14:         case g ◁ AND(g₁, ..., gₘ):
15:           non-deterministically choose  I₁, ..., Iₘ ⊆ [i, j]
16:           if I₁, ..., Iₘ covers [i, j] and g₁ ∈ Goals[I₁] and ... and gₘ ∈ Goals[Iₘ]
       then
17:             Goals[i, j] := Goals[i, j] ∪ {g}
18:   until Goals[i, j] stabilises
19: if (Goals[1, n] ≠ ∅) accept else reject
```

---

rule $g \lhd \text{AND}(g_1, \ldots, g_m)$ can be applied although g is not added to $\text{Goals}[i, j]$. Nevertheless, if the rule $g \lhd \text{AND}(g_1, \ldots, g_m)$ can be applied then there is an execution in which the goal g is added to $\text{Goals}[i, j]$.

At the end, the input is accepted exactly when $\text{Goals}[1, n]$ is not empty, that is, when the algorithm found that there is an attack tree for the full trace t.

Proposition 1 states the main properties of Algorithm 1.

Proposition 1

1. *Executions of* attackTreeSynthesis($\mathcal{L}, t$) *have length in* $poly(size(\mathcal{L}) + |t|)$.
2. *(Soundness) If there is an accepting execution of* attackTreeSynthesis($\mathcal{L}, t$)*, then there is an $\mathcal{L}$-attack tree τ such that $t \in L(\tau)$.*
3. *(Completeness) If there is an $\mathcal{L}$-attack tree τ such that $t \in L(\tau)$, then there is an accepting execution of* attackTreeSynthesis($\mathcal{L}, t$)*.*

Proof. Consider an execution of attackTreeSynthesis($\mathcal{L}, t$). At each iteration of the **repeat-until** loop (lines 2–18), the set $\text{Goals}[i, j]$ is increasing and bounded by finite $\mathcal{G}$. Choosing non-deterministically $I_1, \ldots, I_m \subseteq [i, j]$ consists in choosing $2m$ numbers in $[i, j]$, which can be done in polynomial-time. The rest is polynomial hence Point 1.

Also, the invariant "for every execution of attackTreeSynthesis($\mathcal{L}, t$), $\text{Goals}[i, j]$ is included in the set of goals that derive $t[i, j]$" entails Point 2. Finally, it suffices to consider the execution that chooses the right intervals at line 15 to get Point 3.

By Proposition 1, the attack tree synthesis problem is in NP. To achieve the proof of Theorem 1, it remains to restrict to libraries with bounded-arity AND-rules.

5.4   Libraries with Bounded-Arity AND-Rules

It can be observed that the combinatorics of the unbounded AND operator contributes to the problem's complexity. By bounding the AND operator arity in library $\mathcal{L}$, the resulting subclass of the synthesis problem falls into P.

To see this, observe that bounding the AND operator arity yields a polynomial number of covers, so that line 15 of Algorithm 1 can be replaced by a **for**-loop over all covers that executes a polynomial number of times in the arity m.

6   Conclusion

We have presented a mathematical setting that addresses an attack tree synthesis problem. In this contribution, we rely on a formal trace semantics of attack trees inspired from the path semantics proposed, *e.g.*, in [3,4]. Our setting exploits the ontology of library whose rules describe how a subgoal can be refined into a combination of subgoals; such combinations rely on any of the classic tree operators OR, SAND, and AND. The synthesis problem has two inputs: a library and a trace. It consists in building an attack tree whose refinements are provided by the input library and whose semantics contains the input trace. We have established that the (associated decision) problem is NP-complete. However, the proposed algorithm is only polynomial in the size of the trace. This is good news for the two following reasons. First, traces might be long objects (*e.g.*, log files). Second, the exponential blow up caused by the arity of AND rules in libraries should be tamed in practice: the library is often fixed, and a manually entered AND-rule in this library is unlikely to have a huge arity. We have implemented our algorithm in a humble educative prototype that the interested reader may find at http://attacktreesynthesis.irisa.fr/.

Regarding synthesis, our algorithm can be easily extended to keep track of subtrees: each time a goal is added in Goals, there is a matching subtree that we could build – as done for the classic CYK algorithm to return the syntactic tree of a parsed word. This is classic in dynamic programming and can still be exploited in our case.

Recently, new operators have been proposed to combine subgoals, among which are weak variants of existing operators, as done in [16] and [20]. We claim that our algorithm can be easily extended to deal with these operators.

This contribution opens several perspectives both theoretical and practical.

Theoretical Level. (1) We can investigate the use of first-order formulas in atomic goals $\langle \iota \textbf{ to } \gamma \rangle$, which would encompass the kinds of rules in [14] and [13]. We foresee the need for pattern-matching techniques or Robinson's unification that may impact the theoretical complexity of the problem. (2) We may also relax the problem by not synthesizing a single tree, but a minimal number of trees where each one parses a piece of the input trace. (3) We have to go beyond the case of a single trace, and synthesize a tree whose semantics contains (or equals) an input finite set of traces. This has already been addressed in [10] for the restricted case of OR and SAND-rules only, and regrettably with an incomplete procedure; the authors write that their procedure "either generates a correct tree or aborts" (in contrary, our approach is complete, see Point 3 of Proposition 1).

Practical Level. We foresee two main tracks. The first track regards the lengthy traces arising from concrete log files. Even if our algorithm is polynomial in this parameter, scalability is still an issue. We may explore abstractions of traces (*e.g.,* modulo stuttering equivalence), or subclasses of libraries with efficient parsing methods (*e.g.,* of the type LL(1)). The second track is ambitious and aims at bridging the gap between formal libraries and libraries in practice, such as the knowledge base of adversary tactics MITTRE ATT&CK[2]. We are not aware of any significant advance but of a humble recent degree project [1][3]. This topic should become very hot in the near future.

References

1. Åberg, O., Sparf, E.: Validating the meta attack language using mitre att&ck matrix (2019)
2. Audinot, M.: Assisted design and analysis of attack trees. Ph.D. thesis, Université de Rennes, vol. 1 (2018)
3. Audinot, M., Pinchinat, S., Kordy, B.: Is my attack tree correct? In: Foley, S.N., Gollmann, D., Snekkenes, E. (eds.) ESORICS 2017. LNCS, vol. 10492, pp. 83–102. Springer, Cham (2017). https://doi.org/10.1007/978-3-319-66402-6_7
4. Audinot, M., Pinchinat, S., Kordy, B.: Guided design of attack trees: a system-based approach. In: 31st IEEE Computer Security Foundations Symposium, CSF 2018, Oxford, United Kingdom, July 9–12, 2018, pp. 61–75. IEEE Computer Society (2018). https://doi.org/10.1109/CSF.2018.00012
5. Audinot, M., Pinchinat, S., Schwarzentruber, F., Wacheux, F.: Deciding the non-emptiness of attack trees. In: Graphical Models for Security - 5th International Workshop on Graphical Models for Security, Oxford, UK - July 8, 2018, pp. 25–38 (2018). https://doi.org/10.1007/978-3-319-46263-9_2
6. Bagnato, A., Kordy, B., Meland, P.H., Schweitzer, P.: Attribute decoration of attack-defense trees. Int. J. Secur. Softw. Eng. **3**(2), 1–35 (2012). https://doi.org/10.4018/jsse.2012040101
7. Baier, C., Katoen, J.: Principles of Model Checking. MIT Press, Cambridge (2008)
8. Board, E.A., Board, S.: Election operations assessment - threat trees and matrices and threat instance risk analyzer (TIRA) (2009). https://www.eac.gov/assets/1/28/Election_Operations_Assessment_Threat_Trees_and_Matrices_and_Threat_Instance_Risk_Analyzer_(TIRA).pdf

---

[2] https://attack.mitre.org/.
[3] http://www.diva-portal.org/smash/get/diva2:1350884/FULLTEXT01.pdf.

9. Fraile, M., Ford, M., Gadyatskaya, O., Kumar, R., Stoelinga, M., Trujillo-Rasua, R.: Using attack-defense trees to analyze threats and countermeasures in an ATM: a case study. In: Horkoff, J., Jeusfeld, M.A., Persson, A. (eds.) PoEM 2016. LNBIP, vol. 267, pp. 326–334. Springer, Cham (2016). https://doi.org/10.1007/978-3-319-48393-1_24

10. Gadyatskaya, O., Jhawar, R., Mauw, S., Trujillo-Rasua, R., Willemse, T.A.C.: Refinement-aware generation of attack trees. In: Livraga, G., Mitchell, C. (eds.) STM 2017. LNCS, vol. 10547, pp. 164–179. Springer, Cham (2017). https://doi.org/10.1007/978-3-319-68063-7_11

11. Hong, J.B., Kim, D.S., Takaoka, T.: Scalable attack representation model using logic reduction techniques. In: 2013 12th IEEE International Conference on Trust, Security and Privacy in Computing and Communications, pp. 404–411 (July 2013)

12. Hopcroft, J.E., Motwani, R., Ullman, J.D.: Introduction to Automata Theory, Languages, and Computation. Pearson International Edition, 3rd edn. Addison-Wesley, Boston (2007)

13. Ivanova, M.G., Probst, C.W., Hansen, R.R., Kammüller, F.: Attack tree generation by policy invalidation. In: Akram, R.N., Jajodia, S. (eds.) WISTP 2015. LNCS, vol. 9311, pp. 249–259. Springer, Cham (2015). https://doi.org/10.1007/978-3-319-24018-3_16

14. Jhawar, R., Lounis, K., Mauw, S., Ramírez-Cruz, Y.: Semi-automatically augmenting attack trees using an annotated attack tree library. In: Katsikas, S.K., Alcaraz, C. (eds.) STM 2018. LNCS, vol. 11091, pp. 85–101. Springer, Cham (2018). https://doi.org/10.1007/978-3-030-01141-3_6

15. Kasami, T.: An efficient recognition and syntax-analysis algorithm for context-free languages. Coordinated Science Laboratory Report no. R-257 (1966)

16. Mantel, H., Probst, C.W.: On the meaning and purpose of attack trees. In: 32nd IEEE Computer Security Foundations Symposium, CSF 2019, Hoboken, NJ, USA, June 25–28, 2019, pp. 184–199. IEEE (2019). https://doi.org/10.1109/CSF.2019.00020

17. (NESCOR), N.E.S.C.O.R.: Analysis of selected electric sector high risk failure scenarios, version 2.0 (2015). http://smartgrid.epri.com/doc/NESCOR%20Detailed%20Failure%20Scenarios%20v2.pdf

18. Pinchinat, S., Acher, M., Vojtisek, D.: Towards synthesis of attack trees for supporting computer-aided risk analysis. In: Canal, C., Idani, A. (eds.) SEFM 2014. LNCS, vol. 8938, pp. 363–375. Springer, Cham (2015). https://doi.org/10.1007/978-3-319-15201-1_24

19. Pinchinat, S., Acher, M., Vojtisek, D.: ATSyRa: an integrated environment for synthesizing attack trees. In: Mauw, S., Kordy, B., Jajodia, S. (eds.) GraMSec 2015. LNCS, vol. 9390, pp. 97–101. Springer, Cham (2016). https://doi.org/10.1007/978-3-319-29968-6_7

20. Pinchinat, S., Fila, B., Wacheux, F., Thierry-Mieg, Y.: Attack trees: a notion of missing attacks. In: Graphical Models for Security - 6th International Workshop, GraMSec@CSF 2019, Hoboken, NJ, USA, June 24, 2019, Revised Papers, pp. 23–49 (2019)

21. Poolsapassit, N., Ray, I.: Investigating computer attacks using attack trees. In: Craiger, P., Shenoi, S. (eds.) DigitalForensics 2007. ITIFIP, vol. 242, pp. 331–343. Springer, New York (2007). https://doi.org/10.1007/978-0-387-73742-3_23

22. Saffidine, A., Cong, S.L., Pinchinat, S., Schwarzentruber, F.: The packed interval covering problem is NP-complete. CoRR abs/1906.03676 (2019). http://arxiv.org/abs/1906.03676

23. Schneier, B.: Attack trees: modeling security threats. Dr. Dobb's J. Softw. Tools **24**(12), 21–29 (1999)
24. Sipser, M.: Introduction to the Theory of Computation. PWS Publishing Company, Boston (1997)
25. Vigo, R., Nielson, F., Nielson, H.R.: Automated generation of attack trees. In: IEEE 27th Computer Security Foundations Symposium, CSF 2014, Vienna, Austria, 19–22 July, 2014, pp. 337–350 (2014)
26. Wideł, W., Audinot, M., Fila, B., Pinchinat, S.: Beyond 2014: formal methods for attack tree-based security modeling. ACM Comput. Surv. **52**(4), 1–36 (2019)
27. Younger, D.H.: Recognition and parsing of context-free languages in time n^3. Inf. Control **10**(2), 189–208 (1967)

Asset-Centric Analysis and Visualisation of Attack Trees

Christopher Schmitz[1](✉), André Sekulla[2], and Sebastian Pape[1]

[1] Goethe University Frankfurt, Frankfurt am Main, Germany
{christopher.schmitz,sebastian.pape}@m-chair.de
[2] University of Siegen, Siegen, Germany
andre.sekulla@uni-siegen.de

Abstract. Attack trees are an established concept in threat and risk analysis. They build the basis for numerous frameworks aiming to determine the risk of attack scenarios or to identify critical attacks or attack paths. However, existing frameworks do not provide systematic analyses on the asset-level like the probability of successful or near-successful attacks on specific assets. But these insights are important to enable decision-makers to make more informed decisions. Therefore, a generic approach is presented that extends classical attack tree approaches by asset-specific analyses. For this purpose, the attack steps in the attack trees are annotated with corresponding assets. This allows identifying the attack paths each asset is exposed to. In combination with the standard attack tree parameter "probability of attack success", a set of complementary attack success and protection metrics can be applied on each step of the paths. Furthermore, an integrated visualisation scheme is proposed that illustrates the results in a comprehensible way so that decision-makers can intuitively understand what the metrics indicate. It also includes several features improving usability and scalability. As proof of concept, we have implemented a prototype of our proposed method.

Keywords: Attack trees · Attack graphs · Security metrics · Assets · Visualisation

1 Introduction

Attack trees are an established concept in threat and risk analysis. Security analysts can use them to determine or compare the risk of attack scenarios, to identify the most likely attack paths or to detect the most serious attack steps. However, current attack tree approaches do not link this information to the asset-level. Thus, they do not provide any systematic information on the assets' security or risk level. This includes, for example, the probability that an asset will be subject to a (non-) successful attack but also its impact on the overall risk. This information can be of crucial importance from a decision-making perspective, especially when it comes to the question of how to protect against certain attack scenarios in a resource-efficient way which often requires a prioritisation.

ⓒ Springer Nature Switzerland AG 2020
H. Eades III and O. Gadyatskaya (Eds.): GraMSec 2020, LNCS 12419, pp. 45–64, 2020.
https://doi.org/10.1007/978-3-030-62230-5_3

To address this issue, a generic approach is presented that complements existing attack tree-based risk assessment frameworks, such as the LiSRA framework [20], with meaningful information on the asset-level. This helps to assess the assets' security level in a systematic and less subjective way and helps decision-makers in mitigating the most critical assets first.

These insights are then visualised in a proper way so that decision-makers can intuitively understand possible attack routes as well as the individual attack chances and the risk sensitivity of each asset. This helps to reflect on the implemented security measures in order to better protect the assets at stake and support the analysis of the underlying risk assessment framework.

The approach consists of the following steps: First, the attack steps in the attack trees are annotated with corresponding assets. This link builds the basis for any security-related analysis with respect to these assets. The attack trees are then transformed into the new concept of "asset-centric attack graphs". They illustrate the attack paths leading to each individual asset and show which assets have to be attacked in which sequence to perform a successful attack. In combination with the "probability of attack success", which is a very common parameter for attack trees, new graph metrics are developed that provide meaningful insights on the asset-level [12]. These metrics are developed in such a way that they can be combined in a complementary way. This enables to visualise them in an integrated way so that decision-makers can intuitively understand the assets' security level. Since real-world infrastructures can be very complex and difficult to comprehend it is also shown how the visualisation scheme can cope with large infrastructures and complex attacks scenarios.

The remainder of this paper is organised as follows. After discussing the background and the related work in Sect. 2, Sect. 3 explains how asset-centric attack graphs can be derived from classical attack trees. Furthermore, meaningful graph metrics are proposed. Section 4 then presents the proposed visualisation scheme that describes how all the metrics can be illustrated in an intuitive way. Section 5 gives insights on the prototype implementation and evaluates the fulfilment of the requirements that were specified before. Finally, Sect. 6 concludes and points out future work ideas.

2   Background and Related Work

This section gives a brief introduction on attack trees and attack graphs and also gives an overview of related work in both areas.

2.1   Attack Trees

Attack trees are an established concept in threat and risk analysis initially introduced in 1999 by Schneier [21]. An attack tree illustrates an attack scenario from an attacker's perspective and represents it in a hierarchical, tree-based structure. The attack goal is located in the root node of the tree and is subsequently decomposed into more fine-grained attack steps using logical operations. The leaf nodes finally describe atomic attacker activities. Besides the standard OR and AND operators it is also possible to model more sophisticated operators like "sequential AND" (SAND) described by Jhawar et al. [7]. It is used to consider the sequence of attacker activities.

The principal idea of attack tree-based risk assessment approaches is to analyse the tree nodes with risk-related parameters. Common parameters are the probability of attack success, the costs to perform an attack step or the required skill level. Using bottom-up algorithms these parameters are then propagated up the tree in order to calculate the values for the entire attack tree [12]. There is a large number of approaches determining the risk of attack scenarios like this, for example, the ADTool or the LiSRA framework [11,12,20]. However, only a few approaches consider assets as a central artefact within attack trees [17], and there is no approach that provides systematic analyses of (aggregated) asset classes [12].

2.2 Attack Graphs

An attack graph is an abstraction of attack paths in an infrastructure. The first concept of an attack graph has been proposed by Phillips and Swiler in 1998 [18]. Much work has already been done to define security metrics that can be applied on attack graphs [6,12,13,24]. Several metrics have been defined that are based on the number and the structure of attack paths like the shortest path metric, the number of paths metric, the (normalised) mean of path lengths metric, or the median of path lengths metric [6]. In contrast to these metrics, that only rely on the attack paths, Wang et al. combine path information with the probabilities that specific exploits are executed. In this way, they determine the probability of multi-step attacks [22]. Although this is a specific metric for network security that does not aim to rate or compare certain assets, reachability metrics, in general, build the basis for some of the metrics introduced in the present work. It is shown how reachability metrics can be applied to asset-centric attack graphs. Furthermore, different variations of the standard reachability metric are, amongst other metrics (like the asset risk sensitivity), proposed in this work. The variations indicate, for instance, the probability of near-successfully attack specific assets. The combination of these variations enables an integrated perspective which constitutes one of the central elements of the visualisation scheme. Sawilla and Ou follow a different approach and apply an adapted Google PageRank algorithm on attack graphs in order to rate assets [19]. The assets are associated with vulnerability data from public databases. The algorithm evaluates the assets only in relation to each other. Therefore, it cannot be used to measure the assets' security absolutely. There also exist other approaches that consider assets as central artefacts [3,8,9]. However, they cannot be simply applied on (existing) attack trees but they require in-depth knowledge in threat modelling. Apart from that, systematic analyses of (aggregated) asset classes have not been covered by any of these approaches.

Besides that, a key limitation of many attack graph models is that they lack in scalability which makes it challenging to manage their complexity in user interaction. This is mainly due to the fact that real-world attack scenarios can be very complex. As a consequence, many of the attack graph models are too complex to be objectively evaluated by humans in a reasonable time [4,5,14,15,23]. However, efforts have been made to address this issue. Noel and Jajodia have proposed a technique to collapse attack graph elements through hierarchical aggregation so that attack graphs can be viewed and analysed at different abstraction levels [15]. In 2005, they described a filtering approach that allows the user to filter graph elements so that only the attack subgraphs of interest are shown [14]. Williams et al. represent attack graphs on the basis of treemaps (instead of classical node-link graphs), and they make use of spatial grouping and colour-coding to indicate the level of compromise [23]. Furthermore, they automatically group hosts with similar levels of compromise. Another approach aiming to reduce the complexity of attack graphs has been presented by Homer et al. [4]. They propose a technique to systematically identify and remove "useless" attack paths. Additionally, their approach performs a grouping of similar attack steps. However, these approaches were not designed to be applied to assets or asset hierarchies. In general, most visualisation approaches in information security are "special-purpose representations" [2].

3   Asset-Centric Analysis of Attack Trees

This section first introduces a scenario that is used to explain the approach. Furthermore, two exemplary attack trees are described for this scenario. Afterwards, it is explained how such trees can be annotated with assets. On this basis, the transformation rules are described to transform attack trees into asset-centric attack graphs. These transformations are necessary for all further asset-specific analyses. Finally, the metrics that build the foundation of the assets' analyses are presented.

3.1   Scenario Description

The infrastructure depicted in Fig. 1 is adapted from Homer et al. [4]. It illustrates a realistic network infrastructure which consists of three subnets: a demilitarized zone (DMZ), an internal office IT and an industrial control system (ICS) to control critical infrastructure components of an energy provider. Only the DMZ is directly accessible from the Internet. From there, the internal office IT can be accessed through a firewall. Only the Citrix server, which is located in the office IT, has access to the ICS - more precisely to the data historian that again has direct access to the communication server. The goal of the first attack scenario is to gain access to the communication server to modify its control logic. The scenario is illustrated in attack tree T_1 which is depicted in Fig. 2. It is assumed that three attack paths lead to the communication server. For illustration purposes, we give concrete examples for the attacks required to complete the first attack path. For the other paths, we focus more on the actual routes.

An attacker could run a vulnerability scanner from outside the network to discover vulnerabilities on the webserver (a_1). As a result, he might be able to

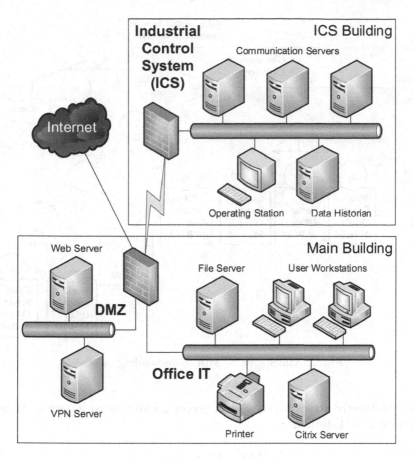

Fig. 1. Exemplary infrastructure

perform a command injection attack on the file server (a_2), and could then access the Citrix server by replacing a binary or shell script on the file server that will be executed on the Citrix server (a_3). From there, the data historian in the ICS could be reached by attacking the remote services (a_8). Due to the direct access to the communication server from the data historian, the attacker could finally execute malicious code on the target (a_9). So the first attack path is:

$$a_1 \rightarrow a_2 \rightarrow a_3 \rightarrow a_8 \rightarrow a_9$$

Alternatively, one could target the VPN server (a_4) and attack the Citrix server from there (a_5). Then, an attacker could perform a_8 and a_9 in the ICS, as described above. Therefore, the second attack path is:

$$a_4 \rightarrow a_5 \rightarrow a_8 \rightarrow a_9$$

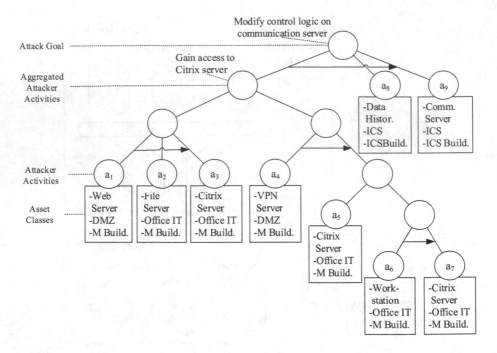

Fig. 2. Attack tree T_1 with corresponding assets

Instead of directly attacking the Citrix server an alternative attack path is to first attack a workstation:

$$a_4 \rightarrow a_6 \rightarrow a_7 \rightarrow a_8 \rightarrow a_9$$

The workstation may not be as protected as the Citrix server but may have more permissions to access the Citrix server than an external connection via the VPN server allows. It is assumed that the attacker has the privileges for lateral movements in the network unless otherwise specified by defining a specific attack in order to gain access to another network or asset in general.

The second attack scenario is represented by attack tree T_2 which is shown in Fig. 3. It is used to demonstrate the scalability for multiple attack trees. Unlike the first tree, it does not target the communication server but the workstation.

3.2 Annotation of Attack Trees with Assets

The attacker activities of an attack tree can be annotated with different assets, e. g. server assets, security zones or buildings. From a modelling perspective, it makes more sense to annotate asset classes instead of specific assets because of their higher abstraction level. For reasons of readability the terms asset is used in the following instead of "asset class". A comprehensive overview of assets can be found in the ISO/IEC 27005 risk management standard that comes up with

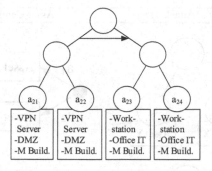

Fig. 3. Attack tree T_2 with corresponding assets

a hierarchical overview of assets. It differentiates between primary assets and supporting assets. Primary assets are the organisation's business processes & activities and sensitive information, such as trade and business secrets. Both of them can be of crucial importance to an organisation's success. More interesting from a security engineering perspective are supporting assets because they need to be protected by security measures in the first place. This also becomes clear from the ISO/IEC 27005 definition: "These assets have vulnerabilities that are exploitable by threats aiming to impair the primary assets of the scope (processes and information)." Therefore, only supporting assets are used for annotation.

The standard defines an asset hierarchy covering a wide range of assets, from hardware over software to location assets that include, for instance, security zones and buildings. However, especially for specific attacks, it makes sense to refine these assets with respect to attack-relevant characteristics to cope with attack scenarios targeting more specific types of attack vectors. For example, the asset smart meter (which is relevant for the electric sector) could be differentiated with respect to the supported remote data transmission standard (GSM/GPRS, WiFi, Bluetooth, Ethernet etc.). This allows that even specific attacks, such as those targeting only smart meters supporting a WiFi transmission, can be precisely assigned to individual assets.

The assigned assets should have the same level of abstraction as the respective attacks. Accordingly, it may be useful to merge similar assets, e. g. comparable workstations that are exposed to similar attacks. A similar host-grouping is applied by Homer et al. in order to reduce complexity [4]. On the other hand, in case of very heterogeneous assets, it makes sense to split these assets into different assets. This enables a more fine-grained analysis. For example, workstations in the ICS might be subject to different attacks than workstations in the office IT.

3.3 Transformation of Attack Trees into Asset-Centric Attack Graphs

Annotated attack trees can be transformed into so-called "asset-centric attack graphs". The general idea of attack graphs is to systematically illustrate all pos-

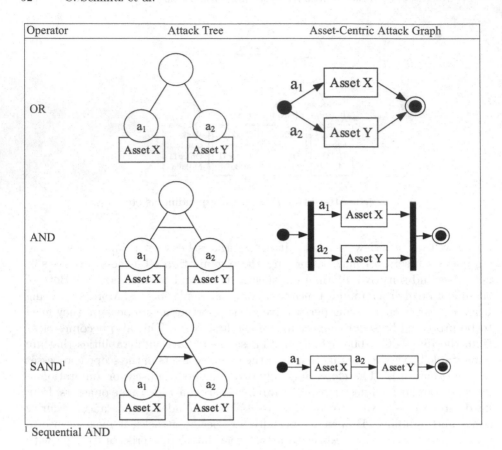

Fig. 4. Transformation of attack tree to attack graph patterns (based on [10])

sible attack paths that are required to achieve the goal of an attack scenario. Asset-centric in this context means that each node represents an asset. Therefore, asset-centric attack graphs show which assets have to be attacked in which sequence to perform a successful attack. Attack paths are thus represented on the level of network topology which typically increases the comprehensibility [4].

The general idea to transform attack trees into attack graphs is already described in literature [10]. The rules to transform an asset-annotated attack tree into an asset-centric attack graph is shown in Fig. 4. If an asset is represented by different nodes in the graph after applying these rules, they must be merged. It is also important to ensure that no cycle is created, as the graphs used in the following are assumed to be acyclic. This can either be ensured by post-annotation checks that indicate which (sub) trees have to be remodelled or by real-time checks which requires a tool-based annotation of assets. After applying the transformation rules on the initial attack trees in Fig. 2 and Fig. 3 the asset-centric attack graph in Fig. 5 is constructed.

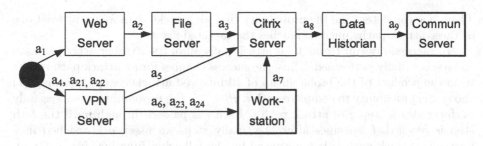

Fig. 5. Asset-centric attack graph focusing on physical assets

The primary purpose of the resulting graph in Fig. 5 is to provide a better understanding of the relation between attacks paths and assets. This is why it concentrates on physical assets (server and workstation assets) only. It must be noted that in case of parallel attack steps of different attack paths the tree does not allow to unambiguously distinguish which attack steps belong to which path (e. g. whether a_6 or a_{23} is a direct successor of a_4). This is different for the data structure used for the analysis. However, the graph still shows the sequence of attack steps required to successfully attack a certain asset. This helps to identify neuralgic points, for instance, that all attacks on the communication server run over the Citrix server and the data historian. It also gives a first indication of how exposed the assets are to attacker activities.

The presented approach could generally directly start with adequately constructed attack graphs without considering attack trees before. However, to extend the scope to the popular concept of attack trees, it makes sense to describe the process starting with attack trees.

3.4   Security Metrics

In this subsection, we introduce security metrics that can be applied on the assets in an attack graph. The probability of attack success is a very common metric for attack trees. The counterpart for the analysis at the asset-level, that is introduced here, is the *probability of successful asset attack*. Another metric is the asset (non-) reachability that describes the probability that an attacker is (not) able to reach the targeted asset at all. Both metrics can be used in combination to derive for each asset how many of the attack attempts can be successfully mitigated. These metrics also allow to derive the probability that an asset is reached but not successfully attacked, in the following referred to as *near-successful asset attack*, although those attacks can even be more challenging than others in practice. Another central metric is the *risk sensitivity* of an asset which measures the maximum impact a specific asset can have on the overall risk.

Successful Asset Attack. To determine the attack success for an asset v one must first calculate the probability for each attack path leading up to this asset.

Then, one can determine the probability that an attacker can follow at least one of these attack paths until he reaches the targeted asset.

To successfully run through an attack path all of its attacker activities have to be successfully performed. Thus, the success chances for an attack path results from the product of the probabilities of all involved attacker step. Equation (1) shows the probability to complete path i. $P(\alpha_{ij})$ is the probability to successfully perform attack step j of attack path i. Path i is passed through until the k-th step is reached. k specifies after how many steps an asset v is reached in a particular attack path i. It is returned by the following function: $k_i^v := f(i, v)$. So $P(s_i^v)$ calculates the probability for the complete path i.

$$P(s_i^v) = P\left(\bigcap_{j=1}^{k_i^v} \alpha_{ij}\right) = \prod_{j=1}^{k_i^v} P(\alpha_{ij}) \qquad (1)$$

Often an asset can be reached via several attack paths so an attacker can try different ways one after another. The probability to successfully perform (the first k steps of) at least one attack path results from the union set of all attack paths I_v containing asset v. This is reflected by the inclusion-exclusion principle, also known as sieve formula presented in Eq. (2) [1].

$$P(S^v) = P\left(\bigcup_{i=1}^{|I_v|} s_i^v\right) = \sum_{t=1}^{|I_v|}(-1)^{t-1}\left(\sum_{1\le i_1<...<i_t\le|I_v|} P(s_{i_1}^v \cap ... \cap s_{i_t}^v)\right) \qquad (2)$$

It defines a summation over all t-element subsets $\{i_1, ..., i_t\}$ for each attack path $\{1, ..., I_v\}$ that contain asset v. It must be noted that the union of attack paths is specified by Eq. (3) ensuring that each attacker activity $\alpha_{ik_i^v}$ is considered only once, even if it appears in several attack paths. The rationale is that a single attacker activity (that is defined from one asset to another) must not be counted multiple times, even if it appears in several paths running in parallel. For example, if the attacker activity a_6 (from the VPN server to the workstation) would occur in both attack trees T_1 and T_2, it would still only be included once in the calculation of the workstation's attack probability. The reason for this is that it is the same attack step by definition.

$$P(s_{i_1}^v \cap ... \cap s_{i_t}^v) = \prod_{\alpha_{ik}\in\{s_{i_1}^v,...,s_{i_t}^v\}} P(\alpha_{ik_i^v}) \qquad (3)$$

Asset Non-reachability. The reachability is calculated similarly to the attack success. The only difference is that an attacker only has to pass the first $k - 1$ attack steps because then he can reach the asset and can continue with $k - th$ step directly targeting the final asset. Therefore, the reachability of an asset v for attack path i is represented by Eq. (4).

$$P(r_i^v) = P\left(\bigcap_{j=1}^{k_i^v-1} \alpha_{ij}\right) = \prod_{j=1}^{k_i^v-1} P(\alpha_{ij}) \qquad (4)$$

The probability that at least one of the $|I_v|$ attack paths are performed successfully is calculated using the sieve formula (see Eq. (5)).

$$P(R^v) = \sum_{t=1}^{|I_v|} (-1)^{t-1} \left(\sum_{1 \le i_1 < ... < i_t \le |I_v|} P(r_{i_1}^v \cap ... \cap r_{i_t}^v) \right) \tag{5}$$

The constraint that each attacker step must not appear multiple times also applies for the reachability as shown in Eq. (6).

$$P(r_{i_1}^v \cap ... \cap r_{i_t}^v) = \prod_{\alpha_{ik} \in \{r_{i_1}^v, ..., r_{i_t}^v\}} P(\alpha_{ik_i^v}) \tag{6}$$

The probability of an asset's non-reachability builds the counterpart that indicates how many per cent of all attacks do not reach the asset v. It is calculated as the complementary probability and is shown in Eq. (7).

$$P(\overline{R^v}) = (1 - P(R^v)) \tag{7}$$

Near-Successful Asset Attack. The probability that an asset is reached but not successfully attacked is derived from both the attack success and the reachability metric. That means the first $k - 1$ attack steps are successful but the the $k - th$ step fails. It is shown in Eq. (8).

$$P(n_i^v) = \prod_{j=1}^{k_i^v - 1} P(\alpha_{ij}) \times \prod_{j=k_i^v}^{k_i^v} (1 - P(\alpha_{ij})) \tag{8}$$

$$= \prod_{j=1}^{k_i^v - 1} P(\alpha_{ij}) \times \left(1 - P(\alpha_{ik_i^v})\right) \tag{9}$$

Finally, $P(n_i^v)$ is inserted into the sieve formula in Eq. (10) with the constraint shown in Eq. (11).

$$P(N^v) = P\left(\bigcup_{i=1}^{|I_v|} n_i^v \right) = \sum_{t=1}^{|I_v|} (-1)^{t-1} \left(\sum_{1 \le i_1 < ... < i_r \le |I_v|} P(n_{i_1}^v \cap ... \cap n_{i_t}^v) \right) \tag{10}$$

$$P(n_{i_1}^v \cap ... \cap n_{i_t}^v) = \prod_{\alpha_{ik_i^v} \in \{r_{i_1}^v, ..., r_{i_t}^v\}} P(\alpha_{ik_i^v}) \tag{11}$$

Additionally, it is possible to derive the asset's self-protection capability from both the *near-successful asset attacks* and the *successful asset attacks*. The self-protection capability is independent of exogenous infrastructural factors, i. e., the self-protection capability of a specific server asset is not influenced by its location in a network topology.

Asset Risk Sensitivity. An asset's risk sensitivity determines how sensitive the overall risk reacts on changes to an asset's vulnerability. So it also serves as a measure of protection efficiency. It is assessed as follows: first, all attacker activities directing to the asset to be analysed are identified. They can be read directly from the asset-centric attack graph (see Fig. 5). The Citrix server, for instance, is exposed to the three attacker activities a_3, a_5 and a_7. These attacker activities are then assumed to be completely secure respectively completely insecure. The overall risk is then simulated for both states. The difference between both risk values (maximum risk range) represents the maximum impact, ceteris paribus, the asset can have on the overall risk. Technically, the insecure state is modelled by temporarily setting the probability of successful asset attack for the $k-th$ attack step required to reach asset v in attack path i to 1. Equation (12) expresses the state more formally.

$$P^v_{insecure} := P(\alpha_{ik^v_i}) = 1 \qquad \forall\, i \in I_v \tag{12}$$

The secure state is modelled similarly but with a probability of a successful asset attack of 0 (see Eq. (13)).

$$P^v_{secure} := P(\alpha_{ik^v_i}) = 0 \qquad \forall\, i \in I_v \tag{13}$$

The approach presented in this paper extends basic attack tree approaches by asset-specific analyses. Such an attack tree approach can be used to simulate the risk for both states (e. g. LiSRA) [20]. Finally, the difference of both risk values determines the risk sensitivity of an asset v, denoted as ρ^v (see Eq. (14)).

$$\rho^v = \Delta Risk(P^v_{secure}, P^v_{insecure}) \tag{14}$$

In Sect. 4 it is shown how the proposed set of complementary metrics can be visualised in an integrated way.

4   Asset-Centric Visualisation of Attack Graphs

This section proposes a visualisation scheme illustrating the metrics presented in Sect. 3.4 in a comprehensible and self-explanatory way. The scheme aims to support decision-makers in analysing attack scenarios and to enable more informed decisions. As already discussed, real-world attack trees and attack graphs are often far too complex to be objectively evaluated by humans in a reasonable time. For example, Homer et al. have automatically generated the attack graph for basically the same attack scenario also used in this work. They have used the popular MulVAL (Multihost Multistage Vulnerability Analysis) attack graph tool suite [16]. Although the scenario does not seem to complex, the resulting graph consists of about 130 nodes [4]. This example demonstrates the need for features (cf. Sect. 4.3) supporting decision-makers to analyse complex infrastructures with a large number of assets and attacks. They are proposed in the following.

4.1   Requirements

The authors have elicited the following key requirements and criteria that have to be fulfilled from a practical viewpoint:

R1 An understandable and comprehensible visualisation of the results. Even users with a lack of technical or security know-how should be able to understand and use the results. This ensures that also less specialised staff from small and medium-sized organisations are able to benefit from the approach. Therefore, the metrics presented must be self-explanatory so that it becomes clear what the metrics indicate.

R2 The most critical threats and attack targets must be identifiable and stand out from less critical threats and attack targets. The user's focus should be immediately directed to the most critical points of the system in order to be able to take measures as quickly and as effective as possible.

R3 Besides that, another key requirement is scalability. A scalable visualisation enables to analyse complex real-world scenarios with large attack trees. Although this aspect is of high practical relevance many attack graph approaches have fundamental scalability problems [15].

4.2   Metrics Visualisation

Figure 6 illustrates an overall view that incorporates the proposed metrics into the asset-centric attack graph.

Attack Success. The attack success metrics introduced in Sect. 3.4 have been developed in such a way that they can be combined in a complementary way. For this purpose, the values of the three core metrics are presented in a bullet-based scheme. Each metric is represented by different coloured bullets (red, green, white). Their values are then mapped to the corresponding number of bullets on a scale with 20 bullets, i. e. a probability of successful asset attack of 0.50 yields 10 bullets. The concept of coloured bullets with a scale of 5 per cent per bullet makes it easy to comprehend and to compare the information at first sight. The colour coding for the metrics is shown in Table 1.

Figure 6 shows the use in practice. The boxes at the bottom of each asset icon show the integrated view. For example, 50% (10 white bullets) of the attacks do not reach the Citrix server. 40% (8 red bullets) of all attacks are successful, whereas 10% (2 green bullets) can be blocked at the asset. Additionally, the relation between red and green bullets of an asset indicates its self-protection capability. Moreover, it can be seen that the percentage of attacks reaching a certain asset (sum of red and green bullets) decreases the deeper the asset is located in the infrastructure and the less inbound bullets paths it has. The same holds for the percentage of successful attacks per asset (number of red bullets), and therefore also for the number of blocked attacks (number of green bullets).

Table 1. Symbols for metrics visualisation

Symbol	Formula	Description
●	$P(S^v)$	Probability that an attacker successfully attacks asset v (successful asset attack)
●	$P(N^v)$	Probability that an attacker reaches but not successfully attacks asset v (near-successful asset attack)
○	$P(\overline{R^v})$	Probability that an attacker does not reach asset v (asset non-reachability)
◐	ρ^v	Risk sensitivity of asset v

Risk Sensitivity. Another metric is the risk sensitivity of an asset that measures the maximum impact an asset can have on the overall risk. It is illustrated with a coloured protection shield at the right top corner of each asset (from green = *low* to red = *high*). The green shields for the two ICS servers in Fig. 6, for instance, indicate that the overall risk reacts less sensitive to changes of the ICS servers' vulnerability than on the vulnerability of the Citrix server which occurs in all attack paths. Although the adverse impact of a compromised ICS server is much higher, far fewer attacks do reach these servers as indicated by the attack success metrics.

Attack Paths. Besides the risk sensitivity and the attack success metrics, it is also essential to understand the attack paths and the attacker activities leading to the respective assets. An attack path connects the assets and illustrates which assets have to be attacked in which sequence. Moreover, the number of inbound and outbound attack paths per asset is illustrated as shown in Fig. 6. They represent to which attacker activities an asset is exposed to and which attacks can be performed from which asset. The number of attacks from asset to asset is represented by the width of the respective edges and is also shown textually. For example, the workstation can be attacked by three different attacker activities - all of them require the VPN server to be successfully attacked first. More detailed information is provided by a mouseover function that displays the concrete attacker activities, their success chances and also refers to the attack trees they originate from.

4.3   Usability and Scalability Features

This section presents features to provide a more usable and scalable view on the security-relevant aspects of the analysed attack scenarios. This is important since it poses a big challenge in practice.

Layered View. The overall view depicted in Fig. 6 provides detailed insights for each asset. Although this detailed view can be reasonable not all details and aspects are always necessary. For complex infrastructures, it can even produce an information overload. Therefore, strong scalability features are needed.

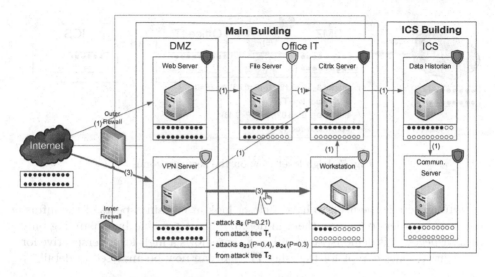

Fig. 6. Detailed view (Colour figure online)

Following the ISO/IEC 27005 definition assets can be structured hierarchically so that, for instance, each Exchange server asset is part of the mail server asset which again is part of the general server asset and so on. Asset hierarchies can also be defined individually. For example, each server type is part of a specific security zone, as long as this definition matches the asset annotation in the attack trees. These hierarchies enable to aggregate all metrics to the next higher level (e. g. from server level to level of security zones). This can be achieved by calculating the median and the standard deviation for the lower level assets. Although the median is not an exact metric it still provides a good overview of the asset's security. Figure 7 shows such a high-level perspective where all metrics at the physical asset level are aggregated to the level of security zones. For the ICS zone this yields to $P(S^{ICS}) = Median(0.15, 0.05) = 0.10$, $P(U^{ICS}) = Median(0.25, 0.10) = 0.175$, and $P(\overline{R^{ICS}}) = Median(0.6, 0.85) = 0.725$. The presentation of the standard deviations is triggered by a mouseover effect.

Additionally, the number of inbound and outbound attack paths to and from each asset is aggregated to the next higher level by summing. For example, the DMZ has 4 inbound attack paths (1 to the webserver and 3 to the VPN server) and 5 outbound attack paths leading to the office IT (1 to the file server, 1 to the Citrix server and 3 to the workstation). This is calculated by summing up the paths for the respective asset.

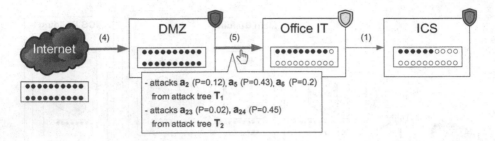

Fig. 7. High-level view on the security zones

Often there is the need to have a closer look at certain aspects of the infrastructure in order to analyse them in detail. This is possible by expanding only these aspects. It is demonstrated in Fig. 8 that shows a high-level perspective for all security zones except for the office IT that can now be analysed in detail.

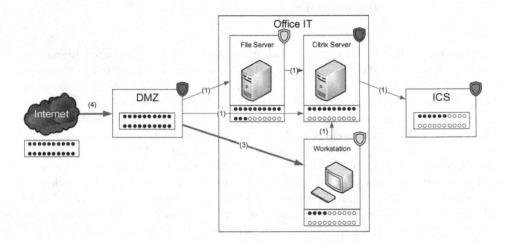

Fig. 8. Focused view on the office IT

Filter Functionality. Also, filtering functions are provided so that the most critical threats stand out from less critical threats and that the user is immediately directed to the neuralgic points. As described before, the visualisation scheme is scalable and supports the analysis of multiple attack scenarios. By default, all scenarios are covered by the analysis. Depending on the target of evaluation it is also possible to display only a subset of scenarios and assets. For example, if a decision-maker wants to analyse the physical security of the ICS building he can display all physical assets as well as the asset "ICS building" and hide all others.

Another filter enables to only display assets with an actual attack vector. Since no attack path in the presented scenario involves the printer or the operating station both assets are not displayed by default.

Additionally, a threshold can be set for each of the metrics so that only those assets with a score above are shown, i. e. a threshold for the probability of successful asset attack of 0.1 would hide all assets with lower attack chances. This filter can also be used complementary to the layered view. Applied to the view of Fig. 8 the workstation would be hidden in this case. This makes it possible to obtain only the necessary and relevant information which is essential especially for complex infrastructures.

Data Reduction. An effective approach for reducing complexity is host-grouping techniques [4]. As described in the section on annotating assets, comparable assets that are exposed to similar attacks should be grouped. For example, the workstation node might represent a grouping of many workstations with comparable configurations. This can significantly reduce the redundancy of data.

5   Prototype Implementation and Evaluation

In this section the developed prototype is described. In addition, it is briefly discussed to what extent the requirements for the visualisation listed above have been met.

5.1   Implementation

The presented approach has also been implemented as a proof of concept in Java. Figure 9 gives an impression of how the GUI looks like. The tool allows importing a single attack tree or an entire directory of attack trees on the client computer. The import function supports the XML format. The XML structure is based on the widely used ADTool that is also supported by the LiSRA framework [11]. The attacker activities of the imported trees can be annotated with assets directly in the tool. In the lower part of the tool there is an exemplary filtering function to exclude certain assets from the analysis by name or by threshold values. Additionally, important analysis results are summarised on the right side.

5.2   Evaluation of the Visualisation Requirements

The fulfilment of the previously defined requirements is briefly discussed in the following, concentrating on the core aspects. The borders are not clearly demarcated. Some explanations also fulfil another requirement to some extent.

R1 The first requirement addresses aspects like understandability and comprehensibility. According to Homer et al., administrators, who typically deal with network structure plans on a regular basis, will find the representation of attack paths on the level of network topology easier to understand than

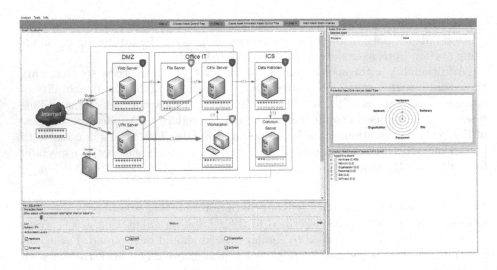

Fig. 9. Prototype implementation

complex attack graphs [4]. Furthermore, the metrics are presented in an integrated way. Their representation allows a quite intuitive interpretation of the values.

R2 The most important information must be immediately clear (see R1) and obvious at first glance. This requirement is ensured by the filtering functionality that hides all non-critical assets and attacks. Furthermore, the proposed metrics are displayed graphically next to the corresponding assets. This allows the metrics to be immediately associated with the correct assets.

R3 To meet the requirement of scalability various features have been integrated. The most important is the layered view. In addition to a very fine-granular view also aggregated views are supported enabling a high-level analysis, as shown in the example of the view for analysing security zones. All metrics are automatically re-calculated according to the chosen abstraction level. Starting from this view, it is possible to navigate through the infrastructure, for instance, by following the critical assets. Additionally, this can be complemented by the filter functionality that allows hiding the non-relevant assets that are out-of-scope or non-critical.

6   Conclusion and Future Work

Attack trees are an established concept in threat and risk analysis that is used to analyse entire attack scenarios and their attacker activities. They enable to identify the most likely attack paths or the most serious attacks. However, there are no attack tree approaches that provide systematic analyses on the asset-level. But this is important from a defenders' perspective to better understand the security and risk of each asset.

Therefore, a novel approach has been proposed that extends attack tree frameworks by linking the attacker activities in the trees to the asset-level. These annotated attack trees can then be transformed into an asset-centric attack graph that illustrates the attack paths for each asset. Together with the standard attack tree parameter "probability of attack success" these paths enable to apply a set of complementary security metrics that give meaningful insights for each asset. To enable these calculations novel metrics like the asset risk sensitivity or the near-successful asset attack have been proposed, partially based on existing reachability metrics. One of the main contributions concerning the security metrics lies in the combination of (partially new) metrics which enable an integrated visualisation. Furthermore, a visualisation scheme has been developed to integrate these complementary metrics into the asset-centric attack graph. All results are presented in such a way that decision-makers can intuitively understand the attack paths as well as the rationale for the individual attack chances and the risk sensitivity of each asset. Since usability and scalability issues pose a big challenge in the visualisation of attack graphs several features have been proposed to cope with complex attack scenarios. The approach has also been implemented in a prototype. The next step will be to conduct a user study to systematically evaluate and improve the approach from a users' perspective.

Acknowledgments. This work was partially supported by European Union's Horizon 2020 research and innovation program from the project CyberSec4Europe (grant agreement number: 830929). We also thank Niklas Paul for his contribution to the prototype implementation.

References

1. Inclusion-exclusion principle. https://mathworld.wolfram.com/Inclusion-Exclusion Principle.html (2020). Accessed 04 May 2020
2. Fink, G.A., North, C.L., Endert, A., Rose, S.: Visualizing cyber security: usable workspaces. In: 2009 6th International Workshop on Visualization for Cyber Security, pp. 45–56 (2009)
3. Holm, H., Shahzad, K., Buschle, M., Ekstedt, M.: P^2 cysemol: predictive, probabilistic cyber security modeling language. IEEE Trans. Dependable Secure Comput. **12**(6), 626–639 (2015)
4. Homer, J., Varikuti, A., Ou, X., McQueen, M.A.: Improving attack graph visualization through data reduction and attack grouping. In: Goodall, J.R., Conti, G., Ma, K.-L. (eds.) VizSec 2008. LNCS, vol. 5210, pp. 68–79. Springer, Heidelberg (2008). https://doi.org/10.1007/978-3-540-85933-8_7
5. Hong, J.B., Kim, D.S., Chung, C.J., Huang, D.: A survey on the usability and practical applications of graphical security models. Comput. Sci. Rev. **26**, 1–16 (2017)
6. Idika, N., Bhargava, B.: Extending attack graph-based security metrics and aggregating their application. IEEE Trans. Dependable Secure Comput. **9**(1), 75–85 (2010)
7. Jhawar, R., Kordy, B., Mauw, S., Radomirović, S., Trujillo-Rasua, R.: Attack trees with sequential conjunction. In: Federrath, H., Gollmann, D. (eds.) SEC 2015. IAICT, vol. 455, pp. 339–353. Springer, Cham (2015). https://doi.org/10.1007/978-3-319-18467-8_23

8. Johnson, P., Vernotte, A., Ekstedt, M., Lagerström, R.: pwnpr3d: an attack-graph-driven probabilistic threat-modeling approach. In: 2016 11th International Conference on Availability, Reliability and Security (ARES), pp. 278–283 (2016)
9. Johnson, P., Lagerström, R., Ekstedt, M.: A meta language for threat modeling and attack simulations. In: Proceedings of the 13th International Conference on Availability, Reliability and Security. ARES 2018, Association for Computing Machinery, New York, NY, USA (2018). https://doi.org/10.1145/3230833.3232799
10. Karray, K., Danger, J.-L., Guilley, S., Abdelaziz Elaabid, M.: Attack tree construction and its application to the connected vehicle. In: Koç, Ç.K. (ed.) Cyber-Physical Systems Security, pp. 175–190. Springer, Cham (2018). https://doi.org/10.1007/978-3-319-98935-8_9
11. Kordy, B., Kordy, P., Mauw, S., Schweitzer, P.: Adtool: security analysis with attack-defense trees. In: Joshi, K., Siegle, M., Stoelinga, M., D'Argenio, P.R. (eds.) Quantitative Evaluation of Systems, pp. 173–176. Springer, Heidelberg (2013)
12. Kordy, B., Piètre-Cambacédès, L., Schweitzer, P.: Dag-based attack and defense modeling: don't miss the forest for the attack trees. Technical report (2014)
13. Lippmann, R.P., Ingols, K.W.: An annotated review of past papers on attack graphs. Technical report, Massachusetts Inst of Tech Lexington Lincoln Lab (2005)
14. Noel, S., Jacobs, M., Kalapa, P., Jajodia, S.: Multiple coordinated views for network attack graphs. In: IEEE Workshop on Visualization for Computer Security, 2005. (VizSEC 05), pp. 99–106. IEEE (2005)
15. Noel, S., Jajodia, S.: Managing attack graph complexity through visual hierarchical aggregation. In: Proceedings of the 2004 ACM Workshop on Visualization and Data Mining for Computer Security, pp. 109–118 (2004)
16. Ou, X., Govindavajhala, S., Appel, A.W.: Mulval: A logic-based network security analyzer. In: USENIX Security Symposium. vol. 8, pp. 113–128. Baltimore, MD (2005)
17. Paul, S., Vignon-Davillier, R.: Unifying traditional risk assessment approaches with attack trees. J. Inf. Secur. Appl. **19**(3), 165–181 (2014). http://www.sciencedirect.com/science/article/pii/S2214212614000180
18. Phillips, C., Swiler, L.P.: A graph-based system for network-vulnerability analysis. In: Proceedings of the 1998 Workshop on New security Paradigms, pp. 71–79 (1998)
19. Sawilla, R.E., Ou, X.: Identifying critical attack assets in dependency attack graphs. In: Jajodia, S., Lopez, J. (eds.) ESORICS 2008. LNCS, vol. 5283, pp. 18–34. Springer, Heidelberg (2008). https://doi.org/10.1007/978-3-540-88313-5_2
20. Schmitz, C., Pape, S.: Lisra: lightweight security risk assessment for decision support in information security. Comput. Secu. **90**, 101656 (2020)
21. Schneier, B.: Attack trees. Dr. Dobb's J. **24**(12), 21–29 (1999)
22. Wang, L., Islam, T., Long, T., Singhal, A., Jajodia, S.: An attack graph-based probabilistic security metric. In: Atluri, V. (ed.) Data and Applications Security XXII, pp. 283–296. Springer, Heidelberg (2008). https://doi.org/10.1007/978-3-540-70567-3_22
23. Williams, L., Lippmann, R., Ingols, K.: An interactive attack graph cascade and reachability display. In: VizSEC 2007, pp. 221–236. Springer, Heidelberg (2008). https://doi.org/10.1007/978-3-540-78243-8_15
24. Yusuf, S.E., Hong, J.B., Ge, M., Kim, D.S.: Composite metrics for network security analysis. Softw. Netw. **2017**(1), 137–160 (2018)

Attacks and Risks Modelling and Visualisation

An Attack Simulation Language
for the IT Domain

Sotirios Katsikeas[1]([✉])[iD], Simon Hacks[1][iD], Pontus Johnson[1][iD],
Mathias Ekstedt[1][iD], Robert Lagerström[1][iD], Joar Jacobsson[2],
Max Wällstedt[2], and Per Eliasson[2]

[1] Division of Network and Systems Engineering, KTH Royal Institute of Technology,
Stockholm, Sweden
{sotkat,shacks,pontusj,mekstedt,robertl}@kth.se
[2] foreseeti AB, Stockholm, Sweden
{joar.jacobsson,max.wallstedt,per.eliasson}@foreseeti.com
https://www.kth.se/nse, http://www.foreseeti.com

Abstract. Cyber-attacks on IT infrastructures can have disastrous consequences for individuals, regions, as well as whole nations. In order to respond to these threats, the cyber security assessment of IT infrastructures can foster a higher degree of security and resilience against cyber-attacks. Therefore, the use of attack simulations based on system architecture models is proposed. To reduce the effort of creating new attack graphs for each system under assessment, domain-specific languages (DSLs) can be employed. DSLs codify the common attack logics of the considered domain.

Previously, MAL (the Meta Attack Language) was proposed, which serves as a framework to develop DSLs and generate attack graphs for modeled infrastructures. In this article, we propose coreLang as a MAL-based DSL for modeling IT infrastructures and analyzing weaknesses related to known attacks. To model domain-specific attributes, we studied existing cyber-attacks to develop a comprehensive language, which was iteratively verified through a series of brainstorming sessions with domain modelers. Finally, this first version of the language was validated against known cyber-attack scenarios.

Keywords: Meta Attack Language · Threat modeling · Attack simulation · Attack graphs · Domain specific language · IT Infrastructure

This work has received funding from the Swedish Civil Contingencies Agency through the research centre Resilient Information and Control Systems (RICS), European Union's H2020 research and innovation programme under the Grant Agreements no. 833481 and no. 832907, the Swedish Energy Agency, and the Swedish Governmental Agency for Innovation Systems (Vinnova).

H. Eades III and O. Gadyatskaya (Eds.): GraMSec 2020, LNCS 12419, pp. 67–86, 2020.
https://doi.org/10.1007/978-3-030-62230-5_4

1   Introduction

Today, our society is heavily dependent on IT infrastructures. Another fact is that cyber-attacks on IT infrastructures can have disastrous consequences for individuals, regions, and whole nations. One example are the recent deliberate disruptions of electrical power and energy systems [3,19], which resulted in real-world catastrophic physical damage, like major power outage or city-wide disruptions of any service that requires electric power. But also, attacks on automated vehicles [20] and internet of things enabled attacks [21,24] are good examples of IT related cyber-attacks.

It is therefore necessary to keep such critical IT infrastructures secure. In order to respond to these threats, the assessment of IT infrastructure's cyber security can foster a higher degree of security and resilience against cyber-attacks.

However, such an assessment is difficult. In order to identify vulnerabilities, the security-relevant parts of the system must be understood and all potential attacks have to be identified [17]. There are three challenges related to these needs: First, it is challenging to identify all relevant security properties of a system. Second, it might be difficult to collect this information. Last, the collected information needs to be processed to uncover all weaknesses that can be exploited by an attacker.

Attack graphs have been previously proposed as a method to assess security on larger system architectures. This approach is gaining in popularity, both in academia and in industry the last years.

Hitherto, we have proposed the use of attack graph simulations based on system architecture models (e.g., [4,9]) to support these challenging tasks. Our approaches facilitate the modeling of systems and simulating cyber-attacks against them, in order to identify the greatest weaknesses. This can be imagined as the execution of a great number of parallel virtual penetration tests. Such an attack simulation tool enables the security assessor to focus on the collection of the information about the system required for the simulations, since the simulation tackles the first and third challenges.

As the previous approaches rely on a static implementation, we propose the use of MAL (the Meta Attack Language) [11]. This framework for domain-specific languages (DSLs) is used to define which information about a system is required and specifies the generic attack logic. Then, MAL automatically generates attack graphs corresponding to security simulations involving the modeled system. Since MAL is a meta language (i.e. the set of rules that should be used to create a new DSL), no particular domain of interest is represented.

Using MAL threat/attack DSLs for many kinds of domains can be defined, as for example industrial control systems, vehicles, IoT, etc. The goal of using DSLs is to make the DSLs as detailed and domain specific as possible in order to be able to get precise results, valid for the specific domains. More specifically, the goal is to capture the specifics of the domains, attack vectors, design strengths and weaknesses. However, these domains also share a lot of common properties and designs. Example of commonalities are that software is executed among all of these domains, execution stacks like virtual machines or operating systems (OS) are used, software communicates over networks, there are accounts with privileges and many more. Therefore, we can conclude that even if we want to capture specifics, in the end, it would be a redundant waste of effort to capture the same fundamental information more than once for all the different DSLs.

We therefore propose to design a core DSL that will cover the basic and common structure of software systems and IT infrastructure. Our goal with this work is to capture the basic architecture for future DSLs. Therefore, this work aims to create and evaluate a MAL-based DSL, named coreLang, that would have a high level of abstraction and will, therefore, be suitable for modeling generic IT infrastructures. Ideally, the aim for corelang is to cover the basics for all possible domains. Then, due to this higher level of abstraction, coreLang could be extended to create other MAL-based DSLs. This is a large task and our current ambition is to get the fundamentals correct for some basic domains (such as normal enterprise IT and control systems). In this paper, the first release of coreLang will be presented. and the open-source code behind the language is publicly available on our GitHub repository[1].

Following, we will present related work before a brief introduction to MAL, the framework that we mainly use in this work, this is done in Sect. 3. Then, in Sect. 4 the language that was developed is presented in detail. To give a better understanding of the capabilities of the language, we created an example model of the IT infrastructure part of the Ukrainian cyber-attack scenario, which is presented in Sect. 5. Finally, the validation and discussion about this work is done in Sect. 6, which is followed by the conclusion.

2   Related Work

This work is related to three domains of previous work: attack/defense graphs, model-driven security engineering, and information technology (IT) security.

First, as already mentioned, attack/defense graphs are widely applied as a formalism for security analysis. Second, there are DSLs for the security analysis of software and system models defined in the domain of model-driven security engineering. Finally, due to the fact that coreLang is designed to be applied in the domain of IT security, the results of existing IT attack studies are utilized for the evaluation of the language.

The concept of attack trees is based on the works by Weiss [25] and Schneier [22,23]. Attack trees were formalized by Mauw & Oostdijk [16] and extended to include defenses by Kordy et al. [13]. As summarized in [14], there are several approaches to elaborating on attack graphs (e.g., [10,26]). Based on the theoretical achievements of previously presented papers, various tools using attack graphs have been developed. These tools largely operate by collecting information regarding existing systems or infrastructures and automatically creating

---

[1] https://github.com/mal-lang/coreLang/tree/stable.

attack graphs based on this information. For example, the topological vulnerability analysis (TVA) tool [18] models security conditions in networks and uses a database of exploits as transitions between security conditions.

A sub-domain of attack graph modeling, that is of more interest to us, focuses on probabilistic attack graphs (e.g., facilitating Bayesian networks). In [6], the authors applied the TVA tool to generate attack graphs, transform generated graphs into dynamic Bayesian networks, and enrich the Bayesian networks using probabilities based on common vulnerability scoring system (CVSS) scores. The CVSS was also utilized by [28] to model uncertainties in attack structures, attacker actions, and alert triggering.

Several DSLs have been built in MAL serving as good examples of the capabilities a MAL-based DSL has and how it can be developed. These languages provide the capability to model a system's design based on its components and their interactions. Furthermore, such languages also facilitate the modeling of security properties such as constraints, requirements, or threats. One example of a MAL-based DSL is vehicleLang [12], which is a DSL for modeling cyberattacks on modern vehicles. Another example is a simplistic core language, that only contains the most common IT entities and attack steps and is included in the presentation of MAL [11]. Finally, another MAL-based DSL that will soon be published but some parts of it were used as inspirational blueprints for developing coreLang, is awsLang, which is a DSL for modeling Amazon Web Services environments [5].

Apart from the languages mentioned before, there exist some security languages which do not support automated analysis purposes [2,15]. They offer only the capability to model security relevant properties. An analysis needs to be conducted manually without any further support.

Approaches using attack graphs and system modeling have been united in some previous works (e.g., P^{2}CySeMoL [9], and securiCAD [4]). The core concept of these methods is to generate probabilistic attack graphs automatically from a given system specification. Attack graphs serve as inference engines to produce predictive security analysis results from system models.

MAL, that will be briefly presented in the next section, is a modeling and simulation framework based on graphical models. It combines attack graphs with conceptual graphical software system modeling techniques.

coreLang does not aim to propose a new way of performing system and attack modeling and simulations but is rather building on top of MAL to provide a DSL solution for the modeling of the general IT domain.

3   MAL

For a detailed overview of the MAL, we refer readers to our original paper, which focuses on core grammar, syntax, formalism, and additional details regarding the MAL [11]. However, for completeness, a short presentation of the MAL is provided below.

First, a DSL created with MAL contains the main elements that are found on the domain under study. Those are called `assets` in MAL. The assets contain

attack steps, which represent the actual attacks/threats that can happen on them.

An attack step can be connected with one or more following attack steps to create an attack path. Those are used to create attack graphs which are facilitated when the simulation is run. Attack steps can be either of the type OR or the type AND, indicating that performing any individual parental attack step is required (OR) or performing all parental attack steps is required (AND) for the current step to be performed. Additionally, each attack step can be associated with specific types of risks. The risks can be any combination of confidentiality (C), integrity (I), and availability (A) and are specified in brackets after the attack step name. Furthermore, defenses are entities that do not allow connected attack steps to be performed if they have the value TRUE. Finally, probability distributions can be assigned to the attack steps in order to represent the effort needed to complete the related attack step.

Assets also have **associations** between each other that describe the relations between them. Inheritance between assets is also possible and each child asset inherits all the attack steps of the parent asset. Additionally, the assets can be organized into categories.

Next, a short example of how a MAL-based DSL looks like follows. On this example, four modeled assets can be seen together with the connections of attack steps from one asset to another. When looking on the code under the **Host** asset, the *connect* attack step is an OR attack step while *access* is an AND attack step. Then the -> symbol denotes the connected next attack step. For example, if an attacker performs *phish* on the **User**, it is possible then to reach *obtain* on the associated **Password** and as a result finally perform *authenticate* on the associated **Host**. In the last lines of the example the **associations** between the assets are defined.

```
category System {
  asset Network {
    | access
      -> hosts.connect
  }

  asset Host {
    | connect
      -> access
    | authenticate
      -> access
    | guessPassword
      -> guessedPassword
    | guessedPassword [Exponential(0.02)]
      -> authenticate
    & access {C,I,A}
  }
```

```
asset User {
  | attemptPhishing
    -> phish
  | phish [Exponential(0.1)]
    -> passwords.obtain
}

asset Password {
  | obtain {C}
    -> host.authenticate
}
}

associations {
  Network [networks]
    * <-- NetworkAccess --> *
    [hosts] Host
  Host [host]
    1 <-- Credentials --> *
    [passwords] Password
  User [user]
    1 <-- Credentials --> *
    [passwords] Password
}
```

4   CoreLang

To model domain specific properties in our language, we relied on brainstorming sessions with people from foreseeti AB which can be considered as domain
experts, since they are in close contact with IT architects and security officers
of many different industries and they provided us with lessons learned from over
five years of development and usage of the securiCAD tool which contains an
attack graph generating DSL. During those sessions, we presented our percep-
tion of the corresponding topic under study and they provided comments back
to us. The comments we got were used as an early indication if we are moving
towards the right direction. These workshops were conducted for two hours on
a weekly basis for five months.

In the end of this development phase, six different main asset categories have
been included in coreLang (see Fig. 1): system, vulnerability, user, identity and
access management (IAM), data resources, and networking. In this section, those
categories and the related design decisions will be explained in detail.

4.1   System

The first category *System* is the collection of assets that usually represent the
computing instances in an environment, and thus are the natural attack surface.

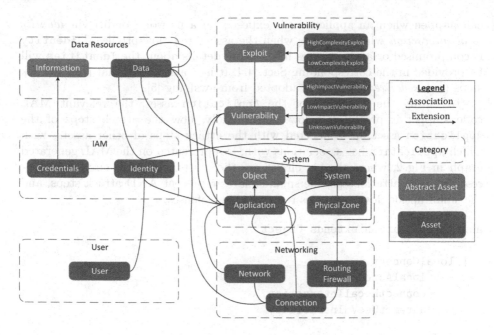

Fig. 1. Overview of assets and their associations in coreLang

First, an asset called `Object` was created (inspired by the object-oriented programming concept) that provides common functionality to all inheriting assets. Basically, an `Object` is the simplest form of an asset that can have a `Vulnerability`. Then, `Object` is specialized into two child assets, `System` and `Application`.

The `System` asset specifies the hardware on which `Applications` can run. After achieving *physical access*, the attacker can try to *authenticate* on it and/or perform a *denial of sevice* attack on all the `Applications` that are executed on it. Except *physical access*, two more levels of access are modeled on a `System`. The first one is the *specific access*, which models the ability to locally connect to the hosted applications after authenticating. Then, there is also the *full access*, which is gained after a "high-privilege" `Identity` authenticates itself or is compromised.

On the other hand, the `Application` asset specifies everything that is executed or can execute other applications. For that reason, the `Application` asset is more complex and includes a wider range of attack steps. With the same way that is modeled for the `System` asset, in order to get *access* on an `Application` two previous attack steps need to be compromised, the first one is some kind of *connect* and second a successful *authentication*. There are three possible ways of "connecting" to an `Application`: i) either via *local connect*, which occurs because any identity with "low-privilege" access on the executing instance is assumed to be able to locally (i.e., on the same host application, using loopback) interact with the executed applications, ii) via *network connect*, which can happen when an application is exposed on a network, or iii) via *identity local interaction* which happens when the associated "low-privilege" Identity is compromised or authenticates itself. More details about the Identities will be provided in the corresponding Sect. 4.4. It is worth noting that some attack steps (e.g. *codeExecution*) were adopted from awsLang [5].

To clarify the definition of the Application asset, the relevant MAL code snippet is presented below. Additionally, how the attack steps of the Application asset are connected with the attack steps of other assets, with which Application has associations with, is represented on the MAL generated graph in Fig. 2, where the big circles are the assets, the small circles are representing OR attack steps, the small squares represent AND attack steps, and the small upside-down triangles represent the defenses.

```
asset Application extends Object
{
  | localConnect
    -> localAccess,
       connectLocalInteraction,
       attemptUseVulnerability

  & localInteraction
    -> appExecutedApps.localConnect,
       attemptUseVulnerability

  | attemptUseVulnerability
    -> vulnerabilities.attemptAbuse

  | networkConnect
    -> networkAccess,
       connectLocalInteraction,
       attemptUseVulnerability

  | accessNetworkAndConnections
   -> networks.access,
      appConnections.applications.networkConnect,
      appConnections.transmit,
      appConnections.transmitResponse

  | authenticate
    -> localAccess,
       networkAccess

  | access {C,I,A}
    -> read,
       modify,
       deny,
```

```
            appExecutedApps.access,
            containedData.attemptAccess,
            accessNetworkAndConnections,
            hostApp.localConnect

    | codeExecution
      -> access,
         executionPrivIds.assume,
         modify

    | read {C}
      -> containedData.attemptRead

    | modify {I}
      -> containedData.attemptAccess

    | deny {A}
      -> containedData.attemptDelete
    ...
}
```

Lastly, this category contains PhysicalZone, which is the location where Systems are physically deployed. If *physical access* is performed on a PhysicalZone, then the attacker is able to *connect* and get *physical access* on the Systems that are part of the PhysicalZone.

4.2   Vulnerability

The basic idea of creating a MAL-based language is to provide a set of already known attack steps to the modeler. However, this incorporates two types of shortcomings. First, we concentrate on known attack steps. But, there are also attack steps that are not known yet. Second, the level of abstraction selected for coreLang is another shortcoming. Because of that, we cannot provide all possible attack steps upfront, as the attack steps are very diverse for different assets.

To overcome these issues, we provide a set of Vulnerabilities and Exploits. On the one hand, these assets can be used as a foundation for other language developers. On the other hand, we provide a standard and abstract set of Vulnerability and Exploit that represent three discrete levels of importance. These can be used by the end-user to model attack steps that are not known at the time of creating the language. Basically, any Object can have a Vulnerability that leads to different levels of *impact* to the vulnerable Object. This Vulnerability can then be facilitated by an Exploit that can have different levels of *complexity*, for example a Low Complexity Exploit can be exploited in order to abuse a High Impact Vulnerability.

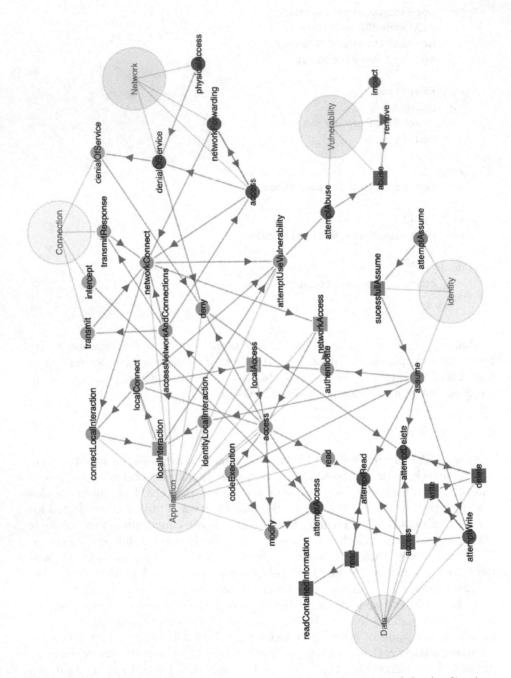

Fig. 2. Graph representing the attack steps, and their connections, of the Application asset in coreLang

4.3   User

This category contains the representation of a User. The User serves as attack surface for *social engineering attacks*. The most apparent attack that is modeled in this asset is the *phishing* attack of the User, which can lead to either *credential theft* or *takeover* of the user's computer. The latter one allows a malicious backdoor connection to be opened to the user's computer, which the attacker can then use to further compromise the same machine or perform lateral movement.

4.4   IAM

Identity and access management (IAM) is an accepted concept to manage different identities representing users and their access to certain applications [27]. Therefore, the IAM category in coreLang is comprised of the Identity asset that represents a user group, and the Credentials asset that can be associated with one or more Identities. After legitimate authentication or an illegitimate compromise of an Identity, the attacker *assumes* its privileges. Thus, both legitimate and illegitimate access is represented. As already mentioned, access to an Identity is usually secured by means of Credentials. Those Credentials can be stolen/guessed by the attacker directly (e.g., due to brute-force) or the User can be convinced to enter them by themselves (e.g., due to social engineering, like phishing, as mentioned previously).

Identities are, however, not only associated with Credentials but also with Users and Objects, like Systems and Applications, as seen in Fig. 1. An Identity associated with a User models the usage of that Identity by a User or by an Application running under the identity's privileges. Additionally, an Identity that is associated with a System or an Application represents the privileges that the Identity has over it.

When it comes to IAM on a System, two different levels of Identity-System associations are modeled. First there is the *Low Privilege Access* which provides individual level/specific access on a System from an Identity. Second, there is the *High Privilege Access*, which is equal to gaining full access on the System as every possible associated Identity. The reason for choosing to have these two levels of privileges is because of the commonly used separation between simple and admin users. In other words, a simple user of a System is only able to access specific parts of the system while an admin user has full access on the System.

On the Application side, there are three different levels of Identity-Application associations modeled. First, there is the *Low Privilege Application Access*, which only provides local interaction with the Application. But, this simple local interaction is the only prerequisite for many Vulnerabilities and, therefore, can result in severe compromise of the whole infrastructure [29]. Second, there is the *Execution Privilege Access*, which represents the fact that every Application is executed with the privileges of an Identity. In this case, if the Application is compromised, then the privileges of the associated Identity should also be compromised. Finally, there is the *High Privilege Application Access*, which models the higher level of privileges over an Application and if such privileges get compromised, all the child/executed applications should also be compromised.

An example in which all three levels of access are implemented is the following: if we assume an operating system and a simple user running a web browser on that operating system then the user will have *Execution Privilege Access* on the web browser, which is an `Application` and will also have *Low Privilege Application Access* on the operating system, which again is an `Application`, then the administrator of that operating system will have *High Privilege Application Access* on it.

4.5 Data Resources

This category groups the assets that are usually communicated. First, the `Information` asset is defined as a conceptually abstract concept that is then incorporated in the `Data` asset. The `Data` asset represents any form of data that can be stored or transmitted. This asset was heavily based on the homonymous asset found on awsLang [5]. An attacker can perform the classical actions of *read*, *write*, and *delete*, which all are modeled as attack steps. Those attack steps can be reached either by compromising the `Identity` that is associated with the `Data` or by compromising the asset that contains those `Data`, as for example the `Connection` or the `Application` asset.

4.6 Networking

The last category is concerned with networking related assets. First, the `Network` asset is defined. An attacker that has *physical access* to a `Network` can perform a *denial of service* attack by physically destroying the network medium. But if the attacker has network *access*, it is able to *network connect* and perform *denial of service* to all the network exposed `Applications` as well as attempt *network forwarding* to other neighbouring `Networks`.

The border of every `Network` is defined by a `RoutingFirewall`, which specifies a border router with firewall capabilities that can interconnect many networks. The `RoutingFirewall` is modeled as a `System` and is therefore subject to possible `Vulnerabilities`. A `Vulnerability` can lead to *full access* which results in bypassing of all the network rules defined by the firewall.

Lastly, there is the `Connection` asset, which specifies the existence of a connection between `Applications` or `Networks` and could consequently be used for lateral movement by an attacker. Each `Connection` that is associated with the `RoutingFirewall` represents a *connection rule* meaning that the firewall allows the forwarding of the associated traffic. If a `Connection` is not associated with the `RoutingFirewall`, then the corresponding traffic is prohibited.

While `Applications` can be associated with connections in a single way, `Networks` have three different types of associations with a `Connection` in regard to the three possible rules that can be found on a firewall. Those are, first the simple *Network Connection*, which models a bidirectional connection rule, second the *Out Network Connection*, which models a uni-directional connection rule that solely allows outgoing traffic of this Network, and third the *In Network Connection* which models the uni-directional connection rule that allows only incoming traffic into that Network.

5   Example Model

As already mentioned, coreLang aims to provide a high level of abstraction in the models created. For that reason, it is suitable for modeling a wide variety of IT infrastructures with a high level of abstraction. To demonstrate the application of coreLang, we use it to model a simplified version of the Ukrainian cyber-attack scenario and the way we interpreted it from an analysis that was published on it [3], that described how the attackers got a foothold on the internal networks.

The model was created in securiCAD [4], which is a software tool developed by foreseeti AB for creating models of IT architectures and performing virtual attack simulations on them, and which also allows to create MAL-based models after the language file is loaded into the tool.

In our case, the example model was created after the main development phase of the language was completed and, therefore, only minor changes were needed in the language to be able to fully represent the modeled scenario. The file of the created model can be found on our GitHub repository and in Fig. 3, the created model is presented. Additionally, the attack path shown in the attack graph, presented in Fig. 4, was the only possible path towards reaching the end goal. In the case where multiple attack paths were calculated, the less time consuming and most probable one would be highlighted on the attack graph.

The attack description below is based on the simulation results which are in accordance to what the analysis reports from that specific cyber-attack state [3].

The simulated attack scenario, which is presented on the generated attack graph in Fig. 4, is the following. First, the attacker performs a *social engineering attack* towards the User by sending a malicious payload file attached on a Microsoft Office Word document sent via email. Then, the User opens the document and executes the payload. Due to a Vulnerability on the Office Word Application, the malicious payload is executed and the vulnerability is *exploited* allowing the attacker to successfully *execute code* and take control of the user's Office Word application. The attacker has *assumed* the privileges of the Identity associated with the Office Word application and, therefore, has *access* on the Application. That, in turn, allows a *local connect* to the Windows operating system, which is an Application. Unluckily enough, the operating system is also vulnerable and the attacker can attempt exploit this also to gain *access* on it. Next, due to poor security policy enforcement, the Credentials for another workstation located in the same office Network is stored in the operating system in a text file and is accessible by the attacker. The attacker can also *access* the office Network and *network connect* to the second workstation. By having the Credentials that attacker is also able to *authenticate* and gain *access* on this workstation. Gaining *access* on this workstation is proven to be resourceful since a VPN client Application is executed on that operating system. Again,

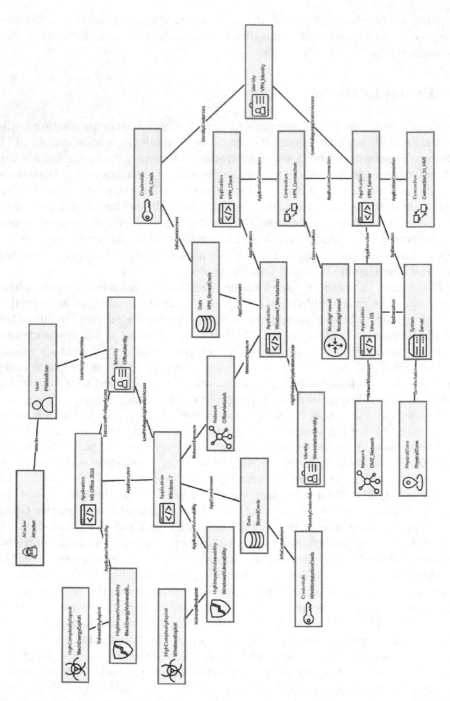

Fig. 3. coreLang model in securiCAD of the IT infrastructure of the Ukrainian cyber-attack example model

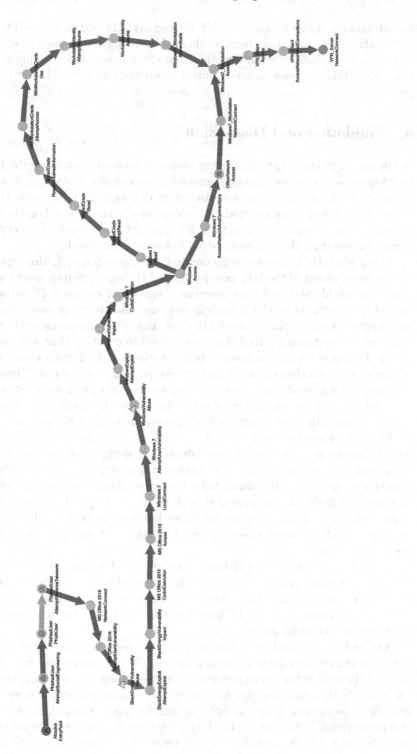

Fig. 4. coreLang generated attack graph for the Ukrainian cyber-attack example model

the attacker was lucky, since the VPN `Credentials` are stored as file on that workstation. By accessing them, is then able to *network connect* on the VPN server on the DMZ `Network` and then use the `Connection` to human-machine interface (HMI) in order to send control commands on the HMI controlling the power grid.

6   Validation and Discussion

According to Hevner et al. [8], five methods can be used to evaluate the produced by research artifacts: observations, analysis, experiments, tests, and descriptions. Because developing coreLang was similar to developing source code, tests were selected as an evaluation method. This decision was made based on the fact that testing is widely used in application development and commonly accepted as a means for ensuring that an application behaves as intended.

In our work, the tests were implemented as use case tests [7]. More specifically, as the development of the language proceeded through different asset categories, some real-world use cases that describe a variety of common IT attacks, that should be supported by the language, were provided to us by our collaborators and domain experts from foreseeti AB. One example of the use cases that we used was a model containing a Red Hat Enterprise Linux server that was running an Oracle Database which was hosting two databases and all the relevant database administrator, database analyst and system administrator users. Then another use case that was used was of a network infrastructure containing a set of network exposed applications and a set of networks where the traffic was managed by specified connection rules that were set up on the routing firewall asset.

In total, we used ten main use case models and a variety of smaller and easier ones to create use case models to evaluate our design was correct. Models for those test use cases were created and simulations were ran. The results of those simulations were then discussed with the same domain experts in evaluation sessions and feedback was provided back to us. If the feedback suggested that improvements or changes are needed in the language to better reflect the reality, an iteration of the development phase for this asset category and evaluation session was done.

By using use cases for validation, we ensure that the generated language fulfills the requirements of having a high level of abstraction while it retains its correctness. Additionally, the language still covers real-world scenarios that are typically requested from the IT infrastructure modelers that will eventually be the users of this language.

Through the evaluation sessions we had, the goal was to use the experiences of our collaborators in order to improve coreLang. Those experiences were related to parts of the models that were previously cumbersome to model using the existing tools and MAL languages, and also experiences about cases that were not at all modelable previously. Some examples of such incomplete modeling cases are IAM and networking. In the case of IAM, the common properties of `Identities` and user groups were not identified, which resulted in increased complexity when modeling IAM. Then, on the other hand, networking was also troublesome to be accurately modeled because no separation between reachability and connectivity was defined in the previous MAL languages.

One problem that occurred during development was caused by the higher level of abstraction that we wanted to retain in the language. Some common IT elements, interactions or relations could not be explicitly modeled. Our solution to this problem was to make assumptions in the design of the language that allow the more specific cases to be modeled with a higher level of abstraction. These assumptions are documented in the language itself. One characteristic example is that on coreLang, there is no asset specifying an operating system nor a guest operating system, both cases can be modeled by having two application assets associated with each other in a hierarchical manner where one is the executor and the other is the executee. This type of recursive design approach can be considered a strength of the language since it allows the modeling of different nested execution cases (e.g. the case of a guest OS running on a VM under a host OS and the case of an OS running an software application) using a single solution.

Another example of such an assumption that was made is related to the three different application privilege levels that are available in the language. More specifically, the use of the two discrete access levels, namely low and high privilege application access, was inspired by the fact that typically an application is either being executed under a simple user's (low) or root/admin's (high) privileges and it always is associated with one type of them, in our case called execution privilege.

Another problem that we had to solve, again related to the level of abstraction, was that it would not be clear to users of the language to understand how exactly each of the included assets should be used in a model. To solve this problem, first, a proper name for each one of the assets was selected, then, second, a short documentation text about each asset was included in the language. Such documentation is also found under each attack step specified in the language to provide useful context information to the user.

7 Conclusion and Future Work

Assessing the cyber security of IT infrastructures is becoming increasingly important as the number of IT security issues and cyber-attacks increases. This article presented coreLang, which is a MAL-based domain specific language for the abstract IT domain.

coreLang supports a high level of modeling abstraction and is therefore suitable for modeling generic IT infrastructures. This higher level of abstraction makes the developed language easier to expand since it is easier to use it as a foundation for many different MAL-based DSLs. Finally, coreLang is an open-source project to which anyone can contribute[2].

---

[2] https://mal-lang.org/coreLang/.

There are several potential directions for future work and future work is something expected since coreLang is still a work in progress and this is the first release.

First, coreLang could be used as a foundation for the creation of extensions that will allow the language to become more specific when needed. Since core-Lang captures the basic IT architecture and has a high level of abstractions it could be used as a foundation for future MAL-based DSLs. For example, some new assets could be added in an extension file that will enhance the language with capabilities for better specific operating system and software modeling.

Second, given the fact that software vulnerabilities are covered in a comprehensive way, an extension could be to add an on par with the common vulnerability scoring system (CVSS) [1] representation of software vulnerabilities. This could be done by creating new vulnerability assets that can be mapped or parameterized, in a one-to-one manner, to all the possible CVSS configurations and therefore allow a realistic representation of vulnerabilities.

Then, another future addition on the language would be to add defenses that are able to either completely stop or make the attacks, that are already modeled, harder to perform. This would allow more flexible models to be simulated without having to change the assets that are placed in the model.

Finally, since there are many common properties of all IT environments, we aimed to develop a well structured boilerplate language that can be reused and extended when environments start to differ. For that reason, if we had specified probabilities and probability values for all the included attack steps the abstraction of the language would have been harmed. Our approach to address this was to not provide probabilities and values but instead consider the definition of correct probabilities and probability values as future work that needs to be done either separately or as a part of the DSL that will built on top of coreLang as their foundation.

References

1. CVSS v3.1 Specification Document. https://www.first.org/cvss/v3.1/specification-document
2. Almorsy, M., Grundy, J.: Secdsvl: a domain-specific visual language to support enterprise security modelling. In: 2014 23rd Australian Software Engineering Conference (ASWEC), pp. 152–161. IEEE (2014)
3. Defense Use Case: Analysis of the cyber attack on the Ukrainian power grid. Electricity Information Sharing and Analysis Center (E-ISAC) (2016)
4. Ekstedt, M., Johnson, P., Lagerström, R., Gorton, D., Nydrén, J., Shahzad, K.: securiCAD by foreseeti: a CAD tool for enterprise cyber security management. In: 2015 IEEE 19th International Enterprise Distributed Object Computing Workshop (EDOCW), pp. 152–155. IEEE (2015)
5. Engström, V., Johnson, P., Lagerström, R.: Automating Cyber Attack Simulations Against Amazon Web Services Environments (To be published) (2020)
6. Frigault, M., Wang, L., Singhal, A., Jajodia, S.: Measuring network security using dynamic bayesian network. In: Proceedings of the 4th ACM workshop on Quality of protection, pp. 23–30. ACM (2008)

7. Hasling, B., Goetz, H., Beetz, K.: Model based testing of system requirements using uml use case models. In: 2008 1st International Conference on Software Testing, Verification, and Validation, pp. 367–376. IEEE (2008)
8. Bichler, M.: Design science in information systems research. WIRTSCHAFTSINFORMATIK **48**(2), 133–135 (2006). https://doi.org/10.1007/s11576-006-0028-8
9. Holm, H., Shahzad, K., Buschle, M., Ekstedt, M.: P²CySeMoL: predictive, probabilistic cyber security modeling language. IEEE Trans. Dependable Secure Comput. **12**(6), 626–639 (2015). https://doi.org/10.1109/TDSC.2014.2382574
10. Ingols, K., Chu, M., Lippmann, R., Webster, S., Boyer, S.: Modeling modern network attacks and countermeasures using attack graphs. In: Computer Security Applications Conference, 2009. ACSAC 2009. Annual, pp. 117–126. IEEE (2009)
11. Johnson, P., Lagerström, R., Ekstedt, M.: A meta language for threat modeling and attack simulations. In: Proceedings of the 13th International Conference on Availability, Reliability and Security, p. 38. ACM (2018)
12. Katsikeas, S., Johnson, P., Hacks, S., Lagerström, R.: Probabilistic modeling and simulation of vehicular cyber attacks : An application of the meta attack language. In: Proceedings of the 5th International Conference on Information Systems Security and Privacy (2019)
13. Kordy, B., Mauw, S., Radomirović, S., Schweitzer, P.: Foundations of attack-defense trees. In: International Workshop on Formal Aspects in Security and Trust, pp. 80–95. Springer, Heidelberg (2010). https://doi.org/10.1007/978-3-642-19751-2_6
14. Kordy, B., Piètre-Cambacédès, L., Schweitzer, P.: Dag-based attack and defense modeling: don't miss the forest for the attack trees. Comput. Sci. Rev. **13**, 1–38 (2014)
15. Lund, M.S., Solhaug, B., Stølen, K.: Model-Driven Risk Analysis: The CORAS Approach. Springer, New York (2010)
16. Mauw, S., Oostdijk, M.: Foundations of attack trees. In: International Conference on Information Security and Cryptology. pp. 186–198. Springer (2005)
17. Morikawa, I., Yamaoka, Y.: Threat tree templates to ease difficulties in threat modeling. In: 2011 14th International Conference on Network-Based Information Systems, pp. 673–678 (2011). https://doi.org/10.1109/NBiS.2011.113
18. Noel, S., Elder, M., Jajodia, S., Kalapa, P., O'Hare, S., Prole, K.: Advances in topological vulnerability analysis. In: Conference For Homeland Security, 2009. CATCH 2009. Cybersecurity Applications Technology, pp. 124–129 (2009). https://doi.org/10.1109/CATCH.2009.19
19. Petermann, T., Bradke, H., Lüllmann, A., Poetzsch, M., Riehm, U.: Was bei einem Blackout geschieht: Folgen eines langandauernden und großflächigen Stromausfalls, vol. 662. Büro für Technikfolgen-Abschätzung (2011)
20. Petit, J., Shladover, S.E.: Potential cyberattacks on automated vehicles. IEEE Trans. Intell. Transport. Syst. **16**(2), 546–556 (2015)
21. Prokofiev, A.O., Smirnova, Y.S., Silnov, D.S.: The internet of things cybersecurity examination. In: 2017 Siberian Symposium on Data Science and Engineering (SSDSE), pp. 44–48 (2017)
22. Schneier, B.: Attack trees. Dr. Dobb's journal **24**(12), 21–29 (1999)
23. Schneier, S.: Lies: Digital Security in a Networked World. Wiley, New York **21**, 318–333 (2000)
24. Stellios, I., Kotzanikolaou, P., Psarakis, M., Alcaraz, C., Lopez, J.: A survey of iot-enabled cyberattacks: assessing attack paths to critical infrastructures and services. IEEE Commun. Surv. Tutorials **20**(4), 3453–3495 (2018)

25. Weiss, J.: A system security engineering process. In: Proceedings of the 14th National Computer Security Conference, vol. 2, pp. 572–581 (1991)
26. Williams, L., Lippmann, R., Ingols, K.: GARNET: A Graphical Attack Graph and Reachability Network Evaluation Tool. Springer, Heidelberg (2008). https://doi.org/10.1007/978-3-540-85933-8_5
27. Witty, R.J., Allan, A., Enck, J., Wagner, R.: Identity and access management defined. Research Study SPA-21-3430, Gartner (2003)
28. Xie, P., Li, J.H., Ou, X., Liu, P., Levy, R.: Using Bayesian networks for cyber security analysis. In: 2010 IEEE/IFIP International Conference on Dependable Systems and Networks (DSN), pp. 211–220. IEEE (2010)
29. Yan, D., Liu, F., Jia, K.: Modeling an information-based advanced persistent threat attack on the internal network. In: ICC 2019–2019 IEEE International Conference on Communications (ICC), pp. 1–7 (2019)

Representing Decision-Makers in SGAM-H: The Smart Grid Architecture Model Extended with the Human Layer

Adam Szekeres$^{(\boxtimes)}$ and Einar Snekkenes

Department of Information Security and Communication Technology,
Norwegian University of Science and Technology - NTNU, Gjøvik, Norway
{adam.szekeres,einar.snekkenes}@ntnu.no

Abstract. The safety and security of critical infrastructures is both a technical and a social issue. However, most risk analysis methods focus predominantly on technical aspects and ignore the impact strategic human decisions have on the behavior of systems. Furthermore, the high degree of complexity and lack of historical data for probability estimations in case of new and emerging systems seriously limit the practical utility of traditional risk analysis methods. The Conflicting Incentives Risk Analysis (CIRA) method concentrates on human decision-makers to address these problems. However, the method's applicability is restricted by the fact that humans are not represented in the Smart Grid Architecture Model (SGAM) which is the industry's most well-known model of the Smart Grid ecosystem. Therefore, the main objective of this paper is to establish a connection between CIRA and SGAM by proposing the SGAM-H, an enhanced version of the original architecture model complemented by the Human Layer. The development and evaluation of the artifact is guided by the Design Science Research methodology. The evaluation presents a working example of applying the CIRA method on a scenario involving intra-organizational risks at a Distribution System Operator. The key benefit of the SGAM-H is that it enables the construction of a common understanding among stakeholders about risks related to key decision-makers, which is a fundamental first step towards forming a more complete picture about potential issues affecting the electric grids of the future.

Keywords: Information security risk analysis · Conflicting Incentives Risk Analysis (CIRA) · Smart Grid Architecture Model (SGAM) · SGAM-H · Human Layer · Stakeholder motivation

1 Introduction

Nation-wide electrification of industries and societies beginning in the 1880s had tremendous economical and societal benefits [7] and the demand for a stable and

---

This work was partially supported by the project IoTSec – Security in IoT for Smart Grids, with number 248113/O70 part of the IKTPLUSS program funded by the Norwegian Research Council.

H. Eades III and O. Gadyatskaya (Eds.): GraMSec 2020, LNCS 12419, pp. 87–110, 2020.
https://doi.org/10.1007/978-3-030-62230-5_5

reliable supply of electricity has exceeded that for any other forms of energy [28]. A properly functioning power grid represents an indispensable infrastructure for modern societies, which supports all aspects of life. While demand for electricity will keep rising in the future (e.g., due to increasing electrification of the transportation sector, growing populations, etc.) international directives and regulations have been pushing toward a shift from dependency on fossil and nuclear power sources to more eco-friendly and sustainable renewables. Most renewable power sources (e.g., wind, solar) are intermittent in nature which requires a paradigm shift from centralized large-scale generation models to flexible, distributed and small-scale solutions [11]. At the same time economic constraints make the complete reconstruction of the power grid highly unfeasible. The envisaged solution is encompassed in the concept of the Smart Grid (SG), which aims at solving the challenges of the future by relying on the physical infrastructure of the past with enhancements from novel information and communication technologies. Thus the SG represents a highly complex system with real-time sensing and control capabilities using a bidirectional flow of electricity and information, enabled by the addition of internet of things (IoT) devices at various parts of the grid. Several stakeholders are involved in SG-related activities including: legislators, governmental agencies, standardizing bodies, data protection authorities, organizations focusing on the generation, transmission, distribution of electricity, equipment manufacturers, software and security providers, researchers and consumers [8].

Developments in SGs are driven by a combination of political, economic and ecological motives. Misaligned incentives are unavoidable when the number of interacting stakeholders is considered in a system of such complexity (both technically and socially). Misaligned incentives are particularly prevalent in information systems where those who are responsible for providing security are not the same people who benefit from the protection or suffer when things go wrong. For example, increasing the dependency of critical infrastructures on public information systems (network convergence) can be an efficient short-term cost saving strategy for utility companies, but it increases society's long-term vulnerability, which will ultimately bear the costs [24]. It has been demonstrated that misaligned incentives, negative externalities and moral hazard arise in a variety of settings within the field of information security [1]. The identification and mitigation of such problems is crucial for ensuring the safety and security of societies depending on SGs and other critical infrastructures.

1.1 Conflicting Incentives Risk Analysis (CIRA)

The Conflicting Incentives Risk Analysis (CIRA) method focuses on the motivation of individual stakeholders to define risks. The lack of relevant historical data in case of emerging and dynamic systems creates a significant challenge for traditional (i.e., relying on frequentist probability estimations) risk analysis methods [37]. Furthermore, deliberate human actions due to misalignment of incentives is rarely at the center of risk analysis procedures. CIRA defines risk as the misalignment between stakeholder incentives. The analysis focuses on the *Risk owner's* (i.e., person at risk) exposure to the actions or inactions of several other stakeholders (*Strategy owners*) who are in the position to choose courses of actions [32]. CIRA combines quantitative methods to characterize risks attributed to key decision-makers, therefore, aims at overcoming some of the problems associated with qualitative risk scoring methods [15].

1.2   Smart Grid Architecture Model (SGAM)

The creation of the Smart Grid Architecture Model (SGAM) was motivated by the need to represent stakeholders, applications and systems that will have to achieve efficient interdependent operations in future SGs. To ensure these goals, developers and standardization bodies of the SG need to have a common understanding or shared model about the systems which will be implemented. To capture the EU-specific requirements the SGAM was designed to tackle the complexity by representing systems in a consistent and comprehensive way. It enables standards gap analysis; visualization and assessment of use cases in a technology-neutral way; comparison of different approaches and road-maps from various viewpoints. Figure 1 presents the SGAM, based on [4]. *Domains* represent the energy conversation chain from generation site to customer premises. *Zones* capture the power system management supported by ICT from the level of processes to markets. *Interoperability layers* represent different levels of abstrac-

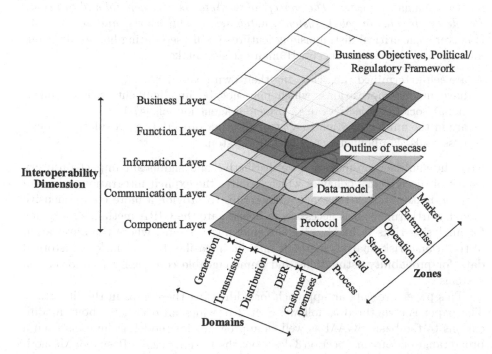

Fig. 1. The Smart Grid Architecture Model (SGAM) based on [4].

tion from the physical hardware to business perspectives highlighting the inter-connectedness and dependencies between entities.

How is it possible to analyse risks arising from human decision-making in a complex system as the SG? Several management failures (management of tree growth, lack of vulnerability and system-health assessment, etc.) contributed to the 2003 Northeast blackout in the US, affecting 55 million people with an estimated economic impact of $6 billion [25]. Organizations responsible for the development and maintenance of the grid need to have the right incentives in place to achieve their goals at a socially optimal level. Are measures in place to protect the privacy of customers despite increased monitoring capabilities enabled by smart meters and other smart home devices [22]? Does information security contribute to the organizational goals or is it perceived as a impediment to smooth operations [48]? Can the SG fulfill the hopes by providing electricity in a safe, reliable and secure way without significantly increasing society's exposure to new threats [19]?

1.3 Problem Statement and Motivation

In order to enable the application of the CIRA method on SG use cases, a connection between the models has to be established. Human decision-makers are not represented in the existing SGAM, which may result in ignoring the impact strategic human decisions have on the grid. The SGAM documentation briefly mentions human-aspects: "*The concept of an Actor is very general and can cover People (their roles or jobs), systems, databases, organizations, and devices*" [4]. However some critical distinguishing features justify separating human decision-makers from the Actor concept. Human decision-makers:

- are self-determined (i.e., choosing their own goals [10]);
- have unique motivations, which may not be in alignment with organiza-tional/societal objectives (e.g., principal-agent models [47]);
- are in the unique position to control all other objects (e.g., regulations, busi-ness goals, components, etc.) within a system.

Ergo, human decision-makers have distinctive and significant impact on every aspect of the system's behavior which requires the explicit integration of human decision-makers into a reference architecture to provide a more comprehensive model. Furthermore, it is necessary to investigate the CIRA method's adequacy for analysing risks in highly complex emerging systems, where the application of traditional risk analysis methods may be infeasible (due to lack of historical data for probability estimations and unmanageable complexity of information systems).

This paper presents an approach for addressing these gaps in the literature. The paper is structured as follows: Sect. 2 provides an overview about modifi-cations to the basic SGAM as well as approaches for modeling humans from a broad range of domains. Section 3 describes the Design Science Research Method-ology (DSRM) which guided the development and evaluation of the paper's arti-fact. The artifact is presented and evaluated by a case study throughout Sect. 4.

Section 5 discusses key findings and Sect. 6 draws conclusions. The paper ends with ideas for further work in Sect. 7.

2 Related Work

This section is divided into two parts. The first part reviews research work which proposes or implements extensions to the generic SGAM to solve specific tasks. A literature search using the search string ("sgam" extend OR extension) appearing anywhere in the articles was conducted on Google Scholar and articles citing the original publication were screened; other relevant articles were identified among references. Studies describing the application of SGAM were excluded. The second part presents approaches for modeling human behavior across various domains to illustrate design decisions about the models.

2.1 Variants of SGAM

The Information System Architecture for e-Mobility (EM-ISA) is an early SGAM variant focusing on electric vehicle (EV) integration into the grid. The model significantly reduces the number of the domains and zones, then proposes the integration of human-machine interfaces into the model to capture interactions between humans (operators) and objects without further specifying human attributes [35]. The Electric Mobility Architecture Model (EMAM) focuses on EV integration as well. In EMAM, the Generation domain is removed and an electric mobility domain is added to the grid plane, while keeping the rest of the original model unchanged. Recognizing the utility of the SGAM for standardisation purposes, two other reference models were developed following similar architecture engineering principles. While the layers of The Smart City Infrastructure Architecture Model (SCIAM) and the Smart Home Architecture Model (SHAM) are the same as those of SGAM, different domains and zones are introduced which may decrease compatibility between models [46]. SGs may differ between countries, therefore it is important to increase compatibility between various implementations. Two state-of-the-art models (the SGAM from EU and the NISTIR 7628 from U.S.) are combined in order to facilitate security analysis from the beginning of the development process [45]. In addition to the previously described variants two more architecture models are described in [43]. The Home and Building Architecture Model (HBAM) utilizes SGAM's layered approach with different zones and domains introduced to capture relevant concepts within scope of smart homes and buildings. The Reference Architecture Model for Industry 4.0 (RAMI 4.0) is regarded as the most sophisticated derivative of the SGAM containing zones and domains relevant for industrial applications and extending the interoperabilty perspectives with an additional layer. Two more reference models have been developed using the SGAM's design principles. The Reference Architecture Model Automotive (RAMA) represents the life-cycle of connected vehicles and the related information technologies and the Maritime Architecture Framework (MAF) models information exchange between various actors in the maritime domain [44].

2.2 Approaches for Modeling Humans

Models in general, are abstract representations of a complex entity or phenomenon capturing its most significant aspects for a pre-specified purpose. Analogies, shared features and other similarities between entities play a key role in modelling activities. For example, pigs and other animals can represent humans in medical experiments due to the high number of shared features (in terms of genetics, physiology and anatomy, etc.) [23]. Investigations in road safety require human models which accurately capture the physical properties of real humans in car crash scenarios [2]. Personas or user archetypes are widely used human models in the software engineering industry. Personas guide the development process by representing future users and their goals in relation to the product [5]. Realism of human models is becoming increasingly important in virtual environments where representations can replace real humans (in communication context [3]) or simulated agents are required to act realistically (in training context [27]). For behavior prediction, a human model must incorporate psychological constructs that are most likely to govern or influence (i.e., mediate and moderate) the behavior of interest. Models reduce real-world complexity, which enables that only a small set of well-defined parameters are required for predictions. The importance of appropriately modeling humans and human behavior has been recognized in a variety of domains. Human performance and mental load models have been developed to represent operator characteristics and to assist the design of human-machine interfaces in the context of industrial control systems [38]. A variety of human behaviors are of interest to the military, therefore a wide range of human models have been developed (at the individual and group level) to support agent-based behavioral simulations [30]. A key challenge is to find the right balance between the model's complexity and its realism [16]. In the context of information security, humans can be represented by a utility function which is the most suitable level of abstraction for game theoretic simulations [20]. People have great impact on the Earth's overall condition, but humans are not yet explicitly represented in Earth system models used for simulating ecological dynamics. The selection of an appropriate human model relies on the modeler's understanding about the strengths and weaknesses of each model [26].

2.3 Summary of Related Work

The reviewed literature demonstrates the SGAM's acceptance among practitioners and researchers and presents several domain- or task-specific variants inspired by the original model. However, the representation of human decision-makers is lacking, which impedes the efficient application of CIRA on SG scenarios. The broad overview on the literature of human modeling approaches highlights that models should be developed according to relevant design considerations (e.g., specifying the model's content in relation to the behavior of interest, complexity-realism trade off, etc.).

3   Methodology

This study is based on the design science research (DSR) paradigm, which provides an organizing framework for the development of purposeful artifacts to solve a specific problem [14]. The DSR methodology defines three cycles which interact with each other during task execution [13]. The *design cycle* represents the core activities (development and evaluation of the artifact in an iterative process) which is embedded in a broader context. The design cycle receives input from two sources. The *relevance cycle* refers to the interaction between the environment (where problems and needs for a new solution arise) and the design cycle (produces solutions). Artifacts from the design cycle are fed back to the environment through the relevance cycle and the artifacts are applied in the context where they were intended to function. Interaction of the design cycle with the supporting knowledge-base defines the *rigor cycle* which provides the necessary tools, methodologies, theories for the development and evaluation of the artifact. Information flows in both directions between the rigor and design cycles as well, thus new knowledge and experience resulting from the construction of the artifact are recorded in the knowledge-base using the most suitable format (presentation, tutorial, academic paper, etc.).

The relevance cycle serves as a starting point for any DSR activity by specifying the context and problems in the domain (i.e., requirements), that the artifact should solve. Furthermore, it defines evaluation criteria for testing the artifact's utility within the environment. The need to represent human stakeholders within the SG has been arising from interactions with other stakeholders (students, conference and project participants). Difficulty of creating a common understanding among stakeholders about CIRA's applicability and relevance was identified as a major barrier to the method's acceptance and adoption. Thus, a more efficient method of conveying meaning was set as a requirement. The second step focuses on the identification of suitable theories, frameworks to meet requirements. Therefore, the rigor cycle was used for the identification of existing frameworks by reviewing the relevant literature, which resulted in identifying the SGAM as an ideal candidate requiring customization. The development activity within the design cycle was used to extract key concepts from CIRA and to create visual representations of its abstract concepts. An important design consideration was to keep a high degree of compatibly with the original SGAM version, therefore an extension is proposed: the SGAM-H enhanced by a Human Layer and its necessary components. The artifact model was built from scratch in Microsoft Visio, to ensure re-usability and mutability (the Visio-based templates reported in [34] were not available online). The final step within the design cycle is the evaluation of the artifact which is achieved through a hypothetical case study (qualitative, descriptive method) demonstrating how key CIRA concepts are mapped onto the Human Layer and how it conveys meaning. The artifact is evaluated in terms of its efficacy, ease of use, completeness and homomorphism (i.e., correspondence with another model) [31].

4   Human Layer

This section presents the Human Layer as an extension of the SGAM, giving rise
to the SGAM-H. The Human Layer's basic elements for constructing and representing the context of risk analysis are introduced. Next, the artifact's efficacy is
demonstrated on a hypothetical case study which applies the CIRA method on
a SG scenario focusing on risks experienced by the CEO of a Distribution System Operator (DSO). Several aspects of the case study were inspired by media
reports [36] and analyses of real-world incidents [25] accompanied by relevant
scientific literature [6] in order to increase its realism. Finally, the artifact is
evaluated along the previously identified criteria.

Figure 2 presents the Human Layer placed on top of the business layer of the
original SGAM. This implementation enables the representation of human stakeholders with their relevant attributes on the architecture model and emphasizes
the critical role that strategic human decisions can have on various aspects of
SGs.

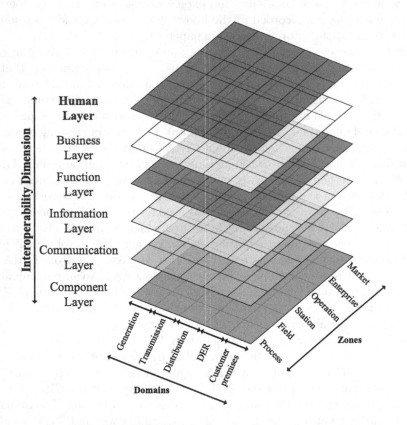

Fig. 2. SGAM-H including the Human Layer.

Figure 3 presents the stakeholder models; components to represent human attributes and other elements of the layer to capture key concepts of CIRA. Two types of stakeholder classes are distinguished by color and related captions: human models in blue represent the risk owner, human models in white represent the class of strategy owners. Post-analysis states are distinguished by a tag above the models to display the risks explicitly (i.e., consequences for the risk owner, incentives for the strategy owner). The sign ($\pm$) represents the direction of utility change following strategy execution. Furthermore, incentives are marked with red fill color on the strategy owner figures. The height of the red coloring from the bottom of the figure matches with the magnitude of the incentive (i.e., an incentive of 50 produces a red fill color up to 50% of the figure's height). Strategy owners' profile information is captured in brackets, to record the information used for the construction of motivational profiles before the analysis. Stakeholders are linked to other entities (e.g., physical hardware, organizations, etc.) by dashed lines. Strategies are represented by continuous lines ending in an arrow, directed from the strategy owner to the risk owner.

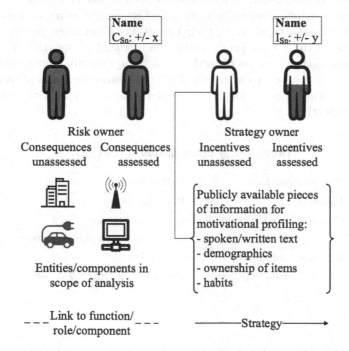

Fig. 3. Components of the Human Layer. (Color figure online)

4.1   Case Study: DSO Risks

This sub-section demonstrates the use of the SGAM-H through a case study in which the CIRA method is applied to a scenario focusing on the risks faced by the organizational leader of a DSO, since the organization has a critical role in the SG ecosystem. Numbering of the subsequent paragraphs follows the steps of the CIRA procedure based on [32].

1. Identification of the Risk Owner. The risk owner is the CEO of a DSO, who is interested in intra-organizational risks which may interfere with the objectives of the organization.

2. Identification of the Risk Owner's Key Utility Factors. The key utility factors (UFs) were identified by relying on the Balanced Scorecard (BSC) method, which was designed to aid managers in evaluating and measuring organizational performance through a set of measures linked to organizational objectives [18]. Four perspectives are distinguished by the BSC method: *Financial, Customers and stakeholders, Learning and growth* and *Internal business processes.* The method enables the development of key performance indicators at various levels (departments, individuals) to achieve better organizational performance. Since utility companies such as DSOs operate as natural monopolies due to high infrastructural costs, their operations differ from purely for-profit organizations. In the not-for-profit sector, the financial perspective is often seen as a constraint rather than an objective, which requires different priorities [21]. Some work has been done to adapt the BSC to the specific needs of utility companies [17,33]. Table 1 presents the risk owner's key utility factors derived from the BSC perspectives.

Table 1. Key utility factors of the CEO.

BSC perspectives	Utility factors
Financial	Revenue
Customers and stakeholders	Customer privacy
	Contribution to public welfare
Learning and growth	Innovation
Internal business processes	Relationship with regulators

3–5. Identification of Strategies that May Influence the Risk Owner's Utility Factors; Identification of Roles and Named Strategy Owners Which Can Execute the Strategies. Steps 3–5 of the procedure are summarized in Table 2. For each utility factor an appropriate strategy was identified by considering key processes and functions at a DSO. The identification of roles and strategy owners is aided by the organizational chart which allocates the responsibilities and tasks to various roles occupied by actual persons. The scenario

Table 2. The risk owners' utility factors (UFs); strategies that impact the risk owner's utility factors; roles and individuals.

Affected UFs	Strategy	Role	Person
Customer privacy	Help a friend (S_1)	Dispatcher	Sigurd
Contribution to public welfare	Fix street lights (S_2)	Operations manager	Emma
Innovation	Recruit research applicants (S_3)	Head of R&D	Hanne
Relationship with regulators	Support system integration (S_4)	CISO	Henry

description for each person illustrates motivational factors at play regarding the dilemmas they face in a given situation.

Sigurd works as a dispatcher at the organization. He is approached by his best friend who suspects that his wife is cheating on him and asks Sigurd to monitor the detailed electricity consumption of their holiday house which he thinks is used as a hideout by her. He has access to the relevant data, and thinks he can fulfil the request without getting into trouble. The legal and financial implications of a privacy breach are of key interest to the risk owner. Emma is responsible for distributing tasks efficiently within her team of technicians working in the field. Citizens are complaining about faulty street lights and dangerously dark streets. She has to decide how to allocate tasks within the team based on existing efficiency measures in place. Hanne works at the R&D department developing new services for customers. Students with novel ideas apply to get work experience at the organization, but she perceives recruitment and training of students as a nuisance since student projects rarely get converted into successful products. She has to decide whether increasing the number of student projects (to fulfill an important societal role) worth lowering her performance indicators. Henry believes that the new agenda to harmonize all data acquisition systems at the organization would create a singularity threat and he believes in security through diversity. He has the final word regarding the new system's implementation in the project.

6. Identification of the Strategy Owners' Utility Factors.

For each strategy owner two types of utility factors are distinguished. Work-related factors are derived from the BSC method's perspectives. Personal utility factors are represented by basic human values [40]. Table 3 presents the key utility factors for each strategy owner.

Table 3. Work-related and personal utility factors for each strategy owner.

Strategy owner	Utility factors					
	Work-related (associated with role)	Personal				
Sigurd	Percentage of successfully located faults and dispatched repair teams within time frame (%)	ST	OC	CO	HE	SE
Emma	Percentage of reconnected electricity customers within time frame (%)					
Hanne	New services ready for market (%)					
Henry	Percentage of resolved cyber-incidents within a time frame (%)					

Note. ST: self-transcendence, OC: openness to change,
CO: conservation, HE: hedonism, SE: self-enhancement.

7. Operationalization of Utility Factors. To operationalize the utility factors, existing work on DSO-specific KPIs was surveyed [6,12] as well as relevant regulations (GDPR [9]). KILE (quality-adjusted revenue frames for energy not delivered) represents customers' costs for interruptions, and is a form of revenue reduction due to interruptions, which aims at incentivizing utility companies to maintain operational reliability [29]. Utility factors capturing personal motivations were operationalized in previous work as publicly observable pieces of information, for the construction of motivational profiles [39–41]. Table 4 presents how each utility factor is operationalized.

8. Weighing of Utility Factors. Table 5 presents each utility factor's contribution to the person's overall utility. For the purpose of demonstration, the CEO's overall utility is entirely composed of work-related utility factors. Employees on the other hand, derive utility from other factors which are not directly linked to their professional role (i.e., human values). Work-life balance is represented by the global ratio between work-related and personal utility factors. Weights (w) of the personal utility factors capture the relative importance of basic human values for the subject. Thus, weights are inferred from psychological profiles based on various publicly available pieces of information (e.g., demographics [41], texts produced by the subject [39], evidence of past choices reflecting value

Table 4. Utility factors operationalized.

Role	Type of utility factor	Utility factor	Operationalized as
Risk owner	Professional	Revenue	R = Revenue cap − KILE (CENS) [29]
		Customer's data privacy (%)	CDP = 1 − (privacy-related penalties/privacy breach cap (0.04 * annual turnover)) [9]
		Contribution to public welfare (%)	PW = resolved public complaints within 1 month/all complaints in a period
		Innovation (%)	INN = number of established research collaborations with universities/number of applications from students
		Relationship with regulators (%)	REG = number of reports accepted without modification/all reports submitted
Strategy owner		Percentage of successfully located faults and dispatched repair teams within time frame (%)	TDISP = number of successful responses within 30 min/all trouble calls received
		Percentage of reconnected electricity customers within time frame (%)	TREST = number of successfully reconnected customers within 24 h/number of customers assigned without electricity supply
		New services ready for market (%)	MARK = new market ready-services/all R&D projects initiated
		Percentage of resolved cyber- incidents within time frame (%)	CYINC = successfully mitigated cyber-incidents within 12 h/all reported
	Personal	Self-transcendence	Publicly available pieces of information for psychological profiling: text analysis [39], demographic features [41], item ownership and habits [40]
		Openness to change	
		Conservation	
		Hedonism	
		Self-enhancement	

trade-offs, habits [40]). Various metrics have been used for quantifying the accuracy/uncertainty of the inferred profiles: R^2 - coefficient of determination (range: 0.19–0.39), PI - prediction interval (Mean: 0.077, SD: 0.794), Pearson correlation coefficients between predicted and ground-truth scores (range: 0.34–0.52) [40]. All the weights sum to 1 for each stakeholder.

Table 5. Weighing of utility factors.

CEO	w	Sigurd	w	Emma	w	Hanne	w	Henry	w
Revenue	0.300	Percentage of successfully located faults and dispatched repair teams within time frame (%)	0.25	Percentage of reconnected electricity customers within time frame (%)	0.30	New services ready for market (%)	0.35	Percentage of resolved cyber-incidents within time frame (%)	0.40
Customer's data privacy (%)	0.175	Self-transcendence	0.18	Self-transcendence	0.12	Self-transcendence	0.10	Self-transcendence	0.11
Contribution to public welfare (%)	0.175	Openness to change	0.14	Openness to change	0.20	Openness to change	0.20	Openness to change	0.10
Innovation (%)	0.175	Conservation	0.17	Conservation	0.09	Conservation	0.05	Conservation	0.18
Relationship with regulators (%)	0.175	Hedonism	0.16	Hedonism	0.12	Hedonism	0.16	Hedonism	0.06
		Self-enhancement	0.10	Self-enhancement	0.17	Self-enhancement	0.14	Self-enhancement	0.15

9. Determination of Each Strategy's Impact on the Utility Factors.

Each strategy owner's decision-making process is modeled in Table 6 with the decisions' impact on the risk owner's utility factors. For simplicity each strategy's influence is limited to a maximum of two utility factors. Real-world choices are determined by the complex trade-offs between utility factors as perceived by the stakeholders in a choice situation (i.e., dilemma). Personal features (represented by the weights of each utility factor) interact with salient features of the immediate situation (i.e., initial and final values- capturing states as opposed to traits). Decisions are motivated/demotivated by the overall gains/losses expected from the execution of a strategy. The decision-making process is modeled as $C = f(P \times S)$, where C is a choice, P refers to personal features and S captures situational features. The formula may include the accuracies with which an analyst can assess the relevant person-situation interactions. The results of the context establishment are depicted on the SGAM-H in Fig. 4.

10. Utility Estimation.

Each stakeholder's overall utility is calculated in Table 7 before and after strategy execution. The weighted sum of each utility factor produces the overall utilities according to the Multi Attribute Utility Theory used in CIRA [32].

11. Calculation of Incentives.

Differences in terms of the overall utilities before and after strategy execution are presented in Table 8. Stakeholders prefer options that increase their utility to options that decrease it, therefore options with positive contribution are selected, whereas options which provide disutility are avoided.

Table 6. Impact of the strategies on utility factors.

	Utility factors	Weights	Initial value	Help a friend (S_1)	Fix street lights (S_2)	Recruit research applicants (S_3)	Support system integration (S_4)
				A	B	C	D
CEO	Revenue	0.3	50	50	48	53	55
	Customer's data privacy (%)	0.175	50	15	50	50	50
	Contribution to public welfare (%)	0.175	50	50	60	50	50
	Innovation (%)	0.175	50	50	50	65	50
	Relationship with regulators (%)	0.175	50	50	50	50	90
Sigurd	Percentage of successfully located faults and dispatched repair teams within time frame (%)	0.25	50	50			
	Self-transcendence	0.18	20	90			
	Openness to change	0.14	50	50			
	Conservation	0.17	50	50			
	Hedonism	0.16	50	50			
	Self-enhancement	0.1	50	50			
Emma	Percentage of reconnected customers within time frame (%)	0.3	90		30		
	Self-transcendence	0.12	50		50		
	Openness to change	0.2	50		50		
	Conservation	0.09	50		50		
	Hedonism	0.12	50		50		
	Self-enhancement	0.17	50		50		
Hanne	New services ready for market (%)	0.35	50			10	
	Self-transcendence	0.1	50			50	
	Openness to change	0.2	50			50	
	Conservation	0.05	50			50	
	Hedonism	0.16	50			20	
	Self-enhancement	0.14	50			50	
Henry	Percentage of resolved cyber-incidents within time frame (%)	0.4	60				30
	Self-transcendence	0.11	50				50
	Openness to change	0.1	50				50
	Conservation	0.18	50				40
	Hedonism	0.06	50				50
	Self-enhancement	0.15	50				50

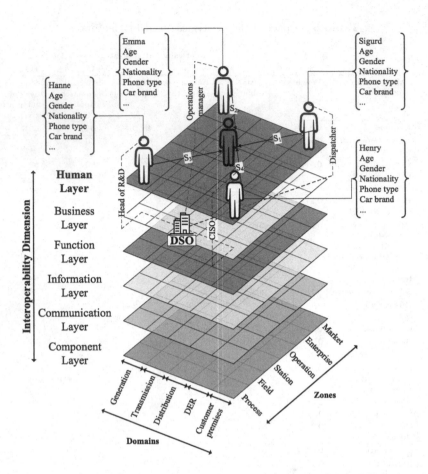

Fig. 4. Summary of context establishment on the SGAM-H.

Table 7. Utility estimation.

Stakeholders	Utility				
	Initial	Final			
		Help a friend (S_1)	Fix street lights (S_2)	Recruit research applicants (S_3)	Support system integration (S_4)
CEO	50	43.875	51.15	53.525	58.5
Sigurd	44.6	57.2			
Emma	62		44		
Hanne	50			31.2	
Henry	54				40.2

Table 8. Change in utilities.

Stakeholders	Change in utilities (incentives)			
	Help a friend (S_1)	Fix street lights (S_2)	Recruit research applicants (S_3)	Support system integration (S_4)
CEO	−6.125	1.15	3.525	8.5
Sigurd	12.6			
Emma		−18		
Hanne			−18.8	
Henry				−13.8

12. Determination of Risks. Risks are expressed and presented to the CEO as incentive-consequence (I-C) pairs in Table 9. Incentives represent the strength of motivation for each strategy owner to select/avoid the related option, consequences capture the risk to the risk owner. Risks that are characterized by a positive incentive and a negative consequence are threat risks. Negative incentive and positive consequence pairs represent opportunity risks, which would be desirable for the risk owner but the strategy owner would have to take a loss to provide the benefit. The assessed risks are shown on the Human Layer in Fig. 5.

Table 9. Risks experienced by the CEO.

Strategy	Incentive	Consequence
Help a friend (S_1)	12.6	−6.125
Fix street lights (S_2)	−18	1.15
Recruit research applicants (S_3)	−18.8	3.525
Support system integration (S_4)	−13.8	8.5

13. Risk Evaluation. The CEO has to subjectively evaluate whether the risks are above or below the acceptability threshold. Risk that are below the acceptance level may not require further action and may only be monitored (e.g., fixing the street lights, recruit students). Risks that are above the threshold require risk treatment. It should be noted that this demonstration relies on crisp numbers, which do not capture appropriately the accuracies/uncertainties associated with each measurement along the chain of inference. Thus, to draw a more accurate picture for real-world applications it is important to understand how

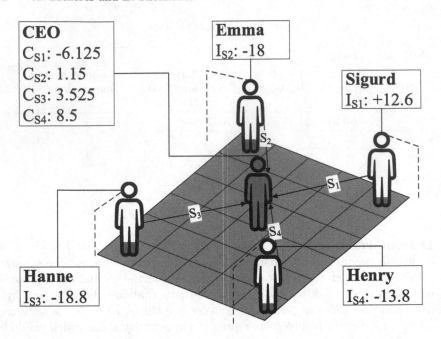

Fig. 5. Risk representation on the Human Layer.

errors propagate. According to [42] the error in a quantity which is derived from other quantities (each measured with some uncertainty) is calculated as:

$$\text{(Measured value of)}\ x = x_{\text{best}} \pm \delta x,$$
$$x_{\text{best}} = \text{best estimate for}\ x,$$
$$\delta x = \text{uncertainty or error in measurement},$$
$$\frac{\delta x}{x_{\text{best}}} = \text{fractional uncertainty}.$$

Since C (choice) is calculated as the product of P and S, the relative error of C can be calculated as the sum of fractional uncertainties in quadrature assuming independent random errors as follows:

$$\frac{\delta C}{C} = \sqrt{\left(\frac{\delta P}{P}\right)^2 + \left(\frac{\delta S}{S}\right)^2}$$

The resulting relative error can be converted into absolute error, and used to compute $C \pm \delta C$ which more accurately captures it's uncertainty.

14. Risk Treatment. Strategy 1 and 4, are above the risk acceptance threshold, therefore certain incentive modifications are necessary to make the options more (for opportunity risks) or less (for threat risks) desirable for the strategy owners.

A risk mitigation for S_1 would be to increase personal accountability in case of privacy violations to make the option less desirable for the strategy owner. Mitigation of S_4 involves the adjustment of the relevant KPI which focuses exclusively on cyber-incident response times by the inclusion of a cross-departmental rating system linked to bonuses which measures cooperation between departments. This can provide incentives to seek mutually beneficial outcomes. The need for alignment between departments requires novel metrics both at the micro and macro levels within the organization.

4.2   Evaluation of the Human Layer

The artifact is qualitatively evaluated across the following criteria by its developers (i.e., internal evaluation by two people): efficacy, ease of use, completeness and homomorphism adhering to the definitions in [31]. A five point grading scale (5-excellent, 4-good, 3-satisfactory, 2-sufficient, 1-unsatisfactory) is used for describing the extent to which the artifact fulfills the evaluation criteria. Efficacy is rated 5 since it successfully establishes a connection between SGAM and CIRA by representing human stakeholder models, thus addressing the identified gap in the literature. Ease of use is rated 3, since the development and construction of the models from scratch required significant effort initially in terms of time spent (several days). After the basic models have been established and with subsequent reuse of the artifacts (i.e., iterative adjustments and updates applied to the models as the case study was developing which involved the identification of relevant literature, extraction of key concepts and customization of the metrics, etc.) it was possible to reduce the effort significantly (below 1 h for each iteration). Completeness is rated 5 since it captures all the relevant elements and relationships between elements identified in CIRA. Homomorphism refers to the correspondence with a reference model (i.e., original SGAM) and is rated 4 since the extension does not interfere with the original model's structure but further adjustments may be necessary to ensure full, unambiguous compatibility with SGAM objects.

5   Discussion

Critical infrastructures designed and built in the previous century are becoming more autonomous and interconnected by the inclusion of IoT devices. Modernisation is driven by a variety of economical, political and ecological motives. Increasing dependency on ICT gives rise to previously unimaginable risks which may endanger the safety, security and privacy of societies at scale. High levels of complexity and lack of historical data about system behavior represent great practical impediments for traditional risk analysis methods. The CIRA method proposes a solution to these problems by focusing on the behavior of fundamental components of any modern system: key decision-makers. Human decision-makers are not appropriately represented on the most well-established model of the SG (SGAM) which may lead to under-recognition of people's influence on the SG.

Consequently, risk analyses may exclusively focus on technical aspects and miss the point, that technology is under the control of human decision-makers with unique motivations. In order to address this imbalance between perspectives, and to enable the creation of a common understanding about the human aspects, this paper proposed the SGAM-H with the Human Layer on top of the SGAM interoperability layers. The extension aimed at keeping compatibility with the original model to a maximum to increase chances of adoption. The extension's efficacy was demonstrated through a case study which applies the CIRA method to a DSO scenario. The case study was inspired by real-world incidents and presented the application of metrics developed for real-world organizations to ensure its realism. The case study presented one threat risk and three opportunity risks to demonstrate the method's applicability. Since the concept of threat risk is more similar to the traditional concept of risk (i.e., an event with negative consequences), the demonstration served the purpose of providing more details about the concept of opportunity risk which has received relatively less attention previously. The artifact has been evaluated along several criteria, thus completing an iteration within the DSR methodology's design cycle. The evaluation has also uncovered some limitations: lack of formal integration of the decision-maker models (and attributes) into existing SGAM models using the Unified Modeling Language (UML); the case study used for demonstration is hypothetical, since access to real-world organizations is limited; the internal, qualitative evaluation represents a weak form of evaluation.

6   Conclusions

The key contributions of this work are as follows: proposal of the SGAM-H augmenting the original SGAM with the Human Layer to create a common understanding among stakeholders operating in the SG ecosystem about the importance of focusing on human-related risks, and to improve risk communication when the CIRA method is applied to SG scenarios. Furthermore, the study contributes by presenting a fully worked-out example of CIRA's application, which may help students and practitioners in better understanding the method's procedures. Recent developments regarding CIRA have been incorporated into the case study (e.g., use of BSC method, operationalization of motivational profiles, differentiation between various aspects of utility, propagation of errors, risk treatment options) and the artifact is evaluated to identify its strengths and weaknesses.

7   Further Work

This study focuses on intra-organizational risks where the CEO is assumed to have the capability to mitigate the identified risks. However, the connection with the other SGAM-layers ensures that relevant stakeholders can be identified from any layer. Stakeholders from other organizations could be identified and elevated from the business layer to analyze inter-organizational risks. Owners of information or physical assets could be identified and elevated to the Human Layer, where the existing connections between assets are inherited by the stakeholders, enabling the identification and specification of strategies that are at the disposal of the strategy owners. This procedure could be a significant step towards replacing the analyst's intuition for strategy identification (step 3). Development of new tools would be required to increase the usability of the Human Layer (e.g., inclusion of interactive functionality would improve user-experience and risk communication capabilities). Furthermore, scalability could be improved by additional software support to enable the representation of more stakeholders on the Human Layer. Simulation-based analyses could be conducted by a more completely populated SGAM model in which the effects of strategic decisions could propagate through the system to simulate and analyze the reactions of other entities (e.g., customers, competitors). Finally, the evaluation can be improved by using more rigorous quantitative evaluation methods, independent of the developers of the artifact (external evaluation). Field experiments with practitioners, or students require the creation of training materials, while application to real-world cases and expert evaluations can be useful to assess user acceptance. It should be investigated how the general idea of a Human Layer can be applied to other domains (e.g., e-health, transportation domains, etc.) to improve understanding about deliberate human behavior and information security risks.

Acknowledgements. We would like to thank the four anonymous reviewers whose comments helped to improve the quality of the paper.

References

1. Anderson, R., Moore, T.: Information security: where computer science, economics and psychology meet. Philos. Trans. Roy. Soc. A Math. Phys. Eng. Sci. **367**(1898), 2717–2727 (2009)
2. Behr, M., et al.: A human model for road safety: from geometrical acquisition to model validation with Radioss. Comput. Meth. Biomech. Biomedi. Eng. **6**(4), 263–273 (2003)
3. Capin, T.K., Noser, H., Thalmann, D., Pandzic, I.S., Thalmann, N.M.: Virtual human representation and communication in VLNET. IEEE Comput. Graphics Appl. **17**(2), 42–53 (1997)
4. CEN-CENELEC-ETSI Smart Grid Coordination Group: Smart grid reference architecture (2012)
5. Cooper, A.: The inmates are Running the Asylum. Macmillan, London (1996)
6. Delgado, I., Aguado, I.: Report on common KPIs D1.4 r2. Project Demonstration 646531, The UPGRID Consortium, Brussels (2016). http://upgrid.eu/wp-content/uploads/2018/01/151104_UPGRID_WP1_D14_KPIs_v14_final.pdf. Accessed 15 Apr 2020
7. Devine, W.D.: From shafts to wires: historical perspective on electrification. J. Econ. Hist. **43**(2), 347–372 (1983)

8. Dragomir, D., Nölle, C., Stomff, S.: Stakeholders' Requirements Analysis Report - D3.1. Project Demonstration 318782, STARGRID project, Brussels (2013). http://stargrid.eu/downloads/2014/07/STARGRID_Stakeholders-Report_D3.1_v1.0_2013_10_11.pdf. Accessed 15 Apr 2020

9. European Parliament, Council of the European Union: Regulation (EU) 2016/679 of the European Parliament and of the Council (GDPR). Official Journal of the European Union (2016), https://eur-lex.europa.eu/legal-content/EN/TXT/HTML/?uri=CELEX:32016R0679#d1e40-1-1. Accessed 15 Apr 2020

10. Gagné, M., Deci, E.L.: Self-determination theory and work motivation. J. Organ. Behav. **26**(4), 331–362 (2005)

11. Gungor, V.C., et al.: Smart grid technologies: communication technologies and standards. IEEE Trans. Industr. Inf. **7**(4), 529–539 (2011)

12. Harder, W.J.: Key Performance Indicators for Smart Grids. Master's thesis, University of Twente, 7522 Enschede, July 2017

13. Hevner, A.R.: A three cycle view of design science research. Scand. J. Inf. Syst. **19**(2), 4 (2007)

14. Bichler, M.: Design science in information systems research. WIRTSCHAFTSIN-FORMATIK **48**(2), 133–135 (2006). https://doi.org/10.1007/s11576-006-0028-8

15. Hubbard, D., Evans, D.: Problems with scoring methods and ordinal scales in risk assessment. IBM J. Res. Dev. **54**(3), 2–1 (2010)

16. Hudlicka, E., Zacharias, G., Psotka, J.: Increasing realism of human agents by modeling individual differences: Methodology, architecture, and testbed. In: Simulating Human Agents, American Association for Artificial Intelligence Fall 2000 Symposium Series, pp. 53–59 (2000)

17. Jürgensen, J.H., Nordström, L., Hilber, P.: A scorecard approach to track reliability performance of distribution system operators. In: 23rd International Conference on Electricity Distribution-CIRED Lyon, 15–18 June 2015. CIRED-Congrès International des Réseaux Electriques de Distribution (2015)

18. Kaplan, R.S., Norton, D.P.: Putting the balanced scorecard to work. Econ. Impact Knowl. **27**(4), 315–324 (1998)

19. Lee, R., Assante, M., Conway, T.: Analysis of the cyber attack on the Ukrainian power grid, Defense Use Case. Electricity Information Sharing and Analysis Center (E-ISAC) 388 (2016)

20. Liu, P., Zang, W., Yu, M.: Incentive-based modeling and inference of attacker intent, objectives, and strategies. ACM Trans. Inf. Syst. Secur. (TISSEC) **8**(1), 78–118 (2005)

21. Martello, M., Watson, J.G., Fischer, M.J.: Implementing a balanced scorecard in a not-for-profit organization. J. Bus. Econ. Res. (JBER) **6**(9), 67–80 (2008)

22. McKenna, E., Richardson, I., Thomson, M.: Smart meter data: Balancing consumer privacy concerns with legitimate applications. Energy Policy **41**, 807–814 (2012)

23. Meurens, F., Summerfield, A., Nauwynck, H., Saif, L., Gerdts, V.: The pig: a model for human infectious diseases. Trends Microbiol. **20**(1), 50–57 (2012)

24. Moore, T.: The economics of cybersecurity: principles and policy options. Int. J. Crit. Infrastruct. Prot. **3**(3–4), 103–117 (2010)

25. Muir, A., Lopatto, J.: Final report on the august 14, 2003 blackout in the united states and canada: causes and recommendations. US-Canada Power System Outage Task Force, Canada (2004)

26. Müller-Hansen, F., et al.: Towards representing human behavior and decision making in earth system models-an overview of techniques and approaches. Earth Syst. Dyn. **8** (2017)

27. Musharraf, M., Khan, F., Veitch, B.: Validating human behavior representation model of general personnel during offshore emergency situations. Fire Technol. **55**(2), 643–665 (2019)
28. National Research Council: Electricity in Economic Growth. The National Academies Press, Washington, DC (1986). https://doi.org/10.17226/900, https://www.nap.edu/catalog/900/electricity-in-economic-growth
29. NVE: KILE - kvalitetsjusterte inntektsrammer ved ikke levert energi, October 2019. https://www.nve.no/reguleringsmyndigheten/okonomisk-regulering-av-nett selskap/om-den-okonomiske-reguleringen/kile-kvalitetsjusterte-inntektsrammer-ved-ikke-levert-energi/, Accessed 15 Apr 2020
30. Pew, R.W., Mavor, A.S. (eds.): Representing Human Behavior in Military Simulations: Interim Report. The National Academies Press, Washington, DC (1997). https://doi.org/10.17226/5714, https://www.nap.edu/catalog/5714/representing-human-behavior-in-military-simulations-interim-report
31. Prat, N., Comyn-Wattiau, I., Akoka, J.: A taxonomy of evaluation methods for information systems artifacts. J. Manag. Inf. Syst. **32**(3), 229–267 (2015)
32. Rajbhandari, L., Snekkenes, E.: Using the conflicting incentives risk analysis method. In: Janczewski, L.J., Wolfe, H.B., Shenoi, S. (eds.) SEC 2013. IAICT, vol. 405, pp. 315–329. Springer, Heidelberg (2013). https://doi.org/10.1007/978-3-642-39218-4_24
33. Sánchez-Ortiz, J., García-Valderrama, T., Rodríguez-Cornejo, V.: Towards a balanced scorecard in regulated companies: a study of the Spanish electricity sector. Electr. J. **29**(9), 36–43 (2016)
34. Santodomingo, R., Uslar, M., Gottschlak, M., Goering, A., Nordstrom, L., Valdenmaiier, G.: The discern tool support for knowledge sharing in large smart grid projects. CIRED Workshop (2016)
35. Schuh, G., Fluhr, J., Birkmeier, M., Sund, M.: Information system architecture for the interaction of electric vehicles with the power grid. In: 2013 10th IEEE International Conference on Networking, Sensing and Control (ICNSC), pp. 821–825. IEEE (2013)
36. Selyukh, A.: NSA staff used spy tools on spouses, ex-lovers: watchdog. U.S, September 2013. https://www.reuters.com/article/us-usa-surveil-lance-watchdog/nsa-staff-used-spy-tools-on-spouses-ex-lovers-watchdog-idUSBRE98Q14G20130927
37. Snekkenes, E.: Position paper: privacy risk analysis is about understanding conflicting incentives. In: Fischer-Hübner, S., de Leeuw, E., Mitchell, C. (eds.) IDMAN 2013. IAICT, vol. 396, pp. 100–103. Springer, Heidelberg (2013). https://doi.org/10.1007/978-3-642-37282-7_9
38. Stassen, H.G., Johannsen, G., Moray, N.: Internal representation, internal model, human performance model and mental workload. Automatica **26**(4), 811–820 (1988)
39. Szekeres, A., Snekkenes, E.A.: Predicting CEO misbehavior from observables: comparative evaluation of two major personality models. In: Obaidat, M.S. (ed.) ICETE 2018. CCIS, vol. 1118, pp. 135–158. Springer, Cham (2019). https://doi.org/10.1007/978-3-030-34866-3_7
40. Szekeres, A., Snekkenes, E.A.: Construction of human motivational profiles by observation for risk analysis. IEEE Access **8**, 45096–45107 (2020)
41. Szekeres, A., Wasnik, P.S., Snekkenes, E.A.: Using demographic features for the prediction of basic human values underlying stakeholder motivation. In: Proceedings of the 21st International Conference on Enterprise Information Systems, volume 2: ICEIS, pp. 377–389. INSTICC, SciTePress (2019)

42. Taylor, J.R.: An introduction to error analysis: The study of uncertainties in physical measurements. University Science Books, Sausalito, California (1997)
43. Uslar, M., Engel, D.: Towards generic domain reference designation: How to learn from smart grid interoperability. DA-Ch Energieinformatik **1**, 1–6 (2015)
44. Uslar, M., et al.: Applying the smart grid architecture model for designing and validating system-of-systems in the power and energy domain: a European perspective. Energies **12**(2), 258 (2019)
45. Uslar, M., Rosinger, C., Schlegel, S.: Security by design for the smart grid: combining the SGAM and NISTIR 7628. In: 2014 IEEE 38th International Computer Software and Applications Conference Workshops, pp. 110–115. IEEE (2014)
46. Uslar, M., Trefke, J.: Applying the smart grid architecture model SGAM to the EV domain. In: EnviroInfo, pp. 821–826 (2014)
47. Waterman, R.W., Meier, K.J.: Principal-agent models: an expansion? J. Public Adm. Res. Theor. **8**(2), 173–202 (1998)
48. Weishäupl, E., Yasasin, E., Schryen, G.: Information security investments: an exploratory multiple case study on decision-making, evaluation and learning. Comput. Secur. **77**, 807–823 (2018)

Breaking the Cyber Kill Chain by Modelling Resource Costs

Kristian Haga[1] , Per Håkon Meland[1,2](✉) , and Guttorm Sindre[1]

[1] Norwegian University of Science and Technology, Trondheim, Norway
{kristian.haga,per.hakon.meland,guttorm.sindre}@ntnu.no
[2] SINTEF Digital, Trondheim, Norway
per.h.meland@sintef.no
https://www.ntnu.no/
https://www.sintef.no/

Abstract. To combat cybercrime, a clearer understanding of the attacks and the offenders is necessary. When there is little available data about attack incidents, which is usually the case for new technology, one can make estimations about the necessary investments an offender would need to compromise the system. The next step would be to implement measures that increase these costs to a level that makes the attack unattractive. Our research method follows the principles of *design science*, where cycles of research activities are used to create artefacts intended to solve real-world problems. Our artefacts are an approach for creating a *resource costs model* (RCM) and an accompanying modelling tool implemented as a web application. These are used to find the required attacker resources at each stage of the cyber kill chain. End user feedback show that structured visualisation of the required resources raises the awareness of the cyberthreat. This approach has its strength and provides best accuracy with specific attacks, but is more limited when there are many possible attack vectors of different types.

Keywords: Cyber kill chain · Costs · Resources · Profiling · Attack tree

1 Introduction

As our use of technology in almost every aspect of life steadily increases, so does our exposure to cybercrime. To combat this growing form of criminality, a clearer understanding of the costs, benefits and attractiveness of cyberattacks is necessary [18]. This is in accordance with *Routine Active Theory* [5], extended to include cybercrime [6,8], which states that crime will occur when all of the following four conditions are met: There exist an *1) accessible and attractive target, 2) the absence of a capable guardian* and the presence of *3) a motivated offender* with *4) the resources required to commit the crime.* For the latter case, it is not just a question of technical skills, but also a requirement that the offender

© Springer Nature Switzerland AG 2020
H. Eades III and O. Gadyatskaya (Eds.): GraMSec 2020, LNCS 12419, pp. 111–126, 2020.
https://doi.org/10.1007/978-3-030-62230-5_6

is able to invest in software development and hardware acquisition, as well as the time it takes to plan, prepare and perform the attack. Alternatively, the offender could bribe an insider or hire someone else to do it through cybercrime-as-a-service [21] being offered by third parties.

We hypothesize that during threat analysis, it is possible to reduce the complexity of the resource requirement to a monetary concern, complemented by a limited set of attacker characteristics. This will allow us to identify the potential offenders and come up with technical and non-technical mitigations that will significantly increase the attacker costs.

The contribution of this paper is a modelling approach that maps resource costs to each stage of a cyberattack, and derives the total cost of the attack. We have utilized principles from Schneier's *attack trees* [32] and the Lockheed Martin's *cyber kill chain* [13], both already widely known in the security community, to structure this approach. A dedicated prototype tool has been developed to simplify and visualise this process, and we have completed the first rounds of iterative evaluation among experts. This tool is able to show calculations interactively and extract potential offenders based on a built-in library from available cybercriminal profile literature. Our goal is to improve the accuracy of threat analysis, and especially increase the understanding and awareness of cyberthreats among sectorial domain stakeholders.

This paper is structured as follows. Section 2 gives an overview of background knowledge and literature, and Sect. 3 explains our method. Results are given in Sect. 4, which are discussed in the light of evaluations in Sect. 5. Finally, Sect. 6 concludes the paper.

2   Background

2.1   The Cyber Kill Chain

Already in 1998, Meadows [23] presented a way of dividing attacks into different stages or phases to make visual representation easier. The next stage would not commence before the previous one had completed, and she used different colours to represent the assumed difficulty of each stage. The stages were not predetermined, but varied according to the nature of the attack. Later on, McQueen et al. [22] defined a set of five fixed stages, *reconnaissance, breach, penetrate, escalation* and *damage*, which were then modelled as a compromise graph in order to find the weakest link(s) in the attack path based on expected time-to-compromise. Hutchins et al. [14] describe different phase-based models from military usage (countering terrorist attacks) and the information security field (between 2008–2010), and present their own version nicked the *intrusion kill chain*. This model was later on renamed and branded as the *cyber kill chain* [13] by Lockheed Martin, and has proven to be widely popular among defenders of IT and enterprise networks [1]. The seven stages of the cyber kill chain are:

 Reconnaissance: Research, identification and selection of target.

Weaponization: Coupling a malware (e.g. remote access trojan) with an exploit into a deliverable payload, e.g. a media file.

 Delivery: Transmission of the weapon to the targeted environment, e.g. an email attachment or USB-drive.

 Exploitation: Triggers malicious code. Ranges from auto-executing within the host's operating system to users triggering execution.

 Installation: Installation of the malware on the victim system, allowing the adversary to maintain presence inside the environment.

 Command and Control (C2): Establishes a channel for the adversary to access the target environment.

 Actions on Objectives: Complete attack objectives, such as data extraction, establish hop point, break integrity or make system unavailable.

According to Hahn et al. [10], a developed cyber kill chain provides the basis for a "systematic study of how the various cyberattack steps and phases can perturb the system layers and eventually impact physical operations". This is subsequently used in their analysis framework to develop security properties and design systems resilient to cyberattacks. As shown by Pols [27], there are many variants of the kill chain found in the literature. Some with different stage types and others with up to eighteen different stages. We chose to focus our work on the original seven stage cyber kill chain due to its popularity.

2.2   Attack Tree Cost Modelling

Attack trees are acyclic graphs used to model threats from the viewpoint of the perpetrator. Schneier's original attack tree paper [32] showed how different costs could be assigned to alternative leaf nodes and how these propagated to define the cheapest way of attack. A fundamental paradigm for this kind of modelling is the assumption of a *rational attacker* [3], meaning that *1) there will be no attack if the attack is unprofitable* and *2) the attacker chooses the most profitable way of attacking*.

There have also been several approaches where costs are used in combination with other attributes. For instance, Buldas et al. [3] include costs, gains, penalties and associated probability values. Further examples of different attributes and references to papers that utilize costs in attack trees is given by Bagnato et al. [2]. Having more attributes enables additional ways of analysing attack trees, for instance Kumar et al. [19] show how to find the minimum time to complete an attack given a specific budget. Jensen et al. [15] present an approach where cost is a function of time instead of a constant cost per atomic attack attempt. Still, the major challenge of assigning accurate attribute values to attack tree nodes is difficult to overcome as attacker-specific information tends to be based on a best guess [31].

A comprehensive overview of more than thirty attack and defence modelling approaches based on directed acyclic graphs can be found in a survey paper by Kordy et al. [17]. A more recent survey focusing on fault and attack trees has been published by Nagaraju et al. [24].

2.3 Cybercriminal Profiling

Shinder and Tittel [33] define a *profile* to be a set of characteristics likely to be shared by criminals who commit a certain type of crime. The use of profiles during criminal investigations can be traced several hundred years back in time, and though this is not an exact science, Nykodym et al. [25] argue that the track record legitimates the concept. However, they also argue that attackers have more advantages in a cyber setting as they do not have to be physically present at the crime scene.

The two main methods for profiling are known as *inductive* and *deductive* [37]. In the former, a profile database is developed based on information from already committed crime, and offender characteristics are correlated with types of crime. In the latter, forensics evidence is gathered from the crime scene and used to deduce the characteristics of the offender. Most of the established literature comes from the digital forensics field and relates to deductive profiling. We have been mostly interested in inductive profiling as a tool to identify potential offenders before any crime is actually committed. Furthermore, it is well established that likely offenders have *motive, means* and *opportunity* (MMO) [26,35] before committing any crime. As attacker costs belongs to the *means* characteristic, the literature becomes more limited. Warikoo et al. [37] have *capability factor* as one of their six profile identification metrics, where available resources for e.g. purchasing malware belongs. Preuß et al. [28] created a small set of profiles based on twelve cybercrime cases between 1998 and 2004. Due to the limited sample size, they could not create a structured set of attributes for these, but found that the principle of *minimum costs and maximum results* were present in all. Casey [4] presents a threat agent library of archetypal cybercriminal agents where *resources* is one of the eight attributes defining them. Casey's work is used to define *Attack Resource Level* in the cyberthreat exchange format *STIX* [16].

3   Method

Our research method follows the principles of *design science*, supporting a pragmatic research paradigm where artefacts are created to solve real-world problems by cycling through research activities related to *relevance, design* and *rigor* [11,34]. The problem we try to address is the challenge of quantifying cyberrisks when there is little reliable historical data about attacks. Our artefacts are 1) an approach for creating a *resource costs model* (RCM), that is used to find the required attacker investments at each stage of the cyber kill chain and 2) an accompanying modelling tool implemented as a web application.

As a part of the relevance cycle, we initially worked with opportunities and problems related to cybersecurity for maritime shipping. We analysed typical vulnerabilities and threats towards eNavigation systems, and made cost estimations for attacking the various underlying technology modules.

During the rigor cycle, past knowledge, as presented in Sect. 2, was examined and we chose to build on practices that already had a significant uptake among practitioners.

Most central to design science research is the design cycle, consisting of artefact construction, evaluation and refinements based on feedback. Initially, we applied "pen-and-paper" variants of the RCM and validated the expressiveness by constructing models of known cyberattacks towards maritime systems. The second iteration produced a *minimum viable product* (MVP) of the tool. Ries [29] defines a MVP as the version of a new product which allows developers to collect the maximum amount of validated learning about customers with the least effort. Our MVP consisted of an info page tutorial and functionality for building basic resource costs models for each attack phase. For the evaluation we recruited eight security experts who modelled a specific use case. These were observed during modelling and debriefed afterwards. The third iteration added the cybercriminal profiling feature, improved the user interface, as well as tweaking flawed features and functions. This evaluation included another eight security professional from the industry and two maritime domain experts.

4   Results

4.1   The Resource Costs Model

In a *resource cost model* (RCM), each stage in the cyber kill chain represents the root node of a *resource tree*, depicted in Fig. 1, which is similar in structure to an attack tree.

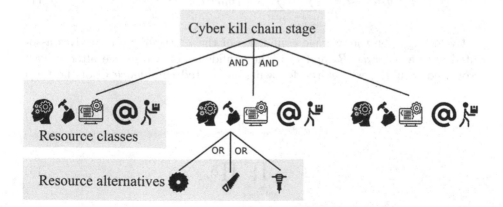

Fig. 1. A resource tree for a single cyber kill chain stage

The second level of the tree defines which resource types are required to complete the parent stage. At this level, all nodes have a conjunctive (*AND*) relationship since an attack would require all necessary resources. A resource can belong to five different classes:

 Skill: Includes domain knowledge, malware development abilities or utilisation of cybercrime tools or guides.

 Tangible: Necessary hardware components or other physical objects. This can range from advanced technology to soldering tools.

 Logic: Commercially available software, data sets or cybercrime tools or services.

 Logic-atomic: Necessary resources that cannot be broken into smaller parts, e.g. an IP-address, email address or a password.

 Behavioral: Actions that must be conducted as a part of the attack, for instance bribing, sending out phishing emails or social engineering.

The third level in the tree, *resource alternatives*, are disjunctive (*OR*) leaf nodes that present ways to realize their parent resource class. Each resource alternative is associated with a cost interval and a confidence value. A confidence close to zero communicates that there is little evidence to support the stated cost interval. At the other end of the scale, a confidence of 1 means that there is exhaustive evidence to back the stated cost interval and that the price of the resource is not subject to great variation.

We can express the total cost interval of the attack T formally by stating that all resources R_j need to have a valid set V of resource alternatives. Let α represent the minimum estimated cost of the cheapest resource alternative and β represent maximum cost of the most expensive resource alternative. From this we can derive the following:

$$T = [(min\ cost = \sum_{\substack{stage\ \in \\ kill\ chain}} \sum_{i \in V} \alpha_i), (max\ cost = \sum_{\substack{stage\ \in \\ kill\ chain}} \sum_{i \in V} \beta_i)] \qquad (1)$$

By letting ϕ be the average confidence of the n resource alternatives associated with a resource R_j and c_i is the confidence of a resource alternative i associated with R_j, we get the following associated confidence C of the total cost:

$$\phi_j = \frac{\sum_{i \in R_j} c_i}{n} \qquad (2)$$

$$C = \prod_{\substack{stage\ \in \\ kill\ chain}} \prod_{R} \phi_j \qquad (3)$$

In order to mitigate an attack, at least a one of the resources throughout the cyber kill chain must be made too expensive for the adversary. However, the adversary only needs a single resource alternative for each of the resources.

4.2   The IRCM Tool

To validate the modelling approach, we have built an interactive installation of the model in the form of a web application called *Interactive Resource Cost Model* (IRCM) tool. This allows the users to model cyberattacks of their choosing, while concurrently deriving the total cost of the attack and probable cybercriminal profiles able to conduct it. An example screenshot from a single resource tree is shown in Fig. 2, while a screenshot of the RCM for the complete cyber kill chain is included in Appendix A.

Fig. 2. A screenshot resource tree from the reconnaissance stage

These examples are taken from the maritime domain, where the *Electronic Chart Display and Information System* (ECDIS) is a central component for ship navigation. It displays the vessels position on a chart and integrates information from a number of sensors, such as radar, gyro, GNSS, echo sounder, weather measurements and the anti-collision systems. Malicious manipulation of this position could cause confusion on the ship bridge and potential course alteration could lead to collisions in congested waters [38]. The examples are loosely based on the demonstrated attack against an air-gapped ECDIS system by Lund et al. [20]. This attack was also structured according to the cyber kill chain, but in contrast to an external attack, it was conducted in cooperation with the Royal Norwegian Navy. Also, no information about resource costs were given, so here we have made our own estimations.

As can be seen in Fig. 2, there are four resources defined for the reconnaissance stage. The first one, *ECDIS documentation*, is a tangible class, and the alternatives are to either *purchase* the documentation from the vendor legally, or *steal* it. The second resource is another tangible class, and represents an operational ECDIS unit that can be used to analyse its operating system, software and network traffic. It can be realized in different ways, by *purchasing a unit from vendor* or the *black market*, or running it as a software *simulation*. These alternatives vary in price, from relatively cheap software (where you pay according to sailing route) to more expensive hardware units in the range of $10 000 - $30 000. The third resource is of class logic-atomic, and represents information about the *ship inventory* used to determine which type and where the ECDIS units are installed. To simplify the model, only a single *bribe insider* alternative is used. The final resource is also of type skill, and represents required knowledge about *vulnerabilities* gained through *scanning and testing*.

Both resources and resource alternatives are created by using the tool input data forms. An example screenshot for the ECDIS resource alternative *purchased from vendor* is shown in Fig. 3.

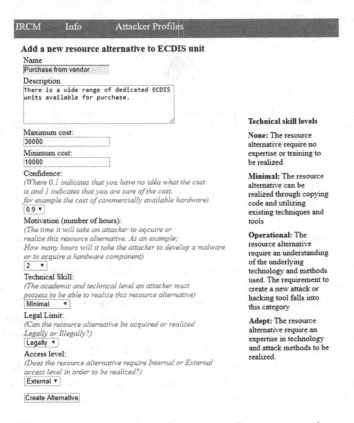

Fig. 3. A screenshot from the resource alternative window

The tool has a built-in database of cybercriminal profiles that the model inductively retrieves candidates from. This database is summarized in Appendix B and has been based on profile definitions we have found in the literature [4,16,30,37]. We found out that mapping total attack cost with assumed *wealth* was not a very useful way of doing this. The wealthiest attacker is not always the most likely one, and attackers have more than one characterizing dimension. Therefore, the tool is able to exclude improbable attacker profiles from the database based on optional information that is assigned to the resources in the RCM. The exclusion rules are based on the following:

- Total minimal *cost* exceeds the financial capacities of the profile [*no cost, low, medium, high*].
- The accumulated time to require all resources exceed its *motivational* limit [*no time, low, medium, high*].
- Any resource alternative that requires a higher *technical skill* level than the profile possesses [*none, minimal, operational, adept*].
- Any resource that requires *moral limits* to be broken [*legally, illegally*].
- Any resource that require an *access level* the profile does not possess [*internal, external*].

The extended ECDIS attack example in Appendix A shows aggregated model information based on input contained in the individual resource tree for each attack stage. The cost interval has a broad range, mostly due to the choice of purchasing ECDIS hardware unit versus other cheaper alternatives in both the *reconnaissance* and *delivery* stages. Besides from these, the overall resource costs related to tangible and skill are relatively low. By analysing the model, we find that there are significant costs related to the *delivery* stage as the attacker would need physical presence at the ship and gain access to the bridge or bribe an insider. It is the air-gapping of the ECDIS that provides the main security measure by making delivery costly. When considering opening up for online software and chart updates, it is clear that additional secure measures will be needed to preserve an expensive attack vector. The confidence value is also very low, but would have been much higher if we had modelled the attack with a specific ECDIS unit in mind where costs are more certain. Also, a higher number of resources will automatically yield a lower confidence, which is natural since acquiring many resources increases uncertainty. The main benefit of the confidence is for attack comparison, which is not shown in these examples. Given the various exclusion rules that have been applied to the model, the most probable attacker profile in this case is *cyber warrior* (described in Appendix B). The cyber warrior profile is not limited by financial requirements of this attack, has a high technical skill level and has little concern for moral limits.

5   Discussion

Hong and Kim [12] have pointed to the inherit challenge with graph-based attack models, namely the ability to scale. A purely tree-based model will generate large, bewildering attack trees for complex attacks. In turn, this creates a conflict between analysis and comprehensibility [7]. Hence, some sort of decomposition is needed. We chose to combine two modelling techniques to amplify their advantages and overcome some of their shortcomings. The cyber kill chain allows us to divide the attack into seven consecutive steps, and by breaking the chain in the early stages we don't have to embellish the later ones. The relatively small resource tree for each of the stages breaks down composite resource requirements into atomic ones, which can be more accurately estimated. This was the main takeaway from the first iteration of the design cycle. Secondly, we experienced that deriving a cost interval, rather than a single estimate, provides more confident information regarding the availability of an attack. A cheap, more available resource alternative set may provide a less stealthy attack than an expensive alternative. By determining both the minimum and maximum cost, we include both the risk willing and risk averse offenders. A large cost interval does not necessarily imply an inaccurate cost estimate, but rather that the evaluated attack can be carried out with a wide span of sophistication and possible impact on the target.

The second iteration involved eight expert end users from a research institute who were observed using the MVP of the tool and debriefed afterwards. Seven out of these eight expressed that the main difficulty was to understand the difference between *resource* and *resource alternative* in the models. We were also able to observe that classifying resources was not straightforward, and the users spent some time navigating between the information page and the modelling interface to check definitions and the tutorial example. Both of these issues improved quickly with hands-on experience and by refining the info page. It was stated during the debrief that "especially interesting is the fact that making only a single resource unavailable, thus breaking the kill chain, will mitigate the entire attack" and all independently agreed that the structured visualisation of the required resources would raise the awareness of the cyberthreat. Some also expressed that many of the resources are impossible to make unavailable, which is true of course. In the MVP, we used *attack trees* as the tree structure term, and this caused some confusion since the RCM focus on resource required to perform the attack and not the attack actions, hence we changed this to *resource tree*.

The third iteration had a focus on inducing criminal profiles from the models and made several improvements to the MVP. We recruited eight professionals from the security industry and two maritime domain experts as end users. Feedback showed that the approach improves the understanding of attacks. The cheapest attack options were considered the most probable, which is helpful when identify mitigation efforts. One of the domain experts encouragingly commented: "It is still a lot of guesswork, but it is systematic guesswork". Being able to document and provide traceability to threat estimations is vital for industries which require safety and security certification of components. More details of these evaluations can be found in the report by Haga [9]. Parallel to this, Walde and Hanus [36] successfully employed the RCM to plan the purchase of necessary components in order to demonstrate a GNSS spoofing attack.

As already mentioned, the wealthiest attacker is not always the most likely one, therefore we are using five identifying attributes as exclusion rules. A known limitation is that none of these say much about the *motive* of the offender, that is *why* she would commit the crime. This has been out of our scope, but could be extended by looking at the attack impact and attacker reward. Those considerations would have to be determined on a case-by-case basis, requiring additional knowledge dimensions. There is a general criticism towards the cyber kill chain that it focuses too much on the perimeter and malware attack vector [27], and we have seen supportive evidence of that too. Therefore, future improvements could be to include other sets of stages more suitable to describe attacks such as for instance related to social engineering, denial-of-service or code injection.

6   Conclusion

Through the iterative nature of design science we have made many improvements to the RCM modelling approach and the accompanying tool. However, we still consider this work to be in progress with many potential improvements related to usefulness and usability. We are also planning to extend the user testing and evaluation, particularly in the field of maritime cybersecurity, but also in other domains to ensure that the artefacts could have a wider usage than just the maritime context. Nevertheless, there is no silver bullet to threat modelling. We are trying to address the real-world problem of missing historical incident data, which is a particular concern for new technology. Attacker costs is one aspect that could be useful during threat estimations, but this must be seen in combination with possible attacker reward as well. In addition, defence costs must be compared with possible loss to make an overall risk assessment.

The RCM has its strength and provides best accuracy with specific attacks; when there are few resources and resource alternatives. Hence, we would not recommend this approach when you want to represent attacks with many possible attack vectors of different types. In such cases, several RCMs could be created and compared, but this quickly becomes a tedious task. As always, the analyst should choose the right tool for the job at hand.

Acknowledgment. The research leading to these results has partially been performed by the Cyber Security in Merchant Shipping Service Evolution (CySiMS-SE) project, which received funding from the Research Council of Norway under Grant No. 295969.

A   Tool screenshots

See Figs. 4 and 5.

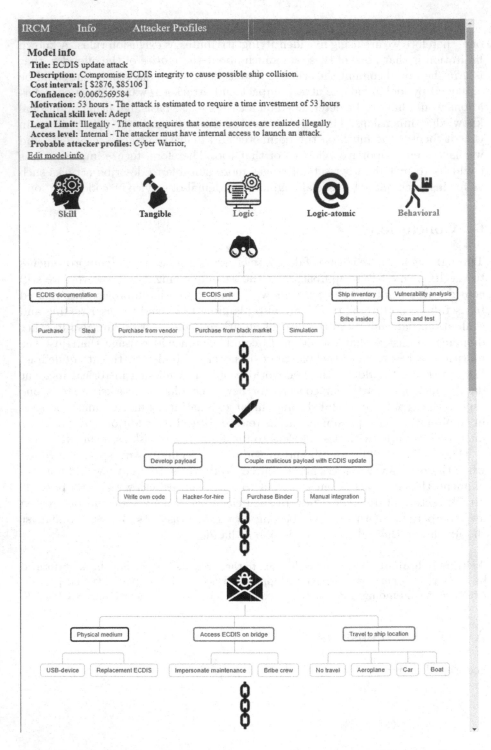

Fig. 4. A screenshot from the first three stages; *Reconnaissance, Weaponization* and *Delivery.*

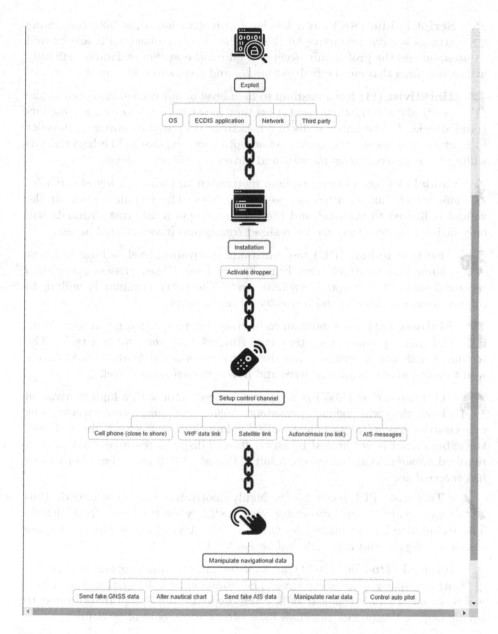

Fig. 5. A screenshot from the last four stages; *Exploitation, Installation, Command and Control* and *Actions on Objectives*

B   Cybercriminal profiles

Script kiddie (SK) has a low level of motivation, thus *time consuming* attacks are not attractive to this profile. The technical skills are limited to *minimal* and the profile only accepts a *minimal* cost. Script kiddies will only utilize resources that can be realized *legally* and have *external* access.

Hacktivist (H) has a medium to high level of motivation anchored in the political cause they represent, thus they may conduct *time consuming*, targeted attacks. The technical skills of a hacktivist is limited to *minimal*. In order to fight for their cause, the hacktivist accepts *some* expenses. The hacktivist is willing to require resources *illegally* and have *external* access level.

Vandal (V) has a low to medium motivation and will only invest a *limited* amount of time in attention seeking attacks. The technical skills of the vandal is limited to *minimal* and the profile accepts a *low* cost. Vandals will only utilize resources that can be realized *legally* and have *external* access.

Petty criminal (PC) has a medium motivation level, willing to invest *some* time in attacks that bring financial gain. They possess *operational* technical skills and accepts a *medium* cost. The petty criminal is willing to require resources *illegally* and has *external* access level.

Mobster (M) has a medium to high level of motivation given that financial gain is possible, thus they may conduct *time consuming* attacks. The technical skills are *operational* and the profile accepts *costly* attacks. Mobsters won't second guess *illegal* resources and have *external* access level.

Cyberwarrior (CW) is a state-sponsored actor with a high motivation level, thus will conduct persistent, *highly time consuming* attacks. The cyberwarrior has *adept* technical skills for launching any attack. In addition, the cyberwarrior is *not limited* by any costs and disposes resources that may be required *illegally*. As an immediate result of the *adept* skill level, the cyberwarrior has *internal* access.

Terrorist (T) tends to be highly motivated and well-funded, thus can conduct *time consuming* and *costly* cyberattacks to front beliefs. The technical skills are limited to *minimal*. The Terrorist is willing to require resources *illegally* and have *external* access level.

Internal - Hostile (IN-H) has a medium motivation level and may launch attacks that require *some* time. The profile knows the system well, which yields an *operational* technical skill. *Some* expenses are acceptable, limited to *legally* acquired resources. Internals have *internal* access level by default.

Internal - Non-hostile (IN-NH) launces cyberattacks by accident, thus *not* motivated at all to invest any time or money in a cyberattack and will only possess resources that can be *legally* realized. Given that accidental cyberattacks are possible yields an *operational* skill level and an *internal* access level.

References

1. Assante, M.J., Lee, R.M.: The industrial control system cyber kill chain. SANSInstitute InfoSec Reading Room **1** (2015)
2. Bagnato, A., Kordy, B., Meland, P.H., Schweitzer, P.: Attribute decoration of attack-defense trees. Int. J. Secure Softw. Eng. (IJSSE) **3**(2), 1–35 (2012)
3. Buldas, A., Laud, P., Priisalu, J., Saarepera, M., Willemson, J.: Rational choice of security measures via multi-parameter attack trees. In: Lopez, J. (ed.) CRITIS 2006. LNCS, vol. 4347, pp. 235–248. Springer, Heidelberg (2006). https://doi.org/10.1007/11962977_19
4. Casey, T.: Threat agent library helps identify information security risks. Intel White Paper **2** (2007)
5. Cohoen, L.E., Felson, M.: Social change and crime rate trends: a routine activity approach. Am. Sociol. Rev. **44**(4), 588–608 (1979)
6. Ekblom, P., Tiley, N.: Going equipped. Br. J. Criminol. **40**(3), 376–398 (2000)
7. Gadyatskaya, O., Trujillo-Rasua, R.: New directions in attack tree research: catching up with industrial needs. In: Liu, P., Mauw, S., Stølen, K. (eds.) GraMSec 2017. LNCS, vol. 10744, pp. 115–126. Springer, Cham (2018). https://doi.org/10.1007/978-3-319-74860-3_9
8. Grabosky, P.N.: Virtual criminality: old wine in new bottles? Soc. Legal Stud. **10**(2), 243–249 (2001)
9. Haga, K.: Breaking the cyber kill chain by modelling resource costs. Master's thesis, NTNU, Trondheim, Norway (2020)
10. Hahn, A., Thomas, R.K., Lozano, I., Cardenas, A.: A multi-layered and kill-chain based security analysis framework for cyber-physical systems. Int. J. Crit. Infrastruct. Prot. **11**, 39–50 (2015)
11. Hevner, A., Chatterjee, S.: Design science research in information systems. In: Design Research in Information Systems, pp. 9–22. Springer, Boston (2010). https://doi.org/10.1007/978-1-4419-5653-8_2
12. Hong, J.B., Kim, D.S.: Performance analysis of scalable attack representation models. In: Janczewski, L.J., Wolfe, H.B., Shenoi, S. (eds.) SEC 2013. IAICT, vol. 405, pp. 330–343. Springer, Heidelberg (2013). https://doi.org/10.1007/978-3-642-39218-4_25
13. Hutchins, E.M.: The cyber kill chain. Technical report, Lockheed Martin (2020). https://www.lockheedmartin.com/en-us/capabilities/cyber/cyber-kill-chain.html. Accessed 12 Apr 2020
14. Hutchins, E.M., Cloppert, M.J., Amin, R.M.: Intelligence-driven computer network defense informed by analysis of adversary campaigns and intrusion kill chains. Leading Issues Inf. Warfare Secur. Res. **1**(1), 80 (2011)
15. Jensen, P.G., Larsen, K., Legay, A., Poulsen, D.: Quantitative evaluation of attack defense trees using stochastic timed automata. In: International Workshop on Graphical Models for Security, pp. 75–90. HAL Id: hal-01640091 (2017)
16. Jordan, B., Piazza, R., Wounder, J.: Stix version 2.0. part 1: Stix core concepts. Technical report, OASIS Committee Specifications 01 (2017) http://docs.oasis-open.org/cti/stix/v2.0/stix-v2.0-part1-stix-core.html. Accessed 13 Apr 2020
17. Kordy, B., Piètre-Cambacédès, L., Schweitzer, P.: Dag-based attack and defense modeling: don't miss the forest for the attack trees. Comput. Sci. Rev. **13**, 1–38 (2014)
18. Kshetri, N.: The simple economics of cybercrimes. IEEE Secur. Privacy **4**(1), 33–39 (2006)

19. Kumar, R., Ruijters, E., Stoelinga, M.: Quantitative attack tree analysis via priced timed automata. In: Sankaranarayanan, S., Vicario, E. (eds.) FORMATS 2015. LNCS, vol. 9268, pp. 156–171. Springer, Cham (2015). https://doi.org/10.1007/978-3-319-22975-1_11

20. Lund, M.S., Hareide, O.S., Jøsok, Ø.: An attack on an integrated navigation system. NECESSE 3(2), 149–163 (2018)

21. Manky, D.: Cybercrime as a service: a very modern business. Comput. Fraud Secur. 2013(6), 9–13 (2013)

22. McQueen, M.A., Boyer, W.F., Flynn, M.A., Beitel, G.A.: Quantitative cyber risk reduction estimation methodology for a small scada control system. In: Proceedings of the 39th Annual Hawaii International Conference on System Sciences (HICSS 2006), vol. 9, pp. 226–226. IEEE (2006)

23. Meadows, C.: A representation of protocol attacks for risk assessment. In: Proceedings of the DIMACS Workshop on Network Threats, pp. 1–10 (1998)

24. Nagaraju, V., Fiondella, L., Wandji, T.: A survey of fault and attack tree modeling and analysis for cyber risk management. In: 2017 IEEE International Symposium on Technologies for Homeland Security (HST), pp. 1–6. IEEE (2017)

25. Nykodym, N., Taylor, R., Vilela, J.: Criminal profiling and insider cyber crime. Comput. Law Secur. Rev. 21(5), 408–414 (2005)

26. Pendse, S.G.: Ethical hazards: a motive, means, and opportunity approach to curbing corporate unethical behavior. J. Bus. Ethics 107(3), 265–279 (2012)

27. Pols, P.: The unified kill chain: Designing a unified kill chain for analyzing, comparing and defending against cyber attacks. Cyber Security Academy (2017)

28. Preuß, J., Furnell, S.M., Papadaki, M.: Considering the potential of criminal profiling to combat hacking. J. Comput. Virol. 3(2), 135–141 (2007)

29. Ries, E.: The lean startup : how constant innovation creates radically successful businesses. Portfolio Penguin (2011)

30. Rogers, M.K.: The psyche of cybercriminals: a psycho-social perspective. In: Ghosh, S., Turrini, E. (eds.) Cybercrimes: A Multidisciplinary Analysis, pp. 217–235. Springer, Heidelberg (2011). https://doi.org/10.1007/978-3-642-13547-7_14

31. Saini, V., Duan, Q., Paruchuri, V.: Threat modeling using attack trees. J. Comput. Sci. Colleges 23(4), 124–131 (2008)

32. Schneier, B.: Attack trees. Dr. Dobb's J. 24(12), 21–29 (1999)

33. Shinder, D.L., Tittel, E.: Chapter 3 - understanding the people on the scene. In: Scene of the Cybercrime, pp. 93–146. Syngress, Burlington (2002)

34. Simon, H.A.: The Sciences of the Artificial, 3rd edn. MIT Press, Cambridge (1996)

35. Van Ruitenbeek, E., Keefe, K., Sanders, W.H., Muehrcke, C.: Characterizing the behavior of cyber adversaries: the means, motive, and opportunity of cyberattacks. In: 40th Annual IEEE/IFIP International Conference on Dependable Systems and Networks Supplemental (DSN 2010), pp. 17–18 (2010)

36. Walde, A., Hanus, E.G.: The feasibility of AIS- and GNSS-based attacks within the maritime industry. Master's thesis, NTNU, Trondheim, Norway (2020)

37. Warikoo, A.: Proposed methodology for cyber criminal profiling. Inf. Secur. J. Global Perspect. 23(4–6), 172–178 (2014)

38. Wingrove, M.: Security flaws open ECDIS to cyber crime. Technical report, Riviera (2018). https://www.rivieramm.com/opinion/opinion/security-flaws-open-ecdis-to-cyber-crime-24334. Accessed 20 Apr 2020

GroDDViewer: Dynamic Dual
View of Android Malware

Jean-François Lalande[✉][iD], Mathieu Simon, and Valérie Viet Triem Tong

CentraleSupélec, Inria, Univ Rennes, CNRS, IRISA, Rennes, France
{jean-francois.lalande,mathieu.simon,valerie.viet_triem_tong}@inria.fr

Abstract. Understanding an Android malware is a difficult task that requires strong skills in reverse engineering. Few tools exist except the well know IDA and Ghidra tools that are more focused on the analysis of binaries. In the Android world, understanding a malware requires to analyze the bytecode of the application, possibly obfuscated or hidden in a benign application that has been modified. At execution time, the malware can download new payloads, compromise the smartphone, and install new apps. We believe that a security analyst would appreciate to visualize and replay an execution of an Android malware. In particular, an analysis that bridges the gap between the bytecode and the events occurring during the execution would help to understand the malware behavior. In this article, we propose GroDDViewer the first tool offering a dual view of the execution of an Android malware. The first view represents the execution at operating system level through the representation of all information flow between files, processes and sockets. The second view represents what happened in the code of the application, during its execution. The benefit of this visualization tool is illustrated on a ransomware sample. In future, we plan to evaluate the tool with a panel of users on a benchmark of malware samples.

Keywords: Malware · Visualization

1 Introduction

Security researchers have different goals when working on Android malware analysis. Faruki et al. have discussed these goals and the associated methodologies [6]. Most contributions try to decide if an application is a malware or not. Few works try to address the problem of understanding the behavior of a malware application. Nevertheless, such an activity is an important task for security analysts of companies or government agencies that are involved in cyber security. Their state of practice is still manual code inspection, which is time-consuming and error-prone without automated support [16]. Any tool supporting this process speeds up the investigation when a malware has to be characterized.

© Springer Nature Switzerland AG 2020
H. Eades III and O. Gadyatskaya (Eds.): GraMSec 2020, LNCS 12419, pp. 127–139, 2020.
https://doi.org/10.1007/978-3-030-62230-5_7

Analyzing and understanding Android malware can have multiple goals. Most of the time it consists in locating a payload, triggering it, for example if it is encrypted. By observing the actions of the malware, the analyst should be able to classify a sample as a locker, a Remote Administration Tool, a ransomware, etc. If the application has been piggybacked [11], the analyst should find out the malicious code. Then, he has to understand what the malicious code is doing, when executed, and we believe that for these tasks, the security analyst needs to be helped by tools, especially visualization tools.

A lot of approaches are based on static analysis but well known contributions such as CopperDroid [17], CrowDroid [5], DroidScope [22], Harvester [4] have focused on extracting malware information from an execution. As mentioned by Faruki et al., such approaches have to face to the difficulty of being sure that the malware has been successfully executed. Thus, new approaches [1, 7] focused on the particular problem of helping the execution of malware that wait for particular conditions to occur. Nevertheless, all these dynamic approaches focus on *how to get* data from an execution (system calls, variable values, network operations, etc.) but not on *how to display* the captured data for the security analyst. Most of the time, online platforms that propose an analysis report give basic textual information about a sample, like virustotal or Andrubis [21]. Such tools can give aggregate view of a huge amount of malware samples analyzed, like one million analysis of Andrubis [12]. Aggregate views are useless for the security analyst that needs to gain information of a particular sample, especially if this sample is a newly discovered one that has never been analyzed before.

In this article, we propose a new visualization approach, GroDDViewer, for helping a malware analyst to gain information about the execution of a malware sample. GroDDViewer gathers information from a static and a dynamic analysis performed by external tools. This way, GroDDViewer offers a dual view of the execution of the malware: one view dedicated to the representation of the attack by all the information flows generated at operating system level between processes, files and sockets, and a second view dedicated to the representation of the executed malicious code. These two views can be manipulated by the analyst and can focus on precise intervals of time. Additionally, GroDDViewer offers a replay feature to animate the two views and *see* the malware operating and executing itself. GroDDViewer is implemented as a standalone Javascript webpage in order to be easily loaded on any platform in a web browser.

The rest of the article is structured as follows. Section 2 presents the approaches related to the visualization of Android malware. Section 3 briefly explains how are collected the data from a malware execution before moving on Sect. 4 that presents the visualization interface of GroDDViewer. We illustrate our tool on a real malware use case in Sect. 5. Finally, Sect. 6 concludes the paper.

2   Related Work

Visual analysis can be used to classify or recognize malware [19]. In [13], the authors use visual similarities of malware's image to discover relationships between malware. In [14], a graphical overview of the similarities of Android malware's code help to identity the shell code shared by different malware samples. These approaches have a different goal because they help to understand the evolution of a family of malware or multiple samples.

For investigating the code and execution traces of a malware, most approaches rely on static or dynamic methods. Static analysis can be used to collect data and build visualization tools that help to classify, browse malware families or study one particular malware. On the other side, few papers focus on the visualization of dynamic analysis. This is surprising, as malware analysts need to collect information from executions, for example API and kernel calls [20]. A complementary approach is to monitor the network during an analysis, which can give good insight of malware activities [23].

We found several approaches that focus on the analysis of one single malware and capture dynamic data and propose visualization results that have similarities with our approach. Trinius et al. [18] propose to use treemaps to visualize system calls and treegraphs to represents the system commands during the time of execution. This work is similar to our approach as is a sort of dual view of a malware (system and command levels) with a dynamic view that helps the user to get what is happening over time. Nevertheless, it is focused on ×86 binaries; thus API calls are realtive to POSIX accesses. With Android malware, more information is available about the Java bytecode that should be exploited. Another works of Gregio *et al.* [8,9] have similar ideas for representing malware's actions with graphs. The visualization that is proposed is dynamic: it displays over time the use of the API calls for manipulating files, processes, network, registers. The chosen visualization is a spiral of actions that represents the whole timeline of the performed actions. We keep this idea in our proposal, but we prefer to use dynamic animation for representing what is happening over time. Indeed, if the malware performs a lot of time the same actions, the timeline visualization should remain compact. Additionally, this approach is again dedicated to x86 binaries and does not handle the specificites of Android. In [15], Quist et al. introduce the visualization of the control flow of the program for executable malware. This approach produces very large graphs but helps to isolate loops, and especially unpacking stages which is of primary interest for x86 malware. Compared to our approach, we intend to use the control flow graph to link observations to the reversed source code of the malware. Thus, we need to have more readability on such kind of representation.

When dealing with a unique malware, well known online platforms give very basic information, mainly in a text based way. The most developed source of information are the blogs web pages that give precise insight for a particular sample. Such analysts use virtualized emulators or real smartphones to execute the malware and can be helped by uncompilers or debuggers like the well known IDA software. Nevertheless, such tools have no advanced display capabilities when a malware operates million of system calls, creates hundreds of files and has thousands of Java classes to understand. The particular nature of Android applications and the way the malware are implemented, as a repackaged benign application where malicious code has been added, pushed us to develop a new visualization interface. Additionally, all the cited approaches are related to the visualization of ×86 malware and do not focus on the particularities of Android malware (except for Paturi et al. [14]).

One recent paper focuses on Android malware: this tool is called "Android Malicious Flow Visualization Toolbox" and is a suite of interactive visualization diagrams that helps to investigate the malicious behavior of an application [16] This contribution is really close to our approach: the investigator works on a specific application in three phases: first, he observes the interactions with the Android system, in particular the sensitive APIs; second, he formulate hypothesis of possible leaks of sensitive data; third, it helps to confirm these leaks by investigating visually the control flow, including broken by the Java exception mechanism. Compared to GroddViewer, the Android Malicious Flow Visualization Toolbox give a more precise insight of the control flow for the analyst. Nevertheless, it lacks a view of flows at operating system level (files, other processes) and it lacks dynamic capabilities to synchronize events that occur during time with the visualization framework.

Another recent paper focuses on the dynamic aspect of an execution: VizMal [3], represents the maliciousness of an application over time with green and red boxes. The decision about the maliciousness of an execution slot is performed using machine learning techniques applied to syscall traces. This approach is complementary to our approach but give few information visually. When a red box is identified, the analyst still have to investigate the code and the operation performed by the malware.

As a conclusion, we believe that our paper is the first to propose a visualization for Android malware combining the view of the code and the operating system events captured during an execution.

3   Material Collection

GroDDViewer leverages existing static and dynamic tools to offer a representation of the attack itself and the malicious code that has been executed during the attack.

First, the malicious behavior is captured by AndroBlare [2], that monitors flows of information at operating system level. AndroBlare intercepts system calls responsible of information flows between files, sockets or processes which enable to observe the malware from the operating system point of view. AndroBlare relies on tainting techniques : the malware APK file is tainted with a mark and each process or object of the system can obtain the mark if a system call generates an information flow from a marked process/object. During the execution, all the interactions that happened between the process created from the APK file and the system are collected in a log. These interactions are process creation, file creation, and socket interactions. We also collect the state of the device file owned by the user before and after an execution in order to be able to show what happened to these files.

The attack is triggered by GroddDroid [1], a framework that detects suspicious codes and controls multiple executions of a malware in order to force the execution of code identified as suspicious. A method of the bytecode may be considered suspicious after a static analysis that computes a score based on its API usage. For example, a method performing a lot of cryptography or using reflection can be considered as suspicious. The analyst should later look at the methods considered as suspicious to confirm or deny their suspiciousness. Grodd-Droid instruments the bytecode to be able to trace the execution of all branches of the control flow. Then, it executes and stimulates the malware in a real smartphone and audits the executed branches. If the suspicious code is not reached, GroddDroid changes branch conditions in order to push the execution towards the malicious code. During such multiple executions, we collect the name and the time of the executed branches in order to be able to give a representation of the executed code at method level, as described later in Sect. 4.

GroDDViewer collects all data from files produced by GroddDroid and Blare. For achieving the visualization, the processing is performed by Javascript scripts that read these files, which avoids to use an HTTP server.

4   Visualizing Malware Execution

4.1   Overview

GroDDViewer offers a dual view of a malware execution: a view of all the information flows at operating system level and a view of the executed malicious bytecode. As shown in Fig. 1, 2, and 4, four main components explain the malware execution:

1. **System Flow Graph** (upper part of Fig. 1) represents all the information flows induced by the malware execution that occurred at system level;
2. **Interactions frequency** (bottom part of Fig. 1): represents the number of information flow events over time;
3. **Method Control Flow and Bytecode View** (Fig. 2 and Fig. 3): represents the control flow of method calls and the bytecode of a method;
4. **User interface navigation** (Fig. 4) represents what is seen on the smartphone from the user perspective, if any, and the events to go from one screen to another one.

Dynamic interactions of the user with these graphical elements provide additional information. For example, the user can click to get additional information such as a file modification or the bytecode source. The selection of time intervals provides a zoom capability on a specific period of time. The replay feature animates the graphs in order to replay events at operating system and bytecode levels. All these features are described in the next sections.

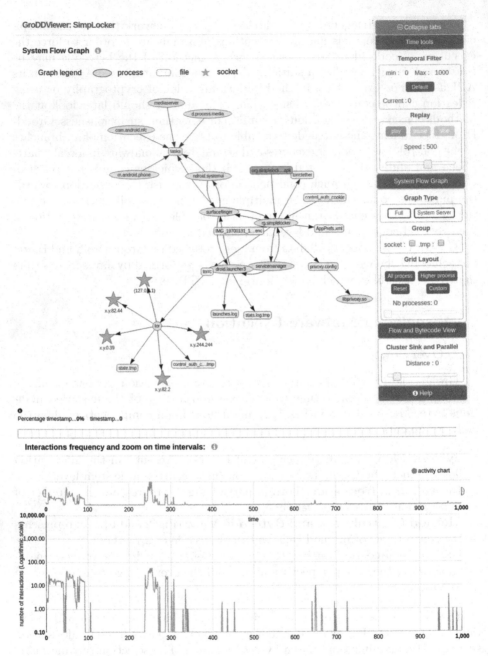

Fig. 1. Overview of GroDDViewer (part 1): System Flow Graph (upper part) – Interactions frequency (bottom part) – Malware investigated: Simplelocker (cf. Section 5). (Color figure online)

4.2   System Flow Graph

Information flows between objects of the operating system represent how the malware contaminates the operating system from the APK file (upper part of Fig. 1). Each edge of the graph may appear multiple times as system calls can be triggered often by the process, for example when writing a file. We record the timestamps of each occurrence which enables to replay the interactions.

A node of the graph can be a process, a socket, or a file. When clicking on a file, the difference of content is displayed between the initial state and final state of the experiment, if the file is a text file. It allows to follow the content modified or created by a malware. If the malware just read information, the edges show a transition from the file to a process.

The toolbar provides additional functionalities to manipulate the System Flow Graph. First, additional nodes can be displayed. The *Full* graph option shows the possible duplicate process nodes. It corresponds to the execution of multiple independent processes that have the same name. The *System Server* graph option shows the subgraph of the System Server process and all connected other processes that have been contaminated by the mark through System Server. As System Server is the central process that delivers Android Services and may asks to other Android process some data, the size of this subgraph can be very large if the malware accesses frequently the Android API. Thus, masking this part of the graph helps to visualize the processes that are accessed by the malware but it may be necessary to reactivate it to learn what the malware tries to access. Second, nodes that have similar extensions can be grouped. It allows to reduce the graph when a malware generates a lot of similar files, for example writes log files or accesses multiple sockets.

Finally, the layout of the processes can be controlled using the *Grid Layout* option. It forces the placement of all, higher or a custom number of processes on a grid. This tool helps to browse the graph when the number of nodes is large.

4.3   Interactions Frequency

At the bottom part of Fig. 1, a frequency graph displays the number of events occurring for information flows at kernel level. Because a simple Java operation can generate a large number of system calls, the number of flows in few milliseconds can be very high. Thus, we discretize the time of experiments in an interval $[0, 1000]$ and we display the number of events on a logarithmic y axis.

The interaction frequency graph also intends to be used for zooming on a precise time interval. Indeed, some malware actions can be concentrated in a particular portion of time: the user selects a new time interval in $[0, 1000]$ on the upperpart of the interaction frequency graph. A new selection of an interval $[x, y]$ has two effects. First, the lower orange graph is updated accordingly. Second, the System Flow graph is updated to display the processes, files and sockets involved during $[x, y]$. This functionality is particularly useful for understanding what the malware is doing on a particular period of time, or where the user shows a pick of activity on the Interaction frequency graph.

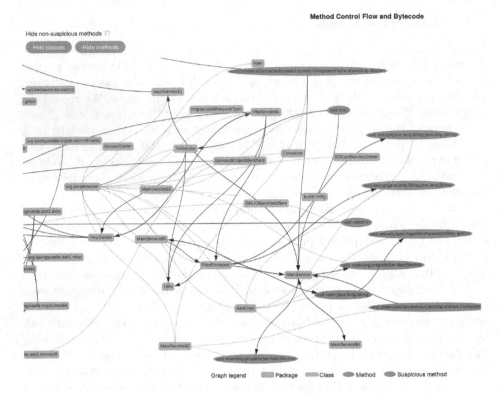

Fig. 2. Overview of GroDDViewer (part 2): Method Control Flow – Malware investigated : Simplelocker (cf. Section 5). (Color figure online)

4.4   Control Flow and Bytecode Views

The dual view of the System Flow Graph is the Method call graph that represents the control flow between methods. We could have displayed the entire control flow, i.e. by representing the control flow of the inside of a method, but the graph would have become difficult to understand. Thus, we define the nodes as methods and the edges represents explicit calls of methods. This way, we obtain a graphic representation of the code of the malware. A path, in such a graph, is a possible nested suite of method calls until a return statement unstack the last call.

As shown in Fig. 2, in order to help the user to browse the graph, we give the possibility to fold/unfold the methods (blue nodes) by packages (orange) and classes (pink). Suspicious classes have a red border and help the user to focus on suspicious methods. Each node of the call graph can be clicked. GroDDViewer displays the bytecode in a popup window, as shown in Fig. 3. This way, the user can analyze the suspicious bytecode and follow the malware developer logic.

Fig. 3. Bytecode visualization

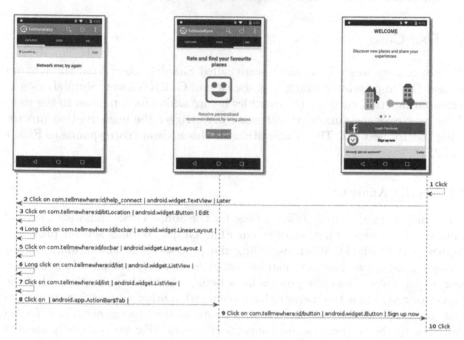

Fig. 4. Automaton of the navigated screens

4.5 User Interface Navigation

GroDDViewer also displays the different screens of the application that appeared during an execution, as shown in Fig. 4. These screenshots are represented as automata where transitions are labeled with the simulated user interaction.

4.6 Dynamic Replay

As the collected data come from an execution of the malware, we also record the timestamps associated to all events: the dates of the observed flows of the System Flow Graph and the dates of the branches of the control flow graph of the bytecode. The collected timestamps are extracted from the kernel (for the System Flow Graph) or from the Android `logcat` command when the malware bytecode is executed. Thus, we have to synchronize the two sources of timestamp to be able to replay events with a precision acceptable from the user perspective.

The Replay feature, located in the Time tools group of the toolbar, replay all events in a dual manner: the System Flow Graph events are animated synchronously with the Method Control Flow graph. This animation helps to see simultaneously the operation at system level, for exemple file creation or socket communication, while the methods of the bytecode are called. It helps to identify the nature of the methods from the nature of the performed action in the system, as illustrated in the use case in Sect. 5.

5   Use Case

We have chosen to study a ransomware called SimpleLocker[1] from the Kharon dataset [10] to present an example of use case of GroDDViewer. SimpleLocker is a ransomware that encrypts the user files before asking for a ransom to the user. If the user pays the ransom, the attacker may trigger the unencryption process using the Tor network. The visualization for this malware corresponds to Figs. 1 and 2.

5.1   Static Analysis

When displaying the GroDDViewer page for the SimpleLocker malware , several things can be noted. First, the System Flow Graph contains several processes (upper part of Fig. 1). When excluding the processes like *m. android.phone* or *servicemanager*, two processes can be noted: *tor* and *libprivoxy.so*. It is uncommon to have more than one process for a benign Android application. Multiple processes reveal that the malware have launched another application. In particular, the graph shows a file *torrc* that is wrote by the process *org.SimpleLocker* and read by the *tor* process. *tor* connects to several IPs: we can easily suspect that this malware tries to communicate with the attacker using the Tor network.

Second, the Method Control Flow and Bytecode View gives an overview of the code (Fig. 2). Two entry points are identified: *onCreate*, the standard way of creating an Android Activity and *onStartCommand* which is used to start an Android Service. Nine methods have been identified as suspicious (red borders). One of the most interesting is *doShellCommands* which name is highly suspicious. Clicking this method shows the bytecode that tries to run shell commands using *java.lang.Runtime*. All other suspicious methods can be inspected but we already know that they have been flagged as suspicious (high score) due to API calls such as encryption, telephony, etc. Other displayed intermediate nodes participate to the paths of calls to reach the suspicious nodes.

---

[1] The visualization of SimpleLocker using GroDDViewer is available at: http:// people.rennes.inria.fr/Jean-Francois.Lalande/talks/GraMSec20/SimpLocker_sample _fd694cf5ca1dd4967ad6e8c67241114c.html.

5.2 Dynamic Analysis

Using the replay capability of GroDDViewer gives an insight about the malware actions. The Interaction frequency graph (bottom part of Fig. 1) shows a lot of interactions on the interval $[0, 100]$. When replaying, this first part corresponds to Android routines and are not linked with the malware execution that starts later. SimpleLocker starts at time $t = 250$: after being unpacked from the .apk file, it deploys local files like *torrc* and *privoxy.config*. Then, a long interaction is observed at time $t = 258$ with a file ending by .enc. This means that some long operations are running for this file. At timestamp 960, operations are finished on this file. At the end of the replay, we also see some interactions between the *tor* process and some IPs.

This first dynamic overview suggests to focus on the interval $t > 240$. Thus, the user can use the zoom functionality to put the replay window on $t \in [240, 1000]$.

Then, the dynamic replay of Method Control Flow graph shows a sequence of calls $onCreate \rightarrow run \rightarrow encrypt$ at times t near 250. It corresponds to the generation of the encrypted file .enc after starting the main activity of the application. Indeed, if the user inspects the executed *encrypt* method, as shown in Fig. 3, the first lines of the bytecode shows the code $\$r1 = new\ org.SimpleLocker.AesCrypt$ followed by $specialinvoke\ \$r1.("jndlasf074hr")$ which corresponds to the call to the constructor of the used AES encryption algorithm with a constant encryption key. When opening the other animated nodes such as *findExistingProc, findProcessIdWithPidOf*, the user may think that it corresponds to the control of the Tor process for handling communication, which is less interesting to investigate.

Thus, the replay shows the encryption occurring at time $t > 250$ with the AES algorithm with a constant key. Unfortunately, as the communication is handled by a native independent process, we cannot inspect using the Method Control Flow graph the details of the execution of the communication protocol.

6 Conclusion

In this paper, we have presented GroDDViewer, an online tool for analyzing, understanding and replaying Android malware. GroDDViewer presents a dual view of malware: the graph of interactions that represents the operations that occured at operating system level and the graph of the methods of the bytecode. The presented use case illustrates how the user can easily gain some knowledge on the execution of a malware. Of course, such a tool cannot replace a manual investigation of the details of the bytecode but ease the understanding of the malware behavior. Future works concern the evaluation of the tool on a large panel of Android malware. Security analysts that conduct regular analysis of new samples will be involved in a campaign with two groups: one using GroDDViewer and not the other. Such a study will help to evaluate finely the obtained benefits.

References

1. Abraham, A., Andriatsimandefitra, R., Brunelat, A., Lalande, J.F., Viet Triem Tong, V.: GroddDroid: a Gorilla for triggering malicious behaviors. In: 10th International Conference on Malicious and Unwanted Software, pp. 119–127. IEEE Computer Society, Fajardo, Puerto Rico, October 2015. https://doi.org/10.1109/MALWARE.2015.7413692
2. Andriatsimandefitra, R., Tong, V.V.T.: Capturing android malware behaviour using system flow graph. In: Au, M.H., Carminati, B., Kuo, C.-C.J. (eds.) NSS 2014. LNCS, vol. 8792, pp. 534–541. Springer, Cham (2014). https://doi.org/10. 1007/978-3-319-11698-3_43
3. Bacci, A., Martinelli, F., Medvet, E., Mercaldo, F.: VizMal: a visualization tool for analyzing the behavior of Android malware. In: 4th International Conference on Information Systems Security and Privacy, vol. 1: ForSE, pp. 517–525. SciTePress, Funchal, Madeira, Portugal, January 2018. https://doi.org/10.5220/0006665005170525
4. Bodden, E.: Harvesting runtime values in android applications that feature anti-analysis techniques. In: Network and Distributed System Security Symposium, pp. 21–24, February 2016. https://doi.org/10.14722/ndss.2016.23066
5. Burguera, I., Zurutuza, U., Nadjm-Tehrani, S.: Crowdroid: behavior-based malware detection system for android. In: 1st ACM Workshop on Security and Privacy in Smartphones and Mobile Devices, p. 15. ACM Press, Chicago, USA, October 2011. https://doi.org/10.1145/2046614.2046619
6. Faruki, P., et al.: Android security: a survey of issues, malware penetration and defenses. IEEE Commun. Surv. Tutorials 17(2), 1–27 (2015). https://doi.org/10. 1109/COMST.2014.2386139
7. Fratantonio, Y., Bianchi, A., Robertson, W., Kirda, E., Kruegel, C., Vigna, G.: TriggerScope: towards detecting logic bombs in android applications. In: IEEE S&P, pp. 1–33, May 2016. https://doi.org/10.1109/SP.2016.30
8. Grégio, A.R.A., Santos, R.D.C.: Visualization techniques for malware behavior analysis. In: Communications, and Intelligence (C3I) Technologies for Homeland Security and Homeland Defense X, vol. 8019, p. 801905, June 2011. https://doi. org/10.1117/12.883441
9. Grégio, A.R.A., et al.: Interactive, visual-aided tools to analyze malware behavior. In: 12th International Conference on Computational Science and Its Applications. LNCS, vol. 7336, pp. 302–313. Salvador de Bahia, Brazil, June 2012. https://doi. org/10.1007/978-3-642-31128-4_22
10. Kiss, N., Lalande, J.F., Leslous, M., Viet Triem Tong, V.: Kharon dataset: android malware under a microscope. In: The Learning from Authoritative Security Experiment Results Workshop. The USENIX Association, San Jose, United States, May 2016
11. Li, L., et al.: Understanding android app piggybacking: a systematic study of malicious code grafting. IEEE Trans. Inf. Forensics Secur. 12(6), 1269–1284, June 2017. https://doi.org/10.1109/TIFS.2017.2656460
12. Lindorfer, M., Neugschwandtner, M.: ANDRUBIS-1,000,000 apps later: a view on current android malware behaviors. In: 3rd International Workshop on Building Analysis Datasets and Gathering Experience Returns for Security. IEEE Computer Society, San Jose, CA, USA, September 2014. https://doi.org/10.1109/BADGERS. 2014.7

13. Long, A., Saxe, J., Gove, R.: Detecting malware samples with similar image sets. In: The 11th Workshop on Visualization for Cyber Security, pp. 88–95, November 2014. https://doi.org/10.1145/2671491.2671500
14. Paturi, A., Cherukuri, M., Donahue, J., Mukkamala, S.: Mobile malware visual analytics and similarities of attack toolkits (malware gene analysis). In: 2013 International Conference on Collaboration Technologies and Systems (CTS), pp. 149–154. IEEE, May 2013. https://doi.org/10.1109/CTS.2013.6567221
15. Quist, D.A., Liebrock, L.M.: Visualizing compiled executables for malware analysis. In: 6th International Workshop on Visualization for Cyber Security, pp. 27–32, Atlantic City, NJ, USA. IEEE, October 2009. https://doi.org/10.1109/VIZSEC. 2009.5375539
16. Santhanam, G.R., Holland, B., Kothari, S.C., Mathews, J.: Interactive visualization toolbox to detect sophisticated android malware. In: IEEE Symposium on Visualization for Cyber Security, pp. 1–8, Phoenix, AZ, USA. IEEE Computer Society, October 2017. https://doi.org/10.1109/VIZSEC.2017.8062197
17. Tam, K., Khan, S., Fattori, A., Cavallaro, L.: CopperDroid: Automatic reconstruction of android malware behaviors. In: 22nd Annual Network and Distributed System Security Symposium, San Diego, California, USA, February 2015. https:// doi.org/10.14722/NDSS.2015.23145
18. Trinius, P., Holz, T., Gobel, J., Freiling, F.C.: Visual analysis of malware behavior using treemaps and thread graphs. In: 6th International Workshop on Visualization for Cyber Security, pp. 33–38, Atlantic City, NJ, USA. IEEE, October 2009. https://doi.org/10.1109/VIZSEC.2009.5375540
19. Wagner, M., et al.: A survey of visualization systems for malware analysis. In: EuroVis, pp. 105–125, Cagliari, Italy, May 2015. https://doi.org/10.2312/eurovisstar. 20151114
20. Wagner, M., et al.: Problem characterization and abstraction for visual analytics in behavior-based malware pattern analysis. In: 11th Workshop on Visualization for Cyber Security, pp. 9–16, Paris, France (2014). https://doi.org/10.1145/2671491. 2671498
21. Weichselbaum, L.: Andrubis: android malware under the magnifying glass. Technical report (2014)
22. Yan, L.K., Yin, H.: DroidScope: seamlessly reconstructing the OS and Dalvik semantic views for dynamic Android malware analysis. In: USENIX Security Symposium, p. 29. USENIX Association, August 2012
23. Zhuo, W., Nadjin, Y.: MalwareVis: entity-based visualization of malware network traces. In: The 9th International Symposium on Visualization for Cyber Security, pp. 41–47, Seattle, WA, USA. ACM Press October 2012. https://doi.org/10.1145/ 2379690.2379696

Models for Reasoning About Security

Attack-Defence Frameworks: Argumentation-Based Semantics for Attack-Defence Trees

Dov M. Gabbay[1], Ross Horne[1(✉)], Sjouke Mauw[1,2], and Leendert van der Torre[1,2]

[1] Department of Computer Science, University of Luxembourg, Esch-sur-Alzette, Luxembourg
ross.horne@uni.lu
[2] SnT, University of Luxembourg, Luxembourg, Luxembourg

Abstract. This position paper connects the areas and communities of abstract argumentation and attack-defence trees in the area of security. Both areas deal with attacks, defence and support and both areas rely on applications dealing with human aggressive activities. The unifying idea we use in this paper is to regard arguments as AND-OR attack trees as proposed by Schneier in the security domain. The core model, which is acceptable for both communities, is a pair $(\mathbf{S}, \twoheadrightarrow)$, where $\mathbf{S}$ is a set of attack trees (the "arguments") and $\twoheadrightarrow$ is a binary relation on attack trees (the "attack" relation). This leads us to the notion of an *attack-defence framework*, which provides an argumentation-based semantics for attack-defence trees and more general attack-defence graphs.

1 Introduction

Argumentation is an interdisciplinary research area concerning the study of conflicts that arise due to competing objectives and views across a range of disciplines. Security is an obvious example of such a discipline where there are human actors with competing interests. The interests and objectives of an attacker seeking to obtain secrets, disrupt services, track users, etc., conflict with those of a defender such as system administrators, software engineers, security guards and others professionals that protect our society both online and offline.

It should be of no surprise that there are immediate parallels between argumentation and methods developed for modelling the relationships between the actions of attackers and defenders in security, notably attack-defence trees [1] and defence trees [2]. In this work we show that it is possible to provide directly a semantics for attack-defence trees by building on models of abstract argumentation. However, on the surface, there are a few differences in modelling styles in argumentation compared to attack-defence trees. Notably, in argumentation, various types of relations can be reduced to a single attack-relation tree formed of *attack* relations, whereas established semantics for attack-defence trees based on multisets collapse such trees of layers of attacks, defences, counter-attacks, etc., to a two-layer structure where there is only one layer of attacks, some of which are countered by a layer of defences. We develop *bipolar* argumentation frameworks [3] that incorporate a notion of support [4] and hence are capable of

H. Eades III and O. Gadyatskaya (Eds.): GraMSec 2020, LNCS 12419, pp. 143–165, 2020.
https://doi.org/10.1007/978-3-030-62230-5_8

modelling in styles favoured by both the argumentation and security communities. This enables us to translate added value in both directions.

From Security to Argumentation. Traditionally, arguments are modelled in a fairly binary fashion: if an argument is attacked by another argument that is not attacked then it is out, hence cannot be an acceptable argument. The source of potential confusions arises in argumentation when there are loops, for example loops may be created in legal arguments where witnesses attack each other. In security, the sources of uncertainty are quite different. They come from the fact that many attacks take resources such as security guards, networking equipment, or botnets, which have associate costs, capacities and likelihoods of success. There may be other factors such as the risk of exposing the identity of the attackers leaving them open to prosecution (the feeling of impunity), balanced against the motives of a profile of attacker. For such reasons, semantics proposed for attack-defence trees typically take into account quantities and qualities in various *attribute domains* that indicate the capability of attacker and defenders to fulfil their actions. This quantitative aspect we translate from the attack-defence trees to argumentation frameworks by making explicit a notion of abstract "weapons" that represent the actions and resources that an attacker or defender can use to perpetrate attacks or hold out against them.

From Argumentation to Security. As mentioned above, much of the attention in the argumentation community revolves around resolving disputes when there are cycles in arguments. Thus the graph structures considered in argumentation are more flexible than the trees stratified into layers of attacks and defences, that form attack-defence trees. While it may be useful for security to incorporate loops, in this work, we take a clearer and simpler first step in that direction. We allow not only trees, but also directed acyclic graphs to appear. Such an extension of attack-defence trees is useful for making explicitly when multiple instances of nodes representing actions of an attacker are in fact the same attack, hence we need not kill all instances to counter that attack, but only the one instance of that action, which of course impacts the resource sensitive analysis [5]. A more adventurous aspect of the modest liberalisation of attack-defence trees that we propose is to forget about the distinction between attacks and defences. We simply have arguments that attack each other, and need not explicitly indicate that the argument is an attack tree associated with an attacker or defender. This allows the modelling of scenarios where two actions of an attacker may be in conflict, for example, enabling a DDoS attack may blow the cover for a stealthy attacker gathering private information from inside the system. Furthermore, a defensive action, such as installing a hypervisor, for separating processes sharing the same underlying hardware may mitigate attacks exploiting vulnerabilities in inter-process communication in software, but may support cache timing side channels at the hardware level. Going further, some nodes may not even be attackers or defenders, they may be engineering requirements such as protocol standards or legal requirements such as clauses of the GDPR regulation that are impacted by a successful attack or by adopting a particular defensive strategy.

Table 1 provides an overview comparing the security and argumentation domains from which this paper draws. Considering the above observations, since these domains were already close we believe that a relatively small step is required to build a general framework accommodating the needs of both communities—in one way we move from

Table 1. Comparison between argumentation and security domains

Argumentation frameworks	Attack-defence trees
Argumentation is a well-developed area with a community formed over 50 years	Strong security community using methods inspired by fault trees which have been in use for over 50 years
Have a range of semantics	May benefit from improved semantics
Mainly concerned with loops	May benefit from handling loops, or at least more general acyclic graphs
Semantics focus on evidence for claims, i.e., proof certificates	Could benefit from more proof theory
Trees are a well-behaved case for this area	Mainly concerned with trees with a stratified structure, formed by alternating layers of attacks and defences
Emphasises attack relations, allowing arbitrary alternations between moves of attackers and defenders in their underlying games	Reduces counter-attacks to a single layer of attacks countered by defences, by using support relations

trees to more general graphs and in the other direction we bring in resource considerations. For example, it is reasonable that the legal domain may have some resource
consideration, e.g., whether an argument stands may take into account the number of
witnesses and their credibility. In the security domain, it is reasonable to lift some constraints on patterns of attacks and defences.

We develop these ideas as follows. In Sect. 2, we provide background on the traditional notion of an argumentation framework and make explicit obvious parallels
and differences compared to attack-defence trees. In Sect. 3, we close the gap between
the models by introducing the notion of attack-defence framework, firstly by defining
what it means for one attack tree to attack another attack tree, and, secondly, by providing an algorithm accommodating the notion of support. In Sect. 4, we discuss the
argumentation-based model introduced in juxtaposition with key examples of attack-
defence trees, and highlight extension and directions enabled.

2 Preliminaries Drawing from Argumentation

We briefly summarise mathematical tools of argumentation on which we build. An
argumentation framework is a pair consisting of a set of arguments S and a relation
$\twoheadrightarrow \subseteq S \times S$ called the attack relation. Argumentation traditionally defines set theoreti-
cally or algorithmically two subsets for an argumentation framework $(S, \twoheadrightarrow)$.

- The **in set** $E^+ \subseteq S$, which is a maximal (with respect to subset inclusion) conflict-
  free set such that: if z is such that $\forall y.(y \twoheadrightarrow z \Rightarrow \exists y' \in E \ s.t. \ y' \twoheadrightarrow y)$ then $z \in E$.
  I.e., any argument attacking an element of E is attacked by another element of E.
  By *conflict-free*, we mean that no two $x, y \in E$ are such that $x \twoheadrightarrow y$.

– The **out set** $E^- = \{y \mid \exists x \in E^+ \ s.t. \ x \twoheadrightarrow y\}$.

If we restrict to acyclic graphs these sets partition the set of arguments, i.e., we have $E^+ \cap E^- = \varnothing$ and $E^+ \cup E^- = S$.

In the acyclic setting, the above sets can be generated algorithmically from $(S, \twoheadrightarrow)$ by calculating $E^+ = \bigcup_i E_i^+$ and $E^- = \bigcup_i E_i^-$, where E_i^+ and E_i^- are defined inductively as follows. We say x is not attacked in S_i if $\neg \exists y \in S_i \ s.t. \ y \twoheadrightarrow x$.

1. **Base case:** Let $S_0 = S$, $E_0^+ = \varnothing$ and $E_0^- = \varnothing$.
2. **Inductive case:** Let $S_{n+1} = S_n \setminus (E_n^+ \cup E_n^-)$.
   Let $E_{n+1}^+ = \{x \in S_{n+1} \mid x \text{ is not attacked in } S_{n+1}\}$.
   Let $E_{n+1}^- = \{x \in S_{n+1} \mid \exists y \in E_{n+1}^+ s.t. \ y \twoheadrightarrow x\}$.

Consider the example argumentation framework in Fig. 1. The argumentation framework depicted is also an attack-defence tree [1], where, in attack-defence tree terminology, the attack relations are *countermeasures*, where an action of an attacker is defeated by an action of a defender, or an action of defender is defeated by a counter-attack of an attacker. In the figure, attack relations are represented by dotted double-headed arrows in order to align with the dotted line notation of attack-defence trees. This notation, at the same time, makes explicit the direction of the attack, as attack relation $\twoheadrightarrow$ indicates. The colours are not necessary for argumentation frameworks; they simply allow ease of reading when there is a clear alternation between two actors the proponent and opponent, i.e., the actions of the attacker and defender.

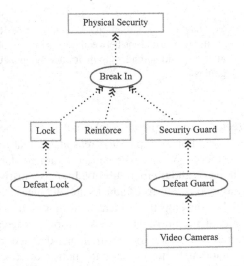

Fig. 1. An argumentation framework which is also an attack-defence tree.

For the example in Fig. 1, the **in set** and **out set** are as follows.

$$E^+ = \{Video\ Camera, Defeat\ Lock, Reinforce, Security\ Guard, Physical\ Security\}$$
$$E^- = \{Defeat\ Guard, Break\ in, Lock\}$$

Thus we say *Physical Security* is an *acceptable argument* with respect to E^+, since any argument that attacks it (i.e., *Break In*) is defeated by some element of E^+, (e.g., *Security Guard*). We note that E^+ is a *maximal admissible* set, which, in argumentation terminology is called the *preferred extension*. Thus the algorithm used to generate E^+ emphasises that the preferred extension is easy to compute in the acyclic setting.

In addition to the notion of attack, we require also a notion of support in order to provide an argumentation-based semantics for attack-defence trees. In order to accommodate support—e.g., the act of supporting a security goal of a system with a range

of network and physical security measures, as is possible using attack-defence trees—
we take a step towards a more general model. We would like to define acyclic *bipolar
argumentation frameworks*, that is a pair of relations on a set of arguments S:

$$(S, \twoheadrightarrow, \rightarrow), \text{ where } \twoheadrightarrow \subseteq S \times S, \rightarrow \subseteq S \times S \text{ and } \twoheadrightarrow \cup \rightarrow \text{ is acyclic}$$

The first relation $x \twoheadrightarrow y$ indicates that x **attacks** y. The second relation $x \rightarrow y$ represents
that x **supports** y. These bipolar argumentation frameworks accommodate conventions
from both argumentation and security.

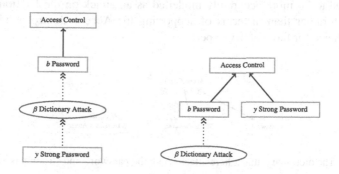

Fig. 2. Modelling counter-defence "Strong Password" as an attack or as a support.

Argumentation Convention: Most argumentation approaches reduce support to attacks
(i.e., eliminate support). This is achieved by reducing $y \rightarrow b$ to $y \twoheadrightarrow \beta \twoheadrightarrow b$ by making
use of auxiliary node β. Thus y supports b by defending against an attacker. See for
example, the bipolar argumentation framework (which happens to be also an attack-
defence tree) to the left of Fig. 2. In that example, the Strong Password y, attacks the
Dictionary Attack β, in order to support the Password b.

Security Convention: One might argue that the above approach drawing directly from
argumentation is not quite the right viewpoint, since the Strong Password does not
actively attack the Dictionary Attack. What really happens is that the Strong Password
strengthens the password to make it more resistant to the Dictionary Attack. This idea
is reflected in the existing multiset semantics for attack-defence trees [1] that elimi-
nates counter-attacks by reducing them to supports. Under such semantics for attack-
defence trees, an argumentation framework with relations as depicted to the left of Fig. 2
might more accurately be modelled, as depicted in the example on the right of Fig. 2. In
that diagram, instead of employing Strong Password as a counter-attack for Dictionary
Attack we employ it as a support for access control.

The use of the support relation from the bipolar argumentation frameworks allows
the fact that the Strong Password really is supporting the Access Control mechanism
rather than attacking the Dictionary Attack to be made explicit. It is a modelling choice
which presentation better respects the situation, a semantics based on argumentation
that accommodates support (to be developed in the next section) would likely distinguish these scenarios, i.e., the diagrams in Fig. 2 may be distinguished by their "in sets"

(which should be a suitable generalisation of preferred extensions). To get a feeling of the intuition behind why this should be the case, observe that in the diagram on the right of Fig. 2 nobody attacks the Dictionary Attack so it should be declared "in" by default, that is $\beta \in E^+$; whereas in the diagram on the left the Dictionary Attack is out by default, since it is attacked by a Strong Password that is not attacked by anyone, hence is in by default. Thus in an extended algorithm accommodating support we expect $y \in E^+$ and $\beta \in E^-$ for the attack-defence tree on the right of Fig. 2.

In contrast, instead of "Strong Password", consider employing an anti-bruteforcing defensive mechanism, such as a CAPTCHA, against a Dictionary Attack. This could be considered to be more accurately modelled as an attack on the Dictionary Attack denoted by β rather than in terms of supporting the Access Control goal. This is a modelling choice for the security expert.

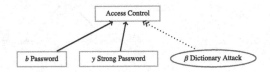

Fig. 3. The dictionary attack here attacks both the password and strong password.

Going further, the diagram in Fig. 3 is an attack-defence tree. This is different from the support relation to the right of Fig. 2, since by attacking directly the access control argument we suggest that both the Password and Strong Password are killed by the dictionary attack. In order to interpret such scenarios, we require richer structure than provided by traditional argumentation frameworks à la Dung [6]. In order to formally present such a semantics, further machinery is defined in the next section.

3   Attack-Defence Frameworks: Trees Attacking Trees

The semantics in this section are built out of those in Sect. 2 and finite sets of multisets of weapons, where weapons are "actions" in attack-defence tree terminology. We start with defining enhanced argumentation frameworks *with joint attacks* (S, R), where S is viewed as a set of weapons (the atomic actions that appear at the leaves of attack trees), and R is more general than just a binary relation over S: we allow the source of the attack to be a multiset of elements of S.

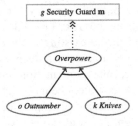

Fig. 4. A joint attack relation as an attack-defence tree.

Thus R is a relation between finite multisets built from S, say Multiset(S), and elements of S, i.e., $R \subseteq$ Multiset(S) $\times S$. We use the notation $a * b * c$ to represent the multiset with three elements, the weapons a, b and c.

Allowing multisets of weapons to attack weapons, allows us to model scenarios such as $o * k\,R\,g$, as depicted in Fig. 4, using an auxiliary node, labeled *Overpower*. Note that while such scenarios are not expressible using traditional argumentation frames, they do appear in several richer models of argumentation, where such attack relation are called *joint attacks* [7,8]. In the attack-defence tree notion in Fig. 4, the fact that multiple actions/weapon/resources must be used together is depicted using an arc between the arrows, which is a *conjunctive refinement* in attack tree terminology [9].

We will use argumentation frameworks with joint attacks to define a semantics for another argumentation framework with more structure, which we call an *attack-defence framework*, since it will generalise attack-defence trees to more general graphical structures, in the spirit of argumentation frameworks.

We denote attack-defence frameworks as a quintuple:

$$(\mathbf{S}, \twoheadrightarrow, \rightarrow, S, :=) \quad \text{where } \twoheadrightarrow \subseteq \mathbf{S} \times \mathbf{S}, \rightarrow \subseteq \mathbf{S} \times \mathbf{S}, \text{ and } := \subseteq \mathbf{S} \times \text{Set(Multiset}(S)).$$

Its arguments $\mathbf{m} \in \mathbf{S}$, denoted in bold, are mapped by functional relation $:=$ to sets of multisets of weapons drawn from the set S (the set of weapons of the argumentation frame with joint attack above). Think of the resources assigned to arguments as basic AND-OR attack trees in the original sense of Schneier [9]. I.e., each node is part of an attack-defence tree consisting of only the actions of the attacker or those of the defender (the connected green or red components only in the example figures). Attack trees allow for actions to be:

- *conjunctively refined*, requiring several actions to be performed to realise the action refined, as denoted using multisets of actions,
- or *disjunctively refined*, where one of the possible actions in the disjunction suffices to realise the action refined, as denoted using the sets of multisets

Thus we take the viewpoint that elements of our attack-defence frameworks represent attack trees, more precisely sets of multisets of weapons regarded as AND-OR attack trees flattened after applying the standard mapping to multisets [10] that reduces the attack tree to a disjunctive normal form. From an argumentation perspective we are essentially assuming that arguments are attack trees. These attack trees represent agents carrying each a variety of weapons, where each of these weapons are elements of S and the sets of multisets represent a choice between a number of combination of weapons that may be employed. Note this viewpoint does not distinguish between agents that are attackers or defenders, agents playing any role maybe be equipped with weapons in this manner.

3.1 Interpreting the Attack Relation of Attack-Defence Frameworks

We first explain how to interpret the attack relation only, for attack-defence frameworks. Consider the following example of an attack tree denoted as a set of multisets: $\mathbf{m} := \{(a_1 * a_2), b_1, b_2\}$, where $a_1, a_2, b_1, b_2 \in S$. The above example may be regarded as the attack tree in Fig. 5, where a node denoted with an arc represents conjunctive refinement, and a node without an arc represents disjunctive refinement.

We now explain the meaning of **m**. We are relying in underlying argumentation frameworks with joint attacks of the form (S, R) in order to provide a semantics for the attack relation.

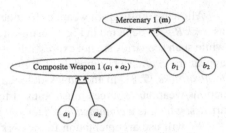

*1) The meaning of **m** is a collection of three weapons. The first weapon is a composite weapon built up of two component weapons a_1 and a_2 denoted by $a_1 * a_2$. Note that $*$ is used to denote a multiset consisting of two elements a_1 and a_2. The second weapon is b_1 and the third is b_2.

Fig. 5. An attack tree denoted by $\{(a_1 * a_2), b_1, b_2\}$. The resources accumulated at each node are indicated in brackets.

*2) So, if we want to attack **m** we need to attack all three components' weapons and leave **m** without weapons. This complements that perspective that, if **m** were to be used to attack another attack tree, there are three options for executing the attack and hence, if it is not the case that all three attack options are defeated, then the attack may be perpetrated.

Expressions like $\{(a_1 * a_2), b_1, b_2\}$ are understood as resource weapons, which can be used for attack or for defence. $(a_1 * a_2)$ is a composite weapon which has two components. So to neutralise the composite weapon $(a_1 * a_2)$ we need to kill at least one of its components, and to attack **m** we must attack each of its weapons.

So, if $\mathbf{n} := \{(\alpha_1 * \alpha_2 * \alpha_3), \delta_1, \delta_2\}$ is the set of weapons of another argument, say Mercenary 2, keen to attack **m**, say Mercenary 1, then for **n** to attack **m** it must attack each of **n**'s weapons. This scenario may be represented using the attack-defence tree in Fig. 6.

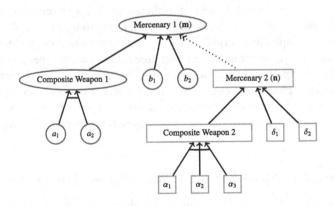

Fig. 6. An attack tree attacking another attack tree.

*3) So, we have:

$$\mathbf{n} \twoheadrightarrow \mathbf{m} \text{ iff } \mathbf{n} \twoheadrightarrow (a_1 * a_2)$$
$$\text{and } \mathbf{n} \twoheadrightarrow b_1$$
$$\text{and } \mathbf{n} \twoheadrightarrow b_2$$

So for $\mathbf{n}$ to attack any single weapon x (such as one of the weapons in $\mathbf{m}$), we need a weapon in $\mathbf{n}$ to attack x. So we follow rule *4):

*4) We interpret disjunctive attacks [11] and attacks on multisets as follows.

$$\{z, y\} \twoheadrightarrow x \text{ iff def. } zRx \vee yRx$$
$$u \twoheadrightarrow z * y \text{ iff def. } uRz \vee uRy$$

where $z * y$ is a weapon with two components. So, for example

$$u \twoheadrightarrow \{(z * y), w\} \text{ iff } (u \twoheadrightarrow (z * y)) \text{ and } uRw) \text{ iff } ((uRz \vee uRy) \wedge uRw).$$

Therefore we have

*5) $\{(\alpha_1 * \alpha_2 * \alpha_3), \delta_1, \delta_2\} \twoheadrightarrow x$ iff $[\delta_1 Rx$ or $\delta_2 Rx$ or $(\alpha_1 * \alpha_2 * \alpha_3)Rx]$, and

*6) $\mathbf{n} \twoheadrightarrow \{(a_1 * a_2), b_1, b_2\}$ iff $\mathbf{n} \twoheadrightarrow (a_1 * a_2)$ and $\mathbf{n} \twoheadrightarrow b_1$ and $\mathbf{n} \twoheadrightarrow b_2$.

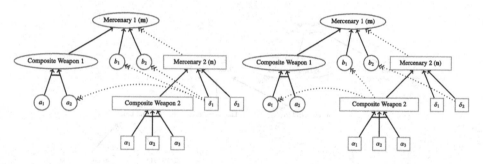

Fig. 7. Two possible joint attack relations realising the attack in Fig. 6.

This gives a full meaning to $\mathbf{n} \twoheadrightarrow \mathbf{m}$ in terms of the underlying argumentation frame *with joint attacks* that can realise the attack relations indicated, where the attack relation is restricted to a multiset of weapons attacking individual weapons.

Thus for the above example in Fig. 6, one such underlying argumentation framework generated from $\mathbf{n} \twoheadrightarrow \mathbf{m}$ is the following relation R_1.

$$\delta_1 \, R_1 \, a_2 \qquad \delta_1 \, R_1 \, b_1 \qquad \delta_1 \, R_1 \, b_2$$

Another example that would also realise the attack $\mathbf{n} \twoheadrightarrow \mathbf{m}$ would be relation R_2 defined as follows.

$$\alpha_1 * \alpha_2 * \alpha_3 \, R_2 \, b_1 \qquad \alpha_1 * \alpha_2 * \alpha_3 \, R_2 \, a_1 \qquad \delta_2 \, R_2 \, b_2$$

These two possible joint attack relations realising the attack in Fig. 6 are depicted by the respective diagrams in Fig. 7, as indicated by the overlaid attack relations from multisets of weapons in attack tree **n** to weapons in **m**. Obviously, this is not an exhaustive list of joint attack relations; indeed there are 54 such joint attack relations realising the attack between the trees in this example. It is sufficient for one of those joint attack relations to be realisable in practice, in order for the attack **n** $\twoheadrightarrow$ **m** to be realisable in practice.

Following the method illustrated above, it is clear that we can give a semantics for the attack relation on attack-defence frameworks, where trees may attack trees in terms of a set of argumentation frameworks with joint attacks.

For a further example consider Fig. 8. Here we have, according to our weapon interpretation the following.

$$\mathbf{b} := \{b_1, b_2\} \quad \beta := \{\alpha_1, \alpha_2\} \quad \mathbf{x} := \{x_1, x_2\}.$$

We get $\{b_1, b_2\} \twoheadrightarrow \{\alpha_1, \alpha_2\} \twoheadrightarrow \{x_1, x_2\}$.

α_1, α_2 are used as weapons to kill $\{x_1, x_2\}$. So the meaning of $\{\alpha_1, \alpha_2\} \twoheadrightarrow \{x_1, x_2\}$ is $(\alpha_1 R x_1 \wedge \alpha_1 R x_2) \vee (\alpha_1 R x_1 \wedge \alpha_2 R x_2) \vee (\alpha_2 R x_1 \wedge \alpha_2 R x_2) \vee (\alpha_2 R x_1 \wedge \alpha_1 R x_2)$.

The meaning of $\{b_1, b_2\} \twoheadrightarrow \{\alpha_1, \alpha_2\}$ is similar, namely $(b_1 R \alpha_1 \wedge b_1 R \alpha_2) \vee (b_1 R \alpha_1 \wedge b_2 R \alpha_2) \vee (b_2 R \alpha_1 \wedge b_2 R \alpha_2) \vee (b_2 R \alpha_1 \wedge b_1 R \alpha_2)$.

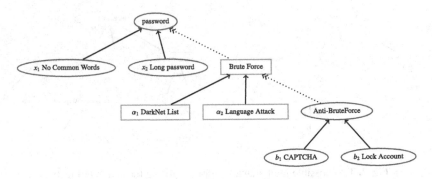

Fig. 8. A variation on Fig. 3, where each node has a choice of weapon to employ.

Putting the above together, an argumentation framework that realises the above constraints is depicted in Fig. 9. That is, we have an attack relation R such that:

$$b_1 \ R \ \alpha_1 \quad b_1 \ R \ \alpha_2 \quad \alpha_1 \ R \ x_1 \quad \alpha_2 \ R \ x_2$$

For the argumentation framework defined by R it is clear that we can ask traditional argumentation questions such as: what is the preferred extension, i.e., the in set E^+, for the realisation of the attack-defence framework in Fig. 8, as given in Fig. 9. The preferred extension is of course the following set.

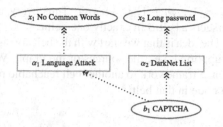

Fig. 9. An example of an argumentation framework realising the attack relations in Fig. 8. Notice that the argumentation framework generated need not be a tree.

$$E^+ = \{b_1, x_1, x_2\}$$

Notice that, since $\mathbf{x} := \{x_1, x_2\}$, for $\mathbf{x}$ to be acceptable it is sufficient that x_1 or x_2 is an acceptable argument. Thus since x_1 and x_2 both happen to be acceptable with respect to E^+, we can claim that $\mathbf{x}$ is acceptable with respect to E^+. Similarly, since $\mathbf{b} := \{b_1, b_2\}$ and b_1 is acceptable with respect to E^+ we have $\mathbf{b}$ is acceptable with respect to E^+ (recall sets represent a disjunctive refinement in attack trees, i.e., a choice of possible attacks, so it is sufficient for one multiset in the set of multisets to be acceptable). In contrast, since $\beta := \{\alpha_1, \alpha_2\}$ and neither α_1 nor α_2 is acceptable with respect to E^+ (equivalently they are both in E^-), β is not an acceptable argument with respect to E^+.

In summary, in this example $\mathbf{b}$ and $\mathbf{x}$ are "in" and β is "out". This is exactly as expected for the traditional argumentation frame, in the sense described in Sect. 2, where we take $\mathbf{b}$, β and $\mathbf{x}$ to be atomic arguments and define the attack relation as $\mathbf{b} \twoheadrightarrow \beta \twoheadrightarrow \mathbf{x}$. The reason, or evidence for the admissibility of $\mathbf{x}$ is however now more fine grained, reflecting the more fine grained nature of the arguments. Since for each underlying argumentation framework E^+ is unique in this acyclic setting, it is sufficient to say "$\mathbf{x}$ is an acceptable argument with respect to the argumentation framework defined by R", where one such R is depicted in Fig. 9.

3.2 Interpreting the Support Relation

But what about support? Here we explain support and provide a semantics in terms of an algorithm rewriting the attack-defence frameworks introduced in this work, inspired by the traditional algorithm for argumentation frameworks at the top of Sect. 2. We make use of the attack tree in Fig. 10 to guide the development of an algorithm suitable for both the security and argumentation communities. The example features Cloudbursting, which is the practice of scaling a service temporarily to the Cloud, so as to cope with spikes of demand and to sit out distributed denial of service attacks (DDoS) [12].

In our algorithm, we make use of the concept of a belt. A *belt (a maximal anti-chain)* for a bipolar argumentation frame is a set $B \subseteq S$ such that:

- For no $x, y \in B$ does $x \twoheadrightarrow y$ or $x \to y$ hold. Hence B is *conflict free*.
- every $z \in S$ is either below or above or in B.

To understand the terminology "maximal anti-chain" used above observe the following. A *maximal chain* in $(S, \twoheadrightarrow)$ is a maximal sequence $x_1, x_2, \ldots x_n$ such that for all $i = 1, \ldots n - 1$, $x_i \twoheadrightarrow x_{i+1}$. Thus every maximal chain containing an argument z intersects a belt B in exactly one point.

The idea is that we start with the belt consisting of all arguments that are not attacked or supported, i.e., the sources of the graph. We then move forwards across the attack-defence framework to another belt reachable by realising the attack and support relation of a node in that belt.

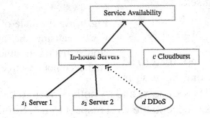

Fig. 10. A bipolar argumentation framework involving support.

We firstly illustrate what our algorithm should do on the attack-defence framework in Fig. 10. To be precise, we specify this attack-defence framework as the following quadruple defined in the bullet points below.

– The abstract arguments, i.e., the nodes of the graph:

{Service Availability, In-house Servers, Server 1, Server 2, Cloudburst, DDoS}

– The attack relation:
$$DDoS \twoheadrightarrow \text{In-house Servers}$$

– The support relation:

In-house Servers $\rightarrow$ Service Availability   Cloudburst $\rightarrow$ Service Availability

Server 1 $\rightarrow$ In-house Servers   Server 2 $\rightarrow$ In-house Servers

– The (initial) resource assignment:

$$\text{Service Availability} := \varnothing$$
$$\text{In-house Servers} := \varnothing$$
$$\text{Server 1} := \{s_1\}$$
$$\text{Server 2} := \{s_2\}$$
$$\text{Cloudburst} := \{c\}$$
$$\text{DDoS} := \{d\}$$

Remark 1. Observe that Service Availability and In-house Servers are initially assigned no resources, as indicated by the empty set. This is because these arguments have no resources inherently, by themselves, instead they inherit their resources via support relations from the arguments Server 1, Server 2, and Cloudburst. Thus if we consider the argumentation frame without the DDoS node, we could represent this scenario using the attack tree consisting of the single node Service Availability, assigned the resources $\{s_1, s_2, c\}$. The advantage of using explicit support relations rather than a single node is that we can employ more fine-grained precision indicating that the in-house servers are affected by the DDoS attack, but Cloudbursting is not affected by a DDoS attack.

Observe also that the sub-framework consisting of "In-house Servers", "Server 1" and "Server 2" could alternatively be modelled by a single node "In-house Servers" with resource assignment $\{s_1, s_2\}$. That modelling decision would not changing the meaning of the tree, since the DDoS attack takes out both servers indiscriminately.

We propose an algorithm that executes as follows on Fig. 10.

Initialisation: The initial belt (those nodes that are not attacked or supported by any other node) is defined as follows:

$$\{\text{Cloudburst, DDoS, Server 1, Server 2}\}$$

Note all of these arguments should correspond to leaves of some attack-defence tree and hence should have resources assigned to them, which is indeed the case for this example.

Step 1: We consider some belt reachable from the initial belt by taking at most one step away from the initial belt, with respect to the attacks and supports. For this example, there is only one choice: the following belt, which is reachable by the attack and support relations in one step:

$$\{\text{Cloudburst, In-house Servers}\}$$

Notice that argument Cloudburst does not advance, if it were to advance we would not have a belt. Firstly, we update the attack-defence framework to reflect the support relations resulting in the attack defence framework where the resources assigned to "Server 1" and "Server 2" are sent to "In-house Servers"—resulting in the new annotation $\{s_1, s_2\}$ for that node.

Secondly, we apply the construction from the previous section to generate an argumentation framework (with joint attacks) based on the weapons given by the resource assignment. I.e., we interpret $d \twoheadrightarrow \{s_1, s_2\}$, thereby generating the relation R_1 consisting of $d\,R_1\,s_1$ and $d\,R_1\,s_2$.

Step 2: As with Step 1 above, we progress to the next belt:

$$\{\text{Service Availability}\}$$

This belt is reachable by two supports from the nodes of the previous belt Cloudburst and In-house Servers, hence we update the resources, assigned to "Service Availability," by sending the resources from "In-house Servers" and "Cloudburst," resulting in the annotation $\{s_1, s_2, c\}$ for the node "Service Availability."

Since there are no attacks for this iteration of the algorithm $R_2 = R_1$.

Output of Algorithm: The result of running the algorithm is an updated *resource assignment* as follows:

$$
\begin{aligned}
\text{Service Availability} &:= \{s_1, s_2, c\} \\
\text{In-house Servers} &:= \{s_1, s_2\} \\
\text{Server 1} &:= \{s_1\} \\
\text{Server 2} &:= \{s_2\} \\
\text{Cloudburst} &:= \{c\} \\
\text{DDoS} &:= \{d\}
\end{aligned}
$$

This is accompanied by the argumentation framework on weapons, with relation R defined as.

$$d \, R \, s_1 \qquad d \, R \, s_2$$

Note that, in general there could be a set of argumentation frameworks with joint attacks generated; but, in this case, there is only a single choice of argumentation framework.

Analysis: Consider the output of the algorithm and observe that, since nothing attacks d or c in R they are both elements of preferred extension E^+. Hence c is acceptable with respect to E^+ in the conventional sense of the argumentation framework defined by R_2. Going further, since the argument Service Availability of the updated attack-defence framework has resource annotation $\{s_1, s_2, c\}$ and c is acceptable with respect to E^+, we can say that "*Service Availability* is an acceptable argument with respect E^+."

We reinterpret the above from the perspective of security. The preferred extension says that if a DDoS attack is active and the option to Cloudbursting is available then we have Service Availability.

3.3   An Algorithm for Attack-Defence Frameworks, in Its General Form

We now distil the general algorithm from the above worked examples.

The input: An attack-defence framework $(\mathbf{S}, \twoheadrightarrow, \rightarrow, S, :=)$. I.e., a bipolar argumentation framework $(\mathbf{S}, \twoheadrightarrow, \rightarrow)$ with a resource assignment $:=$ mapping arguments to sets of multisets of weapons built from the atoms in S.

Remark 2. The attack-defence framework may be generated from an attack-defence tree, by assigning a singleton atomic weapon to each action and the empty set of resources to each node in the attack-defence tree. However, more general acyclic graphs of relations and more detailed resource assignments are also permitted.

The initialisation: We define the initial mapping $:=_0$, belt B_0 and set of joint attack relation $\mathcal{R}_0$ as follows.

- $:=_0 \,=\, :=$
- $B_0 = \{\mathbf{x} \colon \mathbf{x} \in \mathbf{S} \text{ and there is no } \mathbf{y} \in \mathbf{S} \text{ such that } \mathbf{y} \twoheadrightarrow \mathbf{x} \text{ or } \mathbf{y} \rightarrow \mathbf{x}\}$
- $\mathcal{R}_0 = \{\varnothing\}$

The inductive step: Let B_{n+1} be a belt (not necessarily uniquely defined) such that $B_{n+1} \neq B_n$ and for all $\mathbf{y} \in B_{n+1}$ there exists $\mathbf{x} \in B_n$ such that $\mathbf{x} = \mathbf{y}$ or $\mathbf{x} \twoheadrightarrow \mathbf{y}$ or $\mathbf{x} \rightarrow \mathbf{y}$, i.e., every element of B_{n+1} is either in B_n or reachable from B_n. Notice there must be some progress forwards, since at lest one element of B_{n+1} must not be in B_n.

The assignment of sets of multisets of weapons to arguments is updated as follows.

$$\mathbf{y} :=_{n+1} S_n \cup \bigcup \{T : \exists \mathbf{x} \in B_n \ s.t. \ \mathbf{x} \rightarrow \mathbf{y} \wedge \mathbf{x} :=_n T\} \quad \text{where } \mathbf{y} :=_n S_n.$$

The set of relation $\{R_{n+1}^i\}$ is then updated by using the set of joint attack relations on weapons generated by each $\mathbf{x} \twoheadrightarrow \mathbf{y}$ where $\mathbf{x} \in B_n$, $\mathbf{x} \in B_{n+1}$, Recall, that joint attack relations map mutisets of weapons to single weapons. More precisely, we have $\mathcal{R}_{n+1}$ is defined as follows, where $\boxtimes$ is point-wise union of sets of relations:

$$\mathcal{R}_{n+1} = \mathcal{R}_n \boxtimes \{R : \forall \mathbf{x} \in B_n, \forall \mathbf{y} \in B_{n+1} \ s.t. \ \mathbf{x} \twoheadrightarrow \mathbf{y} \wedge \mathbf{x} :=_{n+1} S \wedge \mathbf{y} :=_{n+1} T \wedge$$
$$\forall m \in T, \exists w \in m \ s.t. \ \exists n \in S \ s.t. \ n \ R \ w \}$$

The above defines more formally the joint attack relations generated as described in Sect. 3.1.

The output: Assuming the attack-defence framework is finite and acyclic, the algorithm eventually terminates, returning the assignment and set of joint attack relations at that iteration of the algorithm.

Remark 3. This is just one possible algorithm. Note, some security assessments may require more annotations and different algorithms for advancing from one belt to the next, for interpreting the attack relation, and for interpreting the joint attack relation. We return to this point in our discussion of this model, which occupies the remaining sections of the paper.

4 Reorientation from the Perspective of Attack-Defence Trees

Let us motivate and explain what we are doing in this paper in a Socratic fashion starting bottom up with the security requirements driven by examples of attack-defence trees. This approach enables us to compare existing treatments of attack-defence trees in the security area, with existing treatments of such frameworks in the argumentation area. This enables us to export ideas and technical tools from the argumentation area into the security area.

We take as a starting point an attack-defence tree in Fig. 1 of reference [1], reproduced in the Appendix (Fig. 17). We study this figure and compare it, bit by bit with argumentation frameworks, and try to see how to understand it in a new improved more detailed point of view. Viewed as a bipolar argumentation framework (i.e., a graph formed from attack and support relations) Fig. 17 has the following characteristics.

1. The graph has no cycles. (The handling of cycles is still an open problem in the attack-defence tree context, while it is more central in the argumentation context.)
2. The graph has a single top node (let us call it the goal g) to be defended and it is layered as a tree with layer 1 defending/protecting g and each layer $n + 1$ attacking the previous layer n and or defending layer $n - 1$.

3. The graph uses joint attacks and joint supports
4. The nodes have internal meaningful contents. They are not atomic letter nodes. This should be taken into account when offering semantics for the tree

There are several ways of looking at Fig. 17.

1. As a traditional formal argumentation framework. This works only for limited examples, such as Fig. 1.
2. As a graph for a game between two players (the defender/protector of g and the attacker of g) the levels/layers are moves and countermoves of the players. This view is better but still not exactly right. We shall also discuss this. The graph can be flattened to a mini-max matrix. All defences can put forward in layer 1—consisting of all possible best strategic defensive moves—and the attacker can attack all possible defensive strategies and the net result is the solution. The problem with this view is that we need to address more features of the application, for example the temporal evolution of moves, the availability and cost of resources and the local reasoning and aim of each player and, prospectively, the treatment of cycles.
3. As action counter action temporal sequence between two agents, the one protecting g and the other in principle attacking g. This is a much better view but it needs to be fine-tuned to various applications.

We now ask how do we proceed, and where do we find the connection and use of argumentation in the attack-defence trees context? We start with examples from both areas and step by step, using a Socratic method, add components that converge towards our target theory.

Let us now look at formal argumentation frameworks and find a framework to the formal argumentation community, (Fig. 11) which may be, on the face of it, similar to what Fig. 17 seems to be. We then continue our analysis of Fig. 17. Consider Fig. 11. In this figure we use a single arrow for support "→" and a double arrow for attack "↠". To start our comparison, the nodes in Fig. 11 are explained and exemplified by nodes in Fig. 17 in parentheses below.

Explanation of the nodes of Fig. 11:

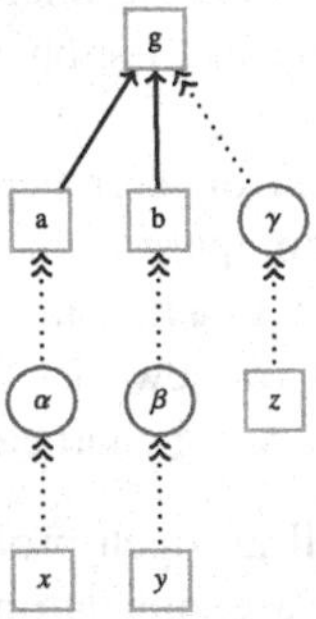

Fig. 11. A scenario with goals, attacks and defences, in terms of attack relations and as an attack defence tree.

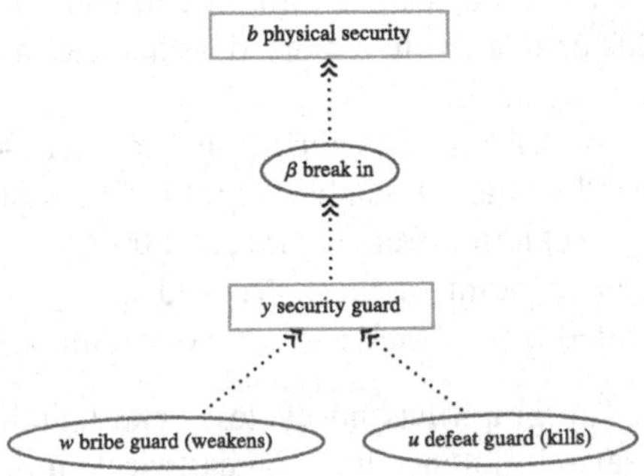

Fig. 12. A subtree of Fig. 17, where some attacks defeat and others weaken.

- g is the goal to protect (Data Confidentiality)
- a, b are supports (Physical Security, Network Security, etc.)
- α, β, γ attack the support (Break In, Dictionary Attack, Corruption)
- x, y, z support a, b, c by attacking the attacks (Security Guard, Strong Password, etc.).

Comparing Fig. 17 and Fig. 11, let us make some observations.

Observation 1. In Fig. 17, consider the subpart of the figure represented by Fig. 2. In this figure the node y does not attack β in the sense of "killing" β but makes b stronger so that it can withstand the attack of β.

In other words, the part of the figure (namely the formal attack and defence sub-figure to the left of Fig. 2) can be transformed to the bipolar argumentation framework to the right of Fig. 2.

Figure 2 represents a bipolar argumentation framework, that is a framework with attack and defence (in argumentation terminology). One of the interpretations of such frameworks, from the argumentation point of view, is that to attack and kill a node b, we need also to kill all of its supporters (i.e., we need to attack y as well). Adopting established terminology [13], the set $\{b, y\}$ forms a *support group*. Indeed this is also the security view of the attack and defence in Fig. 17, in that the attacks must continue on node y = Strong Password. Indeed in Fig. 17, y = Strong Password is attacked by "Strong Password Attacks" (i.e. Find Note, Same Password Different Accounts).

Observation 2. On the other hand, the part of Fig. 17 depicted in Fig. 12 consisting of b, β, y with the additional options, u and w, is different. It has the additional feature that it the security guard is attacked in two possible ways: bribing, which weakens the guard and may be ineffective, and killing, which removes the guard.This observation departs from mainstream argumentation. In argumentation, if a node x attacks a node y (i.e. $x \rightarrow y$), then if x is alive then the attack on y is always successful and x kills y and y is dead. There is no intermediate result such as weakening y, which might be accommodated in a more resource sensitive model.

From the perspective of security, a limitation of lifting directly from argumentation without reworking the semantics is that resource considerations remain limited—all arguments are either "in" or "out" with respect to some joint attack relation. For attack-defence trees, when determining whether an argument such as "data confidentiality" is maintained we consider the resources assigned to an attacker profile. Resources may be specialised equipment or expertise, a budget or time; while profiles of attackers may include cybercriminals, rogue states, script kiddies or cyberterrorists. Only by combining such viewpoints can we estimates the vulnerabilities a system is exposed to and priorities mitigating those attacks with limited security resources.

Instead of calculating whether nodes are in or out we may wish to calculate quantities that remain after being attacked. For instance in Fig. 10, for some attacker and defender profiles, there may not be sufficient budget for the defender to use Cloudbursting, but there is not sufficient motive for the attacker to perpetrate the DDoS attack any way. Bringing in such resource considerations from security would be a contribution to the area of argumentation.

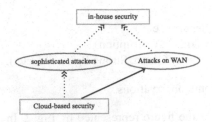

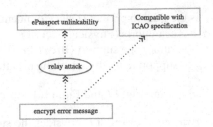

Fig. 13. Scenario where a defensive action supports a new attack.

Fig. 14. Scenario with multiple goals, and goals that are not necessarily security related.

Observation 3. Consider the framework in Fig. 13. This is an acyclic graph rather than a tree. There is no attack-defence node distinction: a "green" node can support a "red" node (colours are meaningless in this model, they simplify making connection with established attack-defence tree notations).

Scenario for Fig. 13: A company with a limited cyber security budget may not have the resources to defend against sophisticated attackers using in house security solutions. Their solution to defeat these sophisticated cyber attacks is to outsource part of their infrastructure to a secure Cloud environment. The dedicated expertise and tools behind the Cloud-based security solution does reduce the risk of the company becoming exposed to certain sophisticated attacks on their in-house infrastructure; however, this move does leave open the organisation to new attacks. Thus, a side-effect of employing Cloud-based security is that new attacks that exploit the fact that certain operations are occurring over a WAN are enabled. Thus the use of certain defences may support new attacks.

Notice that, while we do not have side effects in Fig. 17, it is possible to add examples of side effects. In Fig. 12, killing the guard may activate a Murder Investigation as a side effect and we might not want that.

Observation 4. The scenario in Fig. 14 presents multiple goals, which would not be permitted if we restrict to trees. The privacy goal is to ensure ePassport holders cannot be linked from one session to the next, which is called *unlinkability*. There are attacks on unlinkability, involving relaying messages to remote readers [14]. Note furthermore, that such attacks do not completely compromise unlinkability, e.g., ePassport holders cannot be tracked forever, only in a limited time window, so there are resource considerations here.

The effectiveness of these relay attacks on ePassport unlinkability could be reduced by encrypting error messages that leak information. The added dimension is that the defensive action of encrypting an error message attacks a second goal, which is to satisfy the ICAO specification for ePassports so that the ePassport is compatible with ePassport readers internationally. Thus there may be multiple goals, and not all goals need be security related.

An additional reason for permitting multiple goals and even disconnected acyclic graphs is illustrated in Fig. 9. That figure depicts a graph with multiple sinks which is an attack relation realising that realises another attack relation that formed a tree. Thus by permitting general acyclic graphs we can use graphical nota-tion to depict both attack-defence trees, where arguments may be attack trees, and its semantics given by a set of joint attack relations where the target of each

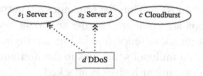

Fig. 15. Diagrammatic representation of the argumentation framework generated algorithmi-cally in Sect. 3.2, which forms a disconnected acyclic graph with no single root node.

attack is an atomic action or weapon. To see why such acyclic graphs need not be connected, observe that the joint attack relation generated by the running example in Sect. 3.2 can be depicted as in Fig. 15. Recall that nothing attacked the Cloudburst argu-ment whose resources were denoted by the weapon c.

Observation 5. In formal argumentation frameworks, a node x attacking several targets attacks all of them in the same way. There is no option for different attacks for different targets. This is not the case in Fig. 17, "defeat lock" attacking the back door is most likely not the same as the one attacking the front door. The attacks are directional.

Observation 6. In Security, there is a stress on resources, hence the use of linear logic in semantics for attack trees [15, 16]. Formal argumentation is based on classical logic.

Observation 7. The structure of an attack-defence framework could be taken further, to provide a still finer semantics for attack-defence trees, by introducing an explicit *con-junctive support relation*. For example, consider the first attack-defence tree in Fig. 16.

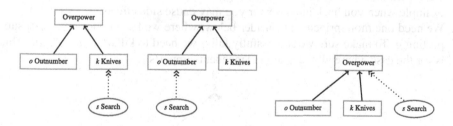

Fig. 16. A case for conjunctive support with two variations.

Existing semantics for attack-defence tree in the literature, and also the semantics in this paper, are not sensitive to the fact that the reason that Overpower is countered is that people were searched upon entry to the building. Indeed, the existing semantics would assign the same meaning to the first tree in Fig. 16 and the two other scenarios.

In terms of the semantics provided, Overpower will be assigned the attack tree denoted by $\{o * k\}$ and a set of two attack relations, say $\{R_1, R_2\}$, will be generated, where

$s\,R_1\,k$ and $s\,R_2\,o$. Thus the semantics are currently indiscriminate about which weapons or actions are countered by the argument Search—it is not necessarily the Knives, as the first attack-defence tree in Fig. 16 might intuitively suggest. As, explained above, established multiset semantics in the literature [1] would also not make it explicit that only the argument Knives is attacked.

The above limitation of the semantics could be resolved by an explicit conjunctive support, which is interpreted in the algorithm by extending the weapons in the nodes supported, using multiset union, by using the resources available to the source node. This would enable the three scenarios in Fig. 16 to be distinguished, since the generated attack relations would be $\{R_1\}$, $\{R_2\}$ and $\{R_1, R_2\}$ respectively.

A further advantage of breaking down all nodes in an attack-defence tree into arguments is that we can refer explicitly to sub-goals of attackers, not just the roots of trees. That is, we can ask questions, such as whether a sub-goal is an acceptable argument with respect to some preferred extension. Recent work on attack trees, has argued for the value of giving sub-goals an explicit status [17].

Remark 4 (Summary of discussion in Sect. 4). We summarise the points learnt from our discussion in this section. To give good argumentation like semantics for Fig. 17 describing a security scenario, we need to enrich argumentation with the following features:

1. And/or attacks and defence (this we have already in argumentation).
2. Allow converting attack to support and support to attacks (this has been done previously [18], but for only the numerical case).
3. Allow for weakening attacks (as well as attacks which fail) in a directional way. (This means that for the same live x and different targets, say for example, $x \twoheadrightarrow y_1, x \twoheadrightarrow y_2$, and $x \twoheadrightarrow y_3$, it is possible that the attack of x on y_1 will succeed, the attack on y_2 will fail and the attack on y_3 will only weaken y_3. Compare this with numerical attacks which change the strength of the target by a numerical factor.)
4. Deal with side effects in the formal argumentation level, because in practice for example when you hack into a server you may cause side effects.
5. We need one more principle: Consider below, where we have nodes $a_1, \ldots, a_n$ supporting g. To make sure we successfully kill g we need to kill *all* of $a_1, \ldots, a_n$. This is for the case where all the a_i are independent supports.

This is not like how it goes in logical and legal argumentation. If we have $a_1 \vdash g, \ldots, a_n \vdash g$, then attacking or falsifying all a_i does not mean that g is false. There may be some new $x \vdash g$.

In the model introduced in this paper, we embody this principal by assigning arguments representing intermediate nodes in an attack tree no resources initially. Since such nodes inherit all their resources from their supports, killing all their supports kills the intermediate argument.

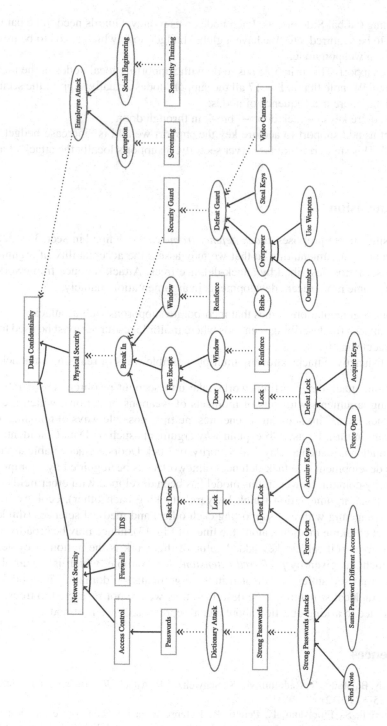

Fig. 17. An ADTree for protecting data confidentiality from reference [1]

6. Running Global Side effects. Each node costs money. Guards need to be paid, Keys need to be acquired, etc. We have a global budget node which needs to be treated as a special weapon node.
7. Local support. This principle has to do with supporting local nodes in the middle of the tree. We note that in Fig. 17 all the support nodes actually support the security of the data. There is a sequence of nodes:

acquire keys $\twoheadrightarrow$ lock door $\twoheadrightarrow$ break in through door.

So let us add support to acquire key the support we add is "increase budget to buy keys". This support is not for server security, it supports locally the attack of acquire keys.

5   Conclusion

This position paper proposes *attack-defence frameworks*, defined in Sect. 3, which build on concepts in argumentation so that we may assess the acceptability of arguments in security scenarios described by attack-defence trees. Attack-defence frameworks borrow from some more recent developments in argumentation, namely:

– bipolar argumentation frames that incorporate support as well as attack,
– joint attacks for describing scenarios where multiple resources must be used together to execute an attack,
– and disjunctive attacks allowing multiple possible ways of realising an attack.

In addition, attack-defence frameworks take into account resource considerations, by annotating arguments with sets of multisets of weapons or actions, which are essentially attack trees. This semantics generates multiple possible ways of realising attacks, which can, in turn, be used to explain *why* arguments such as Data Confidentiality or intermediate goals such as Physical Security, or Lock Doors are acceptable arguments.

The development of attack-defence frameworks has been guided by examples from the security domain. However, this model has been developed with other fields in mind such as legal argumentation (think lawyers attacking each other), ecology (think of species competing with and supporting each other) and medical sciences (think of the side effect of taking medicine along the lines of Fig. 13), hence may be broadly applied. For security specifically, a key added value of this work is the notion of evidence for an argument, as given by *preferred extensions* for example, which is a central notion in the various semantics investigated in the argumentation domain. The model admits general graphical structures to be described thus we are not restricted to trees, nor are we restricted to asking question about a goal represented by a root node.

References

1. Kordy, B., Mauw, S., Radomirović, S., Schweitzer, P.: Attack-defense trees. J. Logic Comput. **24**, 55–87 (2012)
2. Bistarelli, S., Fioravanti, F., Peretti, P.: Defense trees for economic evaluation of security investments. In: First International Conference on Availability, Reliability and Security (ARES 2006), vol. 423 p. 8 (2006)

3. Cayrol, C., Lagasquie-Schiex, M.C.: On the acceptability of arguments in bipolar argumentation frameworks. In: Godo, L. (ed.) ECSQARU 2005. LNCS (LNAI), vol. 3571, pp. 378–389. Springer, Heidelberg (2005). https://doi.org/10.1007/11518655_33
4. Boella, G., Gabbay, D.M., van der Torre, L.W.N., Villata, S.: Support in abstract argumentation. In: Baroni, P., Cerutti, F., Giacomin, M., Simari, G.R., (eds.): Computational Models of Argument: Proceedings of COMMA 2010 of Frontiers in Artificial Intelligence and Applications., Desenzano del Garda, Italy, 8–10 September 2010. vol. 216, IOS Press pp. 111–122 (2010)
5. Wideł, W.: Formal modeling and quantitative analysis of security using attack-defense trees. PhD thesis (2019)
6. Dung, P.M.: On the acceptability of arguments and its fundamental role in nonmonotonic reasoning, logic programming and n-person games. Artif. Intell. **77**, 321–357 (1995)
7. Gabbay, D.M.: Semantics for higher level attacks in extended argumentation frames part 1: overview. Stud. Logica. **93**, 355–379 (2009)
8. Nielsen, S.H., Parsons, S.: A generalization of dung's abstract framework for argumentation: arguing with sets of attacking arguments. In: Maudet, N., Parsons, S., Rahwan, I. (eds.) ArgMAS 2006. LNCS (LNAI), vol. 4766, pp. 54–73. Springer, Heidelberg (2007). https://doi.org/10.1007/978-3-540-75526-5_4
9. Schneier, B.: Attack trees. Dr. Dobb's J. **24**, 21–29 (1999)
10. Mauw, S., Oostdijk, M.: Foundations of attack trees. In: Won, D.H., Kim, S. (eds.) ICISC 2005. LNCS, vol. 3935, pp. 186–198. Springer, Heidelberg (2006). https://doi.org/10.1007/11734727_17
11. Gabbay, D., Gabbay, M.: Theory of disjunctive attacks, part I. Logic J. IGPL **24**, 186–218 (2016)
12. Armbrust, M., et al.: A view of cloud computing. Commun. ACM **53**, 50–58 (2010)
13. Gabbay, D.: Logical foundations for bipolar argumentation networks. J. Logic Comput. **26**, 247–292 (2016)
14. Filimonov, I., Horne, R., Mauw, S., Smith, Z.: Breaking unlinkability of the ICAO 9303 standard for e-Passports using bisimilarity. In: Sako, K., Schneider, S., Ryan, P.Y.A. (eds.) ESORICS 2019. LNCS, vol. 11735, pp. 577–594. Springer, Cham (2019). https://doi.org/10.1007/978-3-030-29959-0_28
15. Horne, R., Mauw, S., Tiu, A.: Semantics for specialising attack trees based on linear logic. Fundam. Inform. **153**, 57–86 (2017)
16. Eades III, H., Jiang, J., Bryant, A.: On linear logic, functional programming, and attack trees. In: Cybenko, G., Pym, D., Fila, B. (eds.) GraMSec 2018. LNCS, vol. 11086, pp. 71–89. Springer, Cham (2019). https://doi.org/10.1007/978-3-030-15465-3_5
17. Mantel, H., Probst, C.W.: On the meaning and purpose of attack trees. In: 2019 IEEE 32nd Computer Security Foundations Symposium (CSF), pp. 184–199 (2019)
18. Barringer, H., Gabbay, D.M., Woods, J.: Temporal, numerical and meta-level dynamics in argumentation networks. Argument Comput. **3**, 143–202 (2012)

A Diagrammatic Approach to Information Flow in Encrypted Communication

Peter M. Hines[✉]

University of York, York, England
peter.hines@york.ac.uk

Abstract. *We give diagrammatic tools to reason about information flow within encrypted communication. In particular, we are interested in deducing where information flow (communication or otherwise) has taken place, and fully accounting for all possible paths.*

The core mathematical concept is using a single categorical diagram to model the underlying mathematics, the epistemic knowledge of the participants, and (implicitly) the potential or actual communication between participants. A key part of this is a 'correctness' or 'consistency' criterion that ensures we accurately & fully account for the distinct routes by which information may come to be known (i.e. communication and / or calculation).

We demonstrate how this formalism may be applied to answer questions about communication scenarios where we have the partial information about the participants and their interactions. Similarly, we show how to analyse the consequences of changes to protocols or communications, and to enumerate the distinct orders in which events may have occurred.

We use various forms of Diffie-Hellman key exchange as an illustration of these techniques. However, they are entirely general; an extended version of this paper [8] provides similar analyses of other protocols.

1 Introduction

This paper is about using categorical diagrams to study (or rather, reconstruct) the flow of information in encrypted communication; it is not about the difficulty of solving mathematical problems on which security is based.

1.1 Key Aims

The main aim of this paper is to introduce tools, based on diagrammatic representations, to ensure that we have fully accounted for *information flow* and *routes to calculating values* in communication generally, and cryptographic protocols specifically. Of course, we do not expect to find within the cryptographic literature examples of protocols where the designers have failed to do this! Rather, we use existing protocols (various forms of Diffie-Hellman key exchange, as a well-understood example) in order to motivated and test our tools.

© Springer Nature Switzerland AG 2020
H. Eades III and O. Gadyatskaya (Eds.): GraMSec 2020, LNCS 12419, pp. 166–185, 2020.
https://doi.org/10.1007/978-3-030-62230-5_9

The utility comes when we use such techniques to reason about incomplete, rather than complete, descriptions of encrypted communication. We analyse situations where – for example – one participant becomes aware of some additional information (say, a secret key, in order to systematically deduce the additional routes to calculating values that this implies. This is considered in Sect. 6.3.

Alternatively, we wish to work backwards – we know that some private information has become more widely known, but no single individual is in a position to have shared this. We show in Sect. 7 how we may fully account for all possible routes by which this information became known.

1.2   Tools Used

Our starting point is the common category-theoretic technique of expressing algebraic identities via commuting diagrams. Drawing such diagrams for the algebra behind cryptographic protocols makes the structure of the underlying mathematics clear (see, for example [14]); this paper also extends such diagrams to represent the participants, and their knowledge.

Mathematically, we do this by moving beyond commuting diagrams, and recovering both the information flow between participants, and distinct routes by which significant values may be computed, as 2-categorical structure.

Based on this, we give a 'correctness' criterion that ensures that potential or actual information flow within the diagram is modelled correctly – i.e. nothing has been 'left out' and we have not overlooked any route by which a participant may come to know some information.

2   Bipartite Diffie-Hellman, Diagramatically

We use, as illustration, the basic bipartite D-H protocol [5,12]; this is very well-known, and summarised in Table 1.

Table 1. A concise summary of D-H key exchange

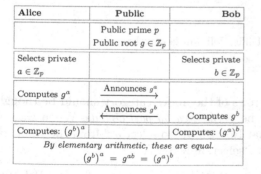
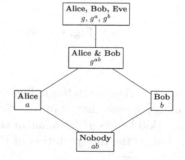

Alice	Public	Bob
	Public prime p	
	Public root $g \in \mathbb{Z}_p$	
Selects private $a \in \mathbb{Z}_p$		Selects private $b \in \mathbb{Z}_p$
Computes g^a	Announces g^a $\longrightarrow$	
	Announces g^b $\longleftarrow$	Computes g^b
Computes: $(g^b)^a$		Computes: $(g^a)^b$
By elementary arithmetic, these are equal. $(g^b)^a = g^{ab} = (g^a)^b$		

The tabular presentation simply distinguishes **public** and **private** information; by contrast, a fine-grained description of the knowledge of the participants

(Alice, Bob, and some putative evesdropper[1] Eve) is given in lattice form, by 'tagging' each algebraic element by a member of the power set lattice $2^{\{A,B,E\}}$ of participants.

2.1   Expressing Algebraic Identities Diagrammatically

A core category-theoretic practice is giving identities as *commuting diagrams*.

Definition 1. *A **diagram** over a category $\mathcal{C}$ is a directed graph with nodes labeled by objects. Each edge is labeled by an arrow whose source/target is given by the labels on the initial/final nodes. A diagram **commutes** when the composites along all paths with the same starting/finishing node are equal.*

Commuting diagrams provide a very efficient and visually appealing way to express algebraic identities. In Fig. 1 we express the identies from Table 1 as a commuting diagram over the following category:

Definition 2. *Given prime $p \in \mathbb{N}$, we define the category $\mathbf{DH_p}$ to have two objects: a singleton object $\{*\}$ and the set $\mathbb{Z}_p = \{0, \ldots, p-1\}$. For all $x = 0, \ldots, p-1$, we have the following arrows:*

- *The **selection** arrows $[x] : \{*\} \to \mathbb{Z}_p$, defined by $[x](*) = x \in \mathbb{Z}_p$.*
- *The **modular exponentiation** arrows $(\_)^x : \mathbb{Z}_p \to \mathbb{Z}_p$, defined in the usual arithmetic manner.*

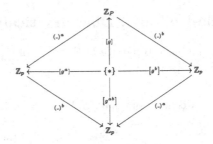

Fig. 1. Bipartite Diffie-Hellman key exchange

Remark 1 (Interpretation). The arrows of the above category should be though of as *operations* that may reliably be *performed by participants*. When we say that "Bob knows g^{ab}", we mean that Bob is able to select g^{ab} from the whole of $\mathbb{Z}_p$. This is the interpretation of the 'selection arrows'.

---

[1] Although it is standard to assume that Eve is an adversary to Alice and Bob, the tools themselves take a more agnostic approach. Our aim is to study information flow generally; we may be more concerned about information flow to Eve, but the models themselves treat her equally to the other participants.

2.2   Combining Algebraic and Epistemic Data

We now combine the algebraic and epistemic aspects of the D-H protocol into a single categorical diagram (Fig. 2), by 'tagging' each arrow by the subset of participants that are able to perform that operation. By treating $2^{\{A,B,E\}}$ as a monoid with composition given by intersection we consider Fig. 2 to be a categorical diagram over the product category $\mathbf{DH_p} \times 2^{\{A,B,E\}}$. Note that this categorical diagram *fails to commute*. We discuss the significance of this in Sect. 3 below, but first provide some much-needed clarification on what, precisely, is being modeled by these diagrams.

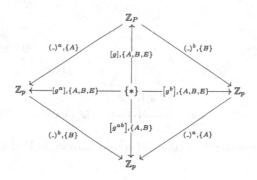

Fig. 2. The Algebraic-Epistemic diagram for Diffie-Hellman key exchange

2.3   What is Being Modeled by A-E Diagrams?

The interpretation of the epistemic tags in an A-E diagram is that an algebraic component (e.g. a private key, public message, shared secret, etc.) is labeled by some representation of 'who knows this value'. What has not been included is *how* or *when* they came to know this. There is therefore no in-built notion of 'event', 'message', 'time-ordering', 'causality' or even 'communication'.

Rather, the information in the diagram simply tells us that a given participant became aware of a given value *at some point*. It may be seen as a retrospective view of some communication protocol. Once the process has completed, who has become aware of what?

This is intentional. We show how, given this restricted information, we may nevertheless reconstruct possible scenarios of how this state of affairs may have arisen (via communications between participants, and participants using the result of these communications to calculate new values). For a well-designed cryptographic protocol, this will be unique, at least up to some inessential re-ordering of events (such as well-known variations of the steps in tri-partite Diffie-Hellman key exchange of Sect. 5). Of more interest is the situation where there is some ambiguity, or simply where something has gone wrong! We may wish account for all routes by which some information became public knowledge (Sect. 7), or to analyse the consequences of some individual having more a priori knowledge than we had anticipated (Sect. 6.3).

3   Information Flow as Failure of Commutativity

The failure of commutativity in Fig. 2 is obvious. Our claim is that this is a feature rather than a bug: non-trivial information flow becomes obvious in this graphical form. Precisely, the points at which commutativity fails are those where either 1/ a public announcement has taken place, or 2/ there exists more than one route to calculating the same result.

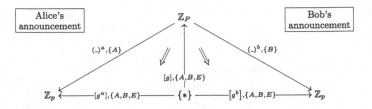

Fig. 3. Announcements as failure of commutativity in D-H key exchange

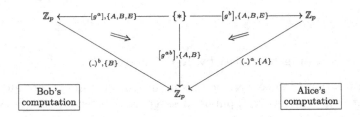

Fig. 4. Failure of commutativity via distinct paths to the same result

Consider the subdiagram of Fig. 2 given in Fig. 3. This fails to commute because $((\_)^a, \{A\}) ([g], \{A, B, E\}) = ([g^a], \{A\}) \neq ([g^a], \{A, B, E\})$. Similarly, $((\_)^b, \{B\}) ([g], \{A, B, E\}) = ([g^b], \{B\}) \neq ([g^b], \{A, B, E\})$.

The underlying cause in both cases is the public announcements: we would see the label $([g^a], \{A\}) = ((\_)^a, \{A\}) ([g], \{A, B, E\})$ in the case where Alice had raised the publicly known root to her secret key, but *kept the result to herself*. Similarly, we see an edge labeled by $([g^b], \{A, B, E\})$, rather than $([g^b], \{B\}) = ((\_)^b, \{B\}) ([g], \{A, B, E\})$ because Bob has *publicly shared the result of his computation*.

Communication between participants clearly causes failure of commutativity; however, there is another significant reason why a diagram may fail to commute. Figure 4 gives another subdiagram of Fig. 2 that also fails to commute, since

$((\_)^b, \{B\})\ ([g^a], \{A, B, E\}) = ([g^{ab}], \{B\}) \neq ([g^{ab}], \{A, B\})$. In a similar way, $((\_)^a, \{A\})\ ([g^b], \{A, B, E\}) = ([g^{ab}], \{A\}) \neq ([g^{ab}], \{A, B\})$.

However, no announcements have taken place in this part of the protocol. Rather commutativity fails because Alice and Bob have separately arrived at the same information (i.e. their shared secret g^{ab}) via two distinct paths. The fact that they both know it (and only they know it) is accounted for by the fact that the label on shared secret is the *join* of the labels of the two paths with the same source and target.

4   Algebraic-Epistemic Diagrams, and a Correctness Condition

The above considerations apply generally, and motivate the following definitions:

Definition 3. *We define an* **Algebraic-Epistemic** *or* **A-E diagram** *to be a categorical diagram giving a representation of the algebraic components of a communication protocol or scenario, together with tags representing who becomes aware of what information.*

Remark 2. This paper uses Diffie-Hellman key exchange as illustration because it is simple and well-understood. The techniques used are general. Other examples are given in [8], with the same interpretations and correctness criteria.

4.1   A Correctness Criterion for A-E Diagrams

We now introduce a general 'correctness' criterion on A-E diagrams.

Definition 4. *A category C is* **poset–enriched** *when each homset $C(X, Y)$ has a partial ordering $\leq_{XY}$ compatible with composition, so $f \leq a \in C(X, Y)$ and $g \leq b \in C(Y, Z)$ implies $gf \leq ba \in C(X, Z)$. (It is common to omit the object subscripts; these are generally clear from the context).*

Every category is enriched over the partial order given by equality on homsets. The product of two poset-enriched categories is also enriched over the product partial order: $(a, b) \leq (c, d)$ iff $a \leq c$ and $b \leq d$. Thus we may assume the category $\mathbf{DH_p} \times 2^{\{A,B,E\}}$ used in Sect. 2.2 to be poset-enriched.

We now give a condition on diagrams over poset–enriched categories that we will claim as a 'correctness criterion' for Algebraic-Epistemic diagrams.

Definition 5. *A diagram $\mathfrak{D}$ over a poset-enriched category C satisfies the* **information flow ordering (IFO) condition**, *or is an* **IFO diagram** *when:*

1. *The underlying diagraph of $\mathfrak{D}$ is acyclic.*
2. *For any edge e and path $p = p_k \ldots p_1$ with the same source and target node, the label on p is $\leq$ the label on e.*

Remark 3 (The general setting). Poset-enriched categories are a very special case of 2-categories, where as well as objects and arrows between objects, we have 'higher-level' notion of 2-morphisms between arrows. We refer to [15] for a good exposition of the general theory, and the diagrammatics we now use.

It is standard to draw 2-morphisms in categorical diagrams as "two-cells", or morphisms between paths; for example, condition 2. is drawn as follows:

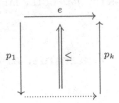

This implies that any pair of edges with the same source and target have the same label; we therefore assume there is at most one edge with a given source/target.

Remark 4 (The IFO condition as a correctness criterion). This 'correctness' is simply about about accurately accounting for information flow between participants, and what this enables them to calculate. Our claim is that if we find that the IFO condition is not satisfied, we have failed to account for one of these.

4.2   Justifying the IFO Condition

An A-E diagram $\mathfrak{D}$ is drawn over a category of the form $\mathcal{C} \times \mathcal{L}$, where $\mathcal{C}$ is the algebraic setting for the protocol, and $\mathcal{L}$ is a meet-semilattice (generally the powerset-lattice 2^P of the participants in the protocol). $\mathcal{C}$ is enriched over the equality relation, so the product category $\mathcal{C} \times 2^P$ is then enriched via the product partial ordering.

The projection onto the first component $\pi_1(\mathfrak{D})$ is an acyclic commuting diagram over $\mathcal{C}$ expressing the relationships between operations performed by participants. By construction, this commutes, and therefore trivially satisfies the IFO condition. The additional lattice labels in $\mathfrak{D}$ itself are 'tags' giving the subset of participants that are able to perform the operation on that edge.

Based on this generic description, the interpretation of the IFO condition is straightforward. Consider (a fragment of) the A-E diagram for some protocol consisting of one edge and one path between nodes H and K, as follows:

$$
\begin{array}{ccccc}
\bullet & \xrightarrow{\ a_2,P_2\ } & \cdots & \xrightarrow{\ a_{n-1},P_{n-1}\ } & \bullet \\
{\scriptstyle a_1,P_1}\uparrow & & & & \downarrow{\scriptstyle a_n,P_n} \\
H & & \xrightarrow{\quad\quad b,Q \quad\quad} & & K
\end{array}
$$

The IFO condition in this simple case states that $\bigwedge_{j=1}^{n} P_j \leq Q$; this is an axiomatisation of the triviality that any individual who is able to perform each of the operations $a_1, \ldots, a_n$ is also able to perform their composite $a_n a_{n-1} \cdots a_1$.

Conversely, consider some diagram consisting of a single edge from node H to node K, and multiple paths $\{\Pi_1, \ldots \Pi_n\}$ with the same source and target, where the meet of the labels along Π_k is denoted R_k, as follows:

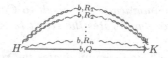

The interpretation of the IFO condition is again straightforward. Every member of $R_1, R_2, \ldots, R_n$ is able to perform b; thus $R_j \leq Q$ for all $j = 1..n$. Using the additional lattice operations of 2^P we may also write this as $\bigvee_{j=1}^{n} R_j \leq Q$. However, the possibility that additional communication / announcements have also taken place prevents us from writing $\bigvee_{j=1}^{n} R_j = Q$; indeed, failure of this condition is a clear signal that additional communication has taken place.

Remark 5 (The IFO condition and deadlock-freeness). A further consequence of the IFO condition is *deadlock-freeness*; for example, it rules out the situation where Alice is waiting for a communication from Bob before she may continue, whilst simultaneously, Bob is waiting for a communication from Alice before he may take his next step.

This is not ruled out by the acyclicity of the underlying graph; communication appears as arrows between the edges of this graph (the partial order relations, drawn as 2-cells) – it is these that we need to ensure do not form closed loops.

This follows from the IFO condition; deadlock would appear as a 'closed loop' of distinct labels on edges, such as $a < b$, $b < c$, and $c < a$. The anti-symmetry axiom $x \leq y$ & $y \leq x \Rightarrow x = y$ for partial orders then implies that $a = b = c$. This contradicts the assumption that a, b and c are *distinct* labels!

5   Tripartite Diffie-Hellman Key Exchange

We now use diagrammatic methods to compare and contrast two approaches to tripartite secret sharing based on Diffie-Hellman key exchange. Multi-partite generalisations of Diffie-Hellman key exchange are well-established (see, for example, [11]). We consider the case where three participants construct a *single shared secret*, and where each pair of the three participants has a *distinct shared secret*. We refer to these as $\binom{3}{3}$ Diffie-Hellman and $\binom{3}{2}$ Diffie-Hellman respectively.

They are of course special cases of the situation where there are n participants, and each subset of k participants constructs a distinct shared secret – what we refer to as the general $\binom{n}{k}$ Diffie-Hellman protocol. This, including its diagrammatics, is considered in [8].

Definition 6 ($\binom{3}{3}$ Diffie-Hellman key exchange). *Let us assume participants $\{Alice, Bob, Carol, Eve\}$ where Eve is the evesdropper, and Alice, Bob, and Carol will construct a mutual shared secret. Alice, Bob and Carol choose* *private keys* $a, b, c \in \mathbb{Z}_p$ *respectively, and their shared secret* $g^{abc} = g^{bca} = g^{cab}$ *is constructed as follows:*

1. *Alice computes* g^a *and communicates the result to Bob.*
2. *Bob computes* g^b *and communicates the result to Carol.*
3. *Carol computes* g^c *and communicates the result to Alice.*

4. *Alice computes* $(g^c)^a = g^{ca}$ *and communicates the result to Bob.*
5. *Bob computes* $(g^a)^b = g^{ab}$ *and communicates the result to Carol.*
6. *Carol computes* $(g^b)^c = g^{bc}$ *and communicates the result to Alice.*

7. *Alice computes* $(g^{bc})^a = y^{abc}$.
8. *Bob computes* $(g^{ca})^b = g^{abc}$
9. *Carol computes* $(g^{ab})^c = g^{abc}$.

It is of course assumed that Eve is party to all communication. We have made a slight break with convention, simply in order to test the formalism, and assumed that for whatever reason, Carol is not party to the communications between Alice and Bob, etc.

The Algebraic-Epistemic diagram for this is given in Fig. 5, and – should it be needed – a step-by-step description of how this diagram is derived is given in [8]. It may be verified that this diagram satisfies the IFO condition, and it is also unambiguous who has communicated what information to whom.

An obvious alternative to three participants calculating a single shared secret is the scenario where each pair of participants has a distinct shared secret via the standard Diffie-Hellman protocol.

Definition 7. *(The* $\binom{3}{2}$ **Diffie Hellman protocol***) We again assume participants* $\{Alice, Bob, Carol, Eve\}$ *where Eve is the evesdropper. Alice, Bob and Carol choose private keys* $a, b, c \in \mathbb{Z}_p$, *and each pair, Alice-Bob, Bob-Carol, and Carol-Alice uses the bipartite D-H protocol to construct a shared secret.*

- *Alice, Bob, and Carol compute* g^a *and* g^b *and* g^c *respectively. They publicly announce their results.*
- *Alice computes* g^{ba} *(shared with Bob) and* g^{ca} *(shared with Carol).*
- *Bob computes* g^{cb} *(shared with Carol) and* g^{ab} *(shared with Alice).*
- *Carol computes* g^{ac} *(shared with Alice) and* g^{bc} *(shared with Bob).*

We jump straight to the A-E diagram for the above protocol, given in Fig. 6. This uses the same colour-coding as above.

Remark 6 (Ordering of steps in tripartite Diffie-Hellman). A notable difference between the step-by-step descriptions of Definitions 6 and 7, and the A-E diagram of Figs. 5 and 6, is that in the tabular description the order of steps is fixed. In the categorical diagrams, it becomes clear how this particular ordering of steps is not essential; rather, the only real restrictions are that a participant

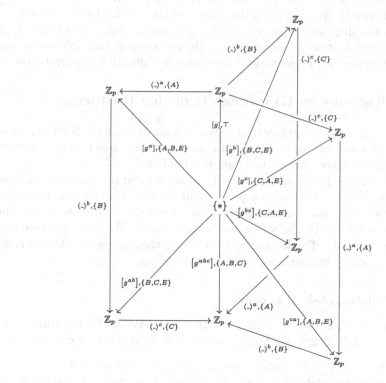

Fig. 5. Algebraic-Epistemic diagram for $\binom{3}{3}$ Diffie-Hellman

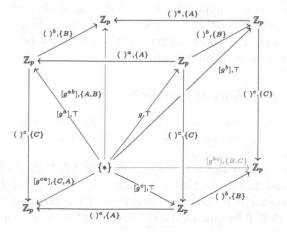

Fig. 6. $\binom{3}{2}$ Diffie-Hellman

can only communicate a value *after* she has calculated it, and a value can only be calculated once the pre-requisites for this calculation have been received.

Based on the diagram we may consider alternative orderings of the steps given in Definition 6; it may be verified that these correspond to alternative, but operationally equivalent, presentations multipartite Diffie-Hellman protocols.

6   A-E Diagrams as Graphical Tools for Protocols

Although a diagrammatic approach may give a path to intuitive descriptions of protocols via pictures, we also wish to show how these pictures provide concrete tools for deducing & reasoning about information flow.

A diagrammatic calculus allows us easily to answer certain questions such as, 'how much information does a given participant have?', 'what are the routes by which an evesdropper may become aware of a given secret?', and 'what are the consequences of this particular value becoming known?'. We first illustrate this using various forms of Diffe-Hellman key exchange, then give general techniques for finding implicit or hidden information via diagrams.

6.1   Manipulating A-E Diagrams

We make some straightforward definitions that will have useful interpretations when applied to A-E diagrams. A key concept is ordering categorical diagrams.

Definition 8. *Let* $(\mathcal{C}, \leq)$ *be a poset-enriched category, and let* $\mathfrak{H}, \mathfrak{K}$ *be diagrams (not necessarily commutative) over* $\mathcal{C}$. *We say* $\mathfrak{H} \leq \mathfrak{K}$ *iff the underlying directed graph of* $\mathfrak{H}$ *is a subgraph[2] of the underlying digraph of* $\mathfrak{K}$, *and for all edges of* $\mathfrak{H}$, *the label in* $\mathfrak{H}$ *is less than or equal to the label of the same edge in* $\mathfrak{K}$. *It is immediate that this a partial order on diagrams over* $\mathcal{C}$.

The above is of course applicable to IFO diagrams. Of particular interest is the poset of IFO diagrams that are above an arbitrary diagram, and whether this poset has a bottom element. In general there may not be a *unique* minimal IFO diagram above an arbitrary diagram.

6.2   Participants' Views of Protocols

A natural example of the ordering of diagrams is given by taking the A-E diagram for a given protocol, and erasing all edges whose 'tag' does not include some participant, or set of participants.

In Fig. 7, we consider the A-E diagram for the $\binom{3}{3}$ Diffie-Hellman protocol, given in Fig. 5, and do this for for the subsets $\{A\}$, $\{A, B\}$, $\{A, B, C\}$ and $\{E\}$. This gives a convenient graphical illustration of the information available to Alice, Alice and Bob, Alice and Bob and Carol, and the evesdropper respectively.

---

[2] We assume an implicit, fixed, embedding in order not to have to consider the graph embedding or graph isomorphism problem. In practice, this embedding is immediate from the interpretation.

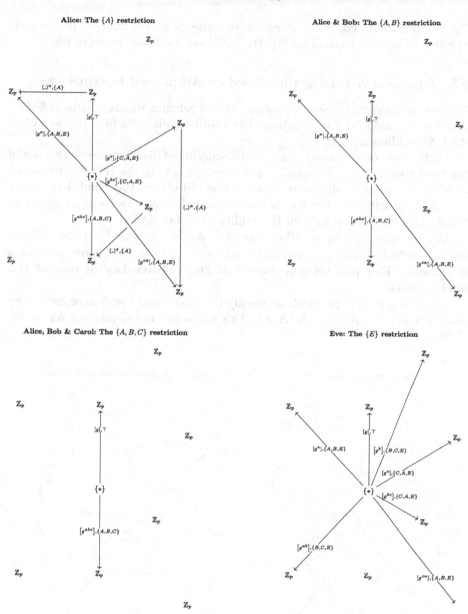

Fig. 7. $\binom{3}{3}$ Diffie-Hellman as seen by various sets of participants

It is immediate that these subdiagrams also satisfy the IFO condition, and similarly that taking any A-E diagram satisfying the IFO condition, and erasing all edges according to a similar criterion, will result in a diagram that again satisfies the IFO condtion. In particular, it is simple to take the diagram of

Fig. 6 and erase all edges not accessible to some (non-evesdropper) participant, to recover the A-E diagram for bipartite D-H key exchange given in Fig. 1.

6.3   Updating A-E Diagrams Based on Additional Information

We now consider the more interesting case of when a diagram is modified to reflect some additional information. The resulting diagram may fail to satisfy the IFO condition.

Under these circumstances, the partial ordering of diagrams becomes a useful practical tool: given a diagram $\mathfrak{D}$ that does not satisfy the IFO condition, we consider the poset of diagrams above it that do satisfy this condition. Under very light assumptions, this will have a bottom element — we may analyse this to establish the consequences of this additional information.

We illustrate this by a rather simple example; we take both the $\binom{3}{3}$ and the $\binom{3}{2}$ Diffie-Hellman protocols and update them both with some additional information: **Eve has become aware of the private key of one of the participants**.

To analyse the $\binom{3}{3}$ protocol, we modify the diagram of Fig. 5 to replace every ocurrence of $(\ )^a, \{A\}$ by $(\ )^a, \{A, E\}$. This will result in the diagram on the lhs of Fig. 8.

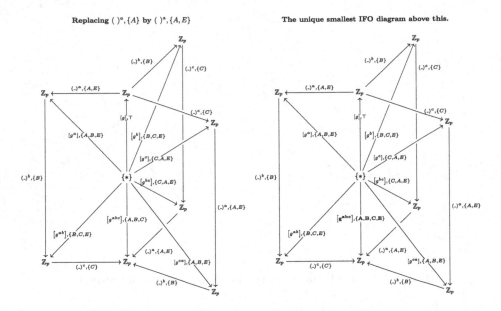

Fig. 8. Eve knows Alice's private key!

This diagram does *not* satisfy the IFO condition; it is missing either some communication or some route to participants calculating a given value. Fortunately, the poset of IFO diagrams above this has a smallest element, given on the rhs of Fig. 8.

This particular case is straightforward; the lhs diagram has failed to satisfy the IFO condition because of the following single subdiagram:

whereas the smallest IFO diagram above this is given by replacing the edge labelled $[g^{abc}], \{A, B, C\}$ with an edge labelled by $[g^{abc}], \{A, B, C, E\}$. This single change corresponds to the observation that Eve now has a route to calculating Alice, Bob and Carol's shared secret.

By contrast, let us now assume that Eve is in fact aware of Bob's secret key in the $\binom{3}{2}$ version of D-H key exchange. We modify the diagram of Fig. 6 to take this into account; we replace each ocurrence of $( )^b, \{B\}$ by $( )^b, \{B, E\}$ and find the minimal A-E above the result. This gives the diagram of Part **(i)** of Fig. 9. Using the techniques of Sect. 6.2, we then consider Eve's view of the result, giving part **(ii)** of Fig. 9. It is clear from the diagrams that Eve now has knowledge of the shared secrets of Alice & Bob, and Bob & Carol. However, she is not able to discover the shared secret of Alice & Carol.

Remark 7. Both the above results are course immediate to anyone even slightly familiar with Diffie-Hellman key exchange. The intention is to demonstrate the reliability of the formalism, before moving on to demonstrate its utility.

7 Ambiguity, Incompleteness, and Algorithmics

In the above diagrammatic manipulations, information about which participant has made a particular announcement is not explicitly included in the A-E diagram for a protocol; this is as described in Sect. 2.3. A key point of this formalism is that it nevertheless may be deduced from the context.

We now move on to situations where we have ambiguous or incomplete information. This is not relevant for analysing existing protocols, which are of course carefully designed to avoid ambiguity, and more applicable to real-world situations involving partial information about public and private communications.

Part (i)

Part (ii)

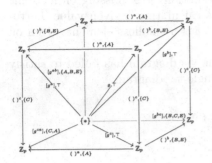
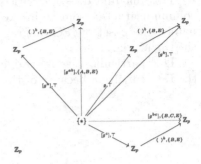

Fig. 9. When Eve knows Bob's private key

Definition 9. *Let $\mathfrak{D}$ be a diagram satisfying the IFO condition. We say that $\mathfrak{D}$ is **triangulated** when every non-identity 2-cell is decomposed into composites of identity two-cells, and non-identity two-cells whose source is a path of length two and whose target is a single edge, such as:*

*We say that a **triangulation** of a diagram $\mathfrak{D}$ is a triangulated diagram $\mathfrak{T}$ with the same nodes as $\mathfrak{D}$, that contains $\mathfrak{D}$ as a sub-diagram.*

No ambiguity can exist about communication/announcements in a triangulated diagram (beyond the inherent ambiguities given in the original data, such as, 'Both A and B know the values x and y; one of them subsequently announces the composite xy.'). For algorithmic purposes the notion of forming triangulations of a given diagram is useful.

Consider the situation described by the following diagram:

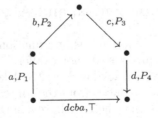

It is inaccurate to declare that, based on this information, some individual or collection of individuals, in $\bigwedge_{j=1}^{4} P_j$ must have publicly announced the result of the composition $dcba$. A counterexample is given by taking $P_1 = \{V, W\}$, $P_2 = \{W, X\}$, $P_3 = \{X, Y\}$, and $P_4 = \{Y, Z\}$, so $\bigwedge_{j=1}^{4} P_j = \bot$.

Instead, when analysing who has shared what information with whom, we require additional edges in that diagram that provide additional *epistemic* data but do not add anything to the underlying *algebraic* structure.

Diagrams $\mathfrak{D}_1$ and $\mathfrak{D}_2$ below give two possible ways in which the composite $dcba$ came to be public knowledge:

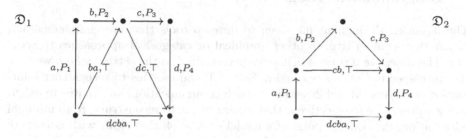

Diagram $\mathfrak{D}_1$ is triangulated; we see that W has publicly announced the composite ba and Z has publicly announced dc, resulting in any participant being able to compute $dcba$.

However, $\mathfrak{D}_2$ is still not triangulated; although we can see that X has publicly announced cb there still remains some ambiguity about how $dcba$ came to be public knowledge. To resolve the ambiguity in $\mathcal{D}_2$, note that it is a sub-diagram of both the following triangulated diagrams:

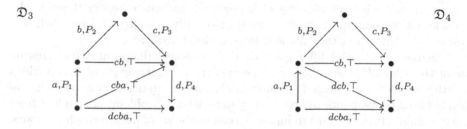

In $\mathfrak{D}_3$, we see that either V or W has announced cba, then either Y or Z has announced $dcba$. Alternatively, in $\mathfrak{D}_4$, we see that either Y or Z has announced dca followed by either U or V announcing $dcba$.

The diagrams $\mathfrak{D}_1, \mathfrak{D}_3, \mathfrak{D}_4$ are of course not the only routes by which $dcba$ may have come to be public knowledge. The two remaining possibilities are left as a straightforward exercise. In general, it is a simple, and easily automated, task to take an A-E diagram and derive the possible ways (if any!) in which communications amongst the participants which may have lead to this situation.

Remark 8. We should be aware that simply drawing such diagrams reflects our own epistemic beliefs; when we tag an edge with the pair $(x, \{U, V\})$ we are making the assumption that, for example, neither U nor V has publicly announced the value x. Triangulating a diagram is a method of making deductions about what actions participants may have taken, *based on a priori assumptions.*

For deducing additional information of which we are not aware (e.g. participant U has communicated the value of x to another participant W), we must combine the above notion of *triangulating diagrams* with the tools derived from considering the poset of diagrams above or below a given diagram.

8   Comparisons and Interactions with Other Diagrammatic Tools

The intention throughout has been to develop tools that are complementary, rather than competitive, to other graphical or categorical approaches to security. The objective has been deliberately restricted to the setting where we take the 'retrospective' view described in Sect. 2.3, and use this to reconstruct information flow – considered generally as both communication, and routes to calculating values. One perspective is that we are trying to reconstruct, from minimal information, the starting point of a model such as [4] that deals with notions of 'sites', 'channels', and 'connections'.

From this viewpoint, it is worthwhile analysing similarities and differences, and potential interactions with other related tools and formalisms. We consider categorical and graphical settings seperately, although there is of course significant overlap between the two.

The closest approach to this current paper – from both a categorical and a graphical viewpoint – is undoubtedly D. Pavlovic's work 'Chasing diagrams in cryptography' [14]. The categorical technique of replacing equations by commuting diagrams is both widespread & powerful, and any category theorist who considers a cryptographic question would naturally start by drawing such diagrams (whether or not they made it into the final work).

The most substantial difference is that [14] uses such diagrammatics to reason about (for example) the difficulty of the underlying algebraic problems on which security is based, and (entirely appropriately for this question), the communication between participants and paths they take to solve problems are explicit from the beginning. It is not hard to imagine some synthesis of his approach and ours, but considering the algebraic problems that must be solved by an attacker would require revisiting the motivation of Footnote 1, that the distinction between a participant and an adversary is sometimes not all that clear.

It is also worth noticing that our notion of 'a route to calculating a significant value' is entirely binary, and something that an participant either does, or does not have. In the long term, this needs to become a more fine-grained notion, and the route to calculating a value must be quantified in terms of its cost in terms of time or resources – something else that is a key concept of [14].

A significant precursor to much modern category theory in security is C. O'Halloran's 1994 DPhil. Thesis, "Category Theory Applied to Information Flow for Computer Security" [13]. This brings in yet another strand of category theory into the security world, by finding interpretations of core concepts such as freeness and universal properties. Although not immediately related, it is surely indirectly connected to both this current paper and other category-theoretic works in the field, and is definitely worth revisiting in light of more modern developments in category theory & security.

A particular curiosity is that categorical/graphical methods seem more firmly established with regard to quantum-mechanical, rather than classical, protocols. The starting point for this is undoubtedly the 'string diagrams' of Abramsky & Coecke's 'A categorical semantics for quantum protocols' [2], along with a great deal of subsequent work. These 'quantum protocols' certainly include crypto-graphic protocols[3].

The use of graphical, rather than specifically categorical, methods in security is much better-established. It is therefore not possible to give a complete account, but it is still worthwhile to give an overview of particularly popular or similar approaches. One of the best-established must be the notion of 'Attack Trees' [16] or 'Threat Trees' [3]. At first sight, these appear completely orthogonal to the approach we take – they are decidedly goal-oriented, and provide a systematic route achieving this goal by splitting it up into smaller steps, then subdividing these, etc. This appears to be in stark contrast to our approach where we have not even specified a goal – rather, we take a retrospective view of 'who knows what', and attempt to deduce all possible paths by which this may have occurred.

However, taking a more goal-oriented view may become essential as we attempt to scale to larger problems. In a real-world setting, we are unlikely to be interested in all the details of *all possible* scenarios that lead to some A-E diagram; instead we would wish to concentrate on some subset of paths that lead to (for example) a crucial shared secret becoming public knowledge. In the long term, this will require a hierarchical approach, and systematic ways of mapping from *models of systems* to *models of threats* such as [10].

Another notable feature of attack trees is that it is commonly to label non-leaf nodes with logical operators – conjunction when all subtasks are required in order to achieve a goal, or disjunction when any single one of them will suffice. This is of course a blunt tool that fails to take into account the cost of achieving a sub-goal, or questions of concurrency & parallelism. A more sophisticated approach is given by considering resource-sensitive logics, such as variations on linear logic [9]. More fundamentally, [6] describes attack trees themselves as formulæ of a form of linear logic, and the notion of specialisation as a form of linear implication.

At this stage, we are left in the rather unsatisfactory situation of having a close connection between *models*, with no similarly obvious connection between what they model. The categorical models of quantum protocols given in [2]are directly based on categorical models of linear logic (precisely, the multiplicative-exponential fragment from Girard's Geometry of Interaction program [7]) found in [1]. This current paper also acknowledges its origins in categorical models of linear logic, although the connection is not as direct.

It is perhaps worth observing that the boolean lattice ordering of participants used throughout this paper is of course a model of a very primitive (boolean)

---

[3] I would like to thank various members of the Oxford school for the folklore that the 'classical communication' in these protocols – although often implicit – should properly be thought of as 2-categorical structure. It is pleasing to be able to claim that the same applies to implicit communication in classical protocols!.

logic, and the crucial partial ordering is the implication of this logic. The connection is likely to become clearer when a more sophisticated notion of labeling and implication is used.

9   Future Directions

Although it is visually appealing to be able to draw A-E diagrams for protocols, the intention is also to develop concrete tools. We have taken the view that they must first be shown to be well-founded, which is why this is a purely theoretical paper. The next question is whether they are both *accurate* and *useful*. So far, we have demonstrated that they give the expected (& indeed, well-established) answer to questions we may pose about communication involving D-H key exchange & other simple protocols.

The next step must be to apply the formalism & tools developed to a wider range of more complex situations, arising from real-world examples, as a step towards validation. Anything but the simplest cases involve non-trivial algorithmics, so a key part of this will involve automating the types of deductions illustrated in this paper, which is work in progress. As our tools are designed for deriving implicit knowledge from incomplete information, testing them on real-world examples seems an essential next step.

Acknowledgements. I have had the good fortune to encounter several cryptographically-minded category theorists, and category-curious cryptographers. Thanks are due to Chris Heunen (Edinburgh), Delaram Kahrobaei (York), Dusko Pavlovic (Hawaii), and Noson Yanofsky (New York). Thanks are also due to Morgan Hines, for help in finding the regular polyhedra in three or more dimensions associated with the protocols in [8].

References

1. Abramsky, S.: Retracing some paths in process algebra. In: Montanari, U., Sassone, V. (eds.) CONCUR 1996. LNCS, vol. 1119, pp. 1–17. Springer, Heidelberg (1996). https://doi.org/10.1007/3-540-61604-7_44
2. Abramsky, S., Coecke, B.: A categorical semantics of quantum protocols. In: Proceedings of the 19th Annual IEEE Symposium on Logic in Computer Science (LICS 2004), pp. 415–425. IEEE Computer Society Press (2005)
3. Amoroso, E.: Fundamentals of Computer Security Technology. Prentice-Hall Inc, USA (1994)
4. Barwise, J., Gabbay, D., Hartonas, C.: On the logic of information flow. Logic J. IGPL 3(7), 7–49 (1998)
5. Diffie, W., Hellman, M.: New directions in cryptography. IEEE Trans. Inf. Theor. 22(6), 644–654 (1976)
6. Eades III, H., Jiang, J., Bryant, A.: On linear logic, functional programming, and attack trees. In: Cybenko, G., Pym, D., Fila, B. (eds.) GraMSec 2018. LNCS, vol. 11086, pp. 71–89. Springer, Cham (2019). https://doi.org/10.1007/978-3-030-15465-3_5

7. Girard, J.-Y.: Geometry of interaction 1. In: Proceedings Logic Colloquium 1988, pp. 221–260. North-Holland (1988)
8. Hines, P.: A diagrammatic approach to information flow in encrypted communication (extended version). arxiv.org/abs/2008.05840 (2020)
9. Horne, R., Mauw, S., Tiu, A.: Semantics for specialising attack trees based on linear logic. Fundamenta Informaticae **153**(1–2), 57–86 (2017)
10. Ivanova, M.G., Probst, C.W., Hansen, R.R., Kammüller, F.: Transforming graphical system models to graphical attack models. In: Mauw, S., Kordy, B., Jajodia, S. (eds.) GraMSec 2015. LNCS, vol. 9390, pp. 82–96. Springer, Cham (2016). https://doi.org/10.1007/978-3-319-29968-6_6
11. Menezes, A.J., van Oorschot, P.C., Vanstone, S.A.: Handbook of Applied Cryptography. CRC Press, Boca Raton (1996). Discrete Mathematics and Its Applications
12. Merkle, R.: Secure communications over insecure channels. Commun. ACM **21**(4), 294–299 (1978)
13. O'Halloran, C.: Category theory applied to information flow for computer security. PhD thesis, Oxford University Computing Laboratory (1994)
14. Pavlovic, D.: Chasing diagrams in cryptography. In: Casadio, C., Coecke, B., Moortgat, M., Scott, P. (eds.) Categories and Types in Logic. Language, and Physics: Essays Dedicated to Jim Lambek on the Occasion of His 90th Birthday, pp. 353–367. Springer, Berlin Heidelberg (2014)
15. Power, J.: 2-categories. Technical report NS-98-7, B.R.I.C.S., p. 18 (1998)
16. Schneier, B.: Attack trees: modeling security threats. Dr. Dobb's J. Softw. Tools **24**(12), 21–29 (1999)

Contextualisation of Data Flow Diagrams for Security Analysis

Shamal Faily[1]([⊠])(iD), Riccardo Scandariato[2], Adam Shostack[3], Laurens Sion[4](iD), and Duncan Ki-Aries[1](iD)

[1] Department of Computing and Informatics, Bournemouth University, Poole, UK
{sfaily,dkiaries}@bournemouth.ac.uk
[2] Chalmers and University of Gothenburg, Gothenburg, Sweden
riccardo.scandariato@cse.gu.se
[3] Shostack and Associates, Seattle, USA
adam@shostack.org
[4] imec-DistriNet, KU Leuven, Leuven, Belgium
laurens.sion@cs.kuleuven.be

Abstract. Data flow diagrams (DFDs) are popular for sketching systems for subsequent threat modelling. Their limited semantics make reasoning about them difficult, but enriching them endangers their simplicity and subsequent ease of take up. We present an approach for reasoning about tainted data flows in design-level DFDs by putting them in context with other complementary usability and requirements models. We illustrate our approach using a pilot study, where tainted data flows were identified without any augmentations to either the DFD or its complementary models.

1 Introduction

Data Flow Diagrams (DFDs) are useful as a sketch that explores how a system and its elements might be exploited; their simplicity makes it possible for different people with different levels of expertise to contribute to the security analysis of a system as it is evolves.

As DFDs become more critical to security design practices, so too is the need to reason about their properties using software tools. Limitations around cognitive ability, expertise and time constrain the effectiveness of modellers when scaling up or making decisions around DFDs [16]. However, their limited semantics makes reasoning with DFDs alone difficult; this leads to an inherent trade-off between using easy to adopt notations and those that afford automated reasoning but are more elaborate [17].

Data flows are analogous with information flows. Information flow analysis (like taint analysis) is a long established technique for reasoning about the interactions of data within entities, and their impact on security as the data flows through the system [4,23]. Unfortunately, visual inspection alone is insufficient for spotting potential issues with data inside data flows. Formal policy specifications and binary instructions provide the context necessary to reason about

© Springer Nature Switzerland AG 2020
H. Eades III and O. Gadyatskaya (Eds.): GraMSec 2020, LNCS 12419, pp. 186–197, 2020.
https://doi.org/10.1007/978-3-030-62230-5_10

tainted information flows, but DFDs lack this level of precision. The options are either (i) adding additional information to the diagram itself, or (ii) providing context via other models aligned with DFDs. In the related work, the first route has been extensively explored [19, 20], so this paper takes the less followed second path. *Usability models* could play a particularly important role in providing such context. For example in [7], usability models describe the main tasks performed by a software system, and the roles associated to those tasks. The models relate to the overall goals and requirements of the system. Just as DFDs provide early insights into how systems might be exploited, usability models indicate where interaction problems might subsequently facilitate exploitation. These different models might be produced independently and, with inter-operable tools, we can reason about the security impact these models have on DFDs, and vice-versa.

Contribution. In this short paper, we present an approach for identifying potential taint in design-level DFDs. Our guiding principle is that, to encourage adoption, DFDs should be no more graphically complex than they currently are. Instead, we should leverage the alignment between DFDs and other usability and requirements models. We present the related work upon which our approach is based in Sect. 2 before presenting the key concepts and algorithms in our approach in Sect. 3. We illustrate our approach in Sect. 4 by using it to identify pre-process and post-process taint in a critical infrastructure pilot study, before discussing the implications of this work in Sect. 5.

2   Related Work and Background

2.1   Reasoning About Data Flow Diagrams in Threat Modelling

Data Flow Diagrams (DFDs) graphically model flows of information (data flows) between human or system actors external to a system (entities), activities that manipulate data (processes), and persistent data storage (data stores) [24]. This notation is often extended with trust boundaries: dotted boxes encompassing DFD elements operating at the same level of privilege. Trust boundaries help identify data flows that cross privilege levels [15].

DFDs have overlapping functions. Diane (a diagram creator) creates a DFD that diagrammatically represents her mental model. On viewing the DFD, Elaine (an engineer) internalises this mental model and requests changes. Dialogue around their differences subsequently brings both mental models closer together. Francis (a formal modeller) crafts a structured representation of a system, from which subsequent reasoning can be performed. This relationship between a mental model, a diagram, and a formal model has not been well explored.

Tuma et al. [21] first examined the potential of using information flow analysis to reason about DFDs. They extended the DFD notation by labelling data flows with assets and their security properties, indicating the source and target of assets, including domain properties and assumptions from the KAOS modelling language [12]. In later work, Tuma et al. [19] further illustrate the potential for using DFDs for design-level information flow analysis. In their approach, a domain specific language is used to model DFDs annotated with security labels. The model is subsequently rendered as a graph and statically analysed.

Antigac et al. [1] examined how certain properties of a DFD can be hotspots for further investigation. For example, a usage hotspot corresponds with 3 DFD elements: data flow d into process p, process p, and data flow d' from p. Antigac et al. showed how such hotspots bridge the gap between different models, and provide a basis for subsequent model transformation without fundamentally changing the visual semantics of DFDs.

2.2   Security and Software Design Meta-Models

Meta-models specify how model concepts are associated. In doing so, they guide analysts in collecting and analysing model data, and guide tool builders in constructing tools to support them. The software engineering community has examined the relationship between software and requirement modelling approaches and security, as summarised by [14]. These approaches do not, however, account for the role played by usability data and models. The **IRIS (Integrating Requirements and Information Security)** meta-model was devised to provide guidance on how early-stage design concepts from usability as well as security and requirements engineering might be aligned [7]. A sub-set of the IRIS concepts relevant to this paper is provided in Fig. 1.

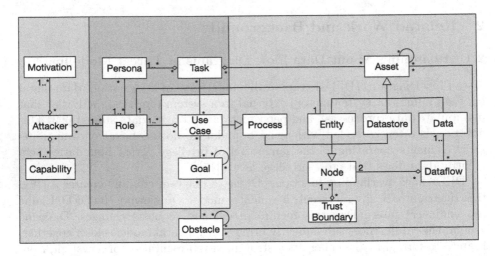

Fig. 1. A UML class diagram showing the IRIS concepts related to threat modelling (red), usability (blue) and requirements modelling (grey). (Color figure online)

Coles et al. [2] demonstrated how use cases and assets provide the concepts necessary to threat model with data flow diagrams, and how – in addition to modelling system goals – the KAOS modelling language [12] is also suitable for modelling attack trees as obstacles. To make attacker assumptions more explicit,

IRIS supports the specification of attackers. Attackers need not be intrinsically malicious, but they will have some motivations as drivers for carrying out an attack, and capabilities that provide the knowledge and resources necessary to mount and sustain any threat. IRIS draws its taxonomy of motivations from [13], and capabilities from [10]. An additional motivation of productivity was also added to better reflect non-malicious attackers who intentionally or unintentionally commit harm to get their job done.

To leverage the outputs of user research in security design, two popular usability modelling concepts are supported by IRIS. Personas are specifications of archetypical user behaviour [3]; they not only capture user goals and expectations, but their construction and usage helps elicit security requirement [8]. Tasks are narrative scenarios that describe both the personas and the broader system – including use cases – in context.

3   Approach

Our approach focuses on how *tainted* data flows cast doubt on the safety of the data they carry. Unlike traditional taint analysis on program source code, the origins of data flow taint in our approach could be human error resulting from human entities and processes, or issues resulting from the DFDs and associated specifications. These problems could have an indeterminate impact on affected endpoints, thereby warranting further investigation. Aligning DFDs with usability and requirements models provides context to assist such an investigation.

Assuming the pre-requisite models exist, our approach validates them using the analysis checks described in Sect. 3.2. Because of its alignment with the DFD concepts as shown in Fig. 1, our approach relies on the IRIS meta-model. DFD processes are analogous with use cases, and actors in use cases could be human or system entities. DFDs directly link to usability models because use cases, as processes, put tasks in context. DFDs are also indirectly linked because roles constituting use case actors are also fulfilled by personas – who interact in tasks – putting these roles in context.

3.1   Dataflow Specification

DFDs are graphs, but can be specified as a set of data flow types. In our approach, a data flow consists of a label, names of the DFD elements data flows from and to, and the types of these elements, where *NODE* is either an *entity*, a *process*, or a *datastore*. Data flows also specify the information assets (as *DATA*) they carry. Using Z [22], we can express a data flow formally, where the predicate part of the schema contains the well-formedness constraints:

DataFlow _____

label, from, to : *STRING*

fromType, toType : *NODE*

assets : $\mathbb{P} \, DATA$

_____

assets $\neq \varnothing$

$((fromType = entity) \wedge (toType = process)) \vee$

$((fromType = process) \wedge (toType = entity)) \vee$

$((fromType = datastore) \wedge (toType = process)) \vee$

$((fromType = process) \wedge (toType = datastore)) \vee$

$((fromType = process) \wedge (toType = process))$

3.2   Pre-process and Post-process Analysis

For each entity in the DFD, our approach first visits the entity's data flows using the *dataFlows* recursive graph traversal function described in Algorithm 1. The function populates a persistent array of unique data flow sequences (*allSeqs*), and a persistent set of previously visited DFD elements (*visited*).

Algorithm 1: Identification of data flows

```
   Input  : currentNode - NODE, prefix - seq DataFlow
   Data: allSeqs - seq(seq DataFlow), visited - ℙ NODE, nodeFlows - ran Node ↔ DataFlow
 1 Function dataFlows(currentNode, prefix) is
 2 |   visited.add(currentNode);
 3 |   dfs ← nodeFlows currentNode;
 4 |   if dfs = ∅ then
 5 |   |   if prefix.length > 0 then
 6 |   |   |   allSeqs.append(prefix);
 7 |   |   end
 8 |   else
 9 |   |   while df ← dfs do
10 |   |   |   newPrefix ← prefix;
11 |   |   |   newPrefix.append(df);
12 |   |   |   if df.to ∈ visited then
13 |   |   |   |   allSeqs.append(newPrefix);
14 |   |   |   else
15 |   |   |   |   dataFlows df.to newPrefix;
16 |   |   |   end
17 |   |   end
18 |   end
19 |   return;
20 end
```

Each sequence in *allSeqs* is then enumerated to identify and log potential data *pre-process* and *post-process* taint as described in Algorithm 2. The types mentioned in the algorithm can be found in Fig. 1, with the exception of *VALUE*, where *VALUE* ::= *Low* | *Medium* | *High*.

Algorithm 2: Taint analysis

Input : dfSeq - seq *DataFlow*
Data: contextualisedTask - ran *UseCase ↔ Task*, taskAsset - ran *Task ↔ Asset*,
   personaRoles - ran *Persona ↔ Role*, taskPersonas - ran *Task ↔ Persona*,
   roleAttackers - ran *Role ↔ Attacker*, allAttackerRoles - ran *roleAttackers*~,
   attackerMotivation - ran *Attacker ↔ Motivation*, attackerCapability -
   ran *Attacker ↔ Capability*, taskDemand - ran *Task ↔ Value*, goalConflict -
   ran *Task ↔ Value*, processExceptions - ran *UseCase ↔ Obstacle*, obstructedGoals -
   ran *Obstacle ↔ Goal*, obstacleAssets - ran *Obstacle ↔ Asset*, nameToProcess -
   String ↦ UseCase, logPreProcessTaint - logs taint to process resulting from named
   task, logPostProcessTaint - logs taint to process resulting from named obstructed goal

```
1  Function analyseDataFlows(dfSeq) is
2      while df ← dfSeq do
           /* Check for pre-process taint                                          */
3          if df.fromType = entity ∧ df.toType = process ∧ df.fromName ∈ Role then
4              while t ← contextualisedTask (nameToProcess df.toName) do
5                  if df.assets ∩ taskAssets t then
6                      while r ← (personaRoles (taskPersonas t) ∩ allAttackerRoles) do
7                          while a ← roleAttackers r do
8                              if (Productivity ∈ attackerMotivation a) ∧ (Low Time ∈
                                 attackerCapability a) ∧ ( (taskDemand t ∩
                                 {Medium,High}) ∨ (goalConflict t ∩ {Medium,High}) )
                                 then
9                                  │ logPreProcessTaint (nameToProcess df.toName) t;
10                             end
11                         end
12                     end
13                 end
14             end
15         end
           /* Check for post-process taint                                         */
16         if df.fromType = process then
17             while o ← processExceptions df.fromName do
18                 if (obstacleAssets o ∩ df.assets) ≠ ∅ then
19                     while g ← obstructedGoals o do
20                         if isObstacleObstructed o = true then
21                             │ logPostProcessTaint (nameToProcess df.fromName) g;
22                         end
23                     end
24                 end
25             end
26         end
27     end
28     return;
29 end
```

Pre-process taint checks (lines 3–15) identify instances where means, motives, and opportunity are present for human errors and violations. The checks are performed on data flows going from human entities to processes contextualised as tasks; these processes are use cases linked to tasks as indicated in Figure 1. Tasks become a possible source of human error when three conditions hold. First, roles fulfilled by personas in a task are shared with roles fulfilled by attackers. Second, attackers have a non-malicious motive and are constrained in the means available; we define such attackers as motivated by productivity and, as a capability, a limited amount of time. Finally, affected tasks are demanding to the affected personas, or in tension with their personal goals.

Post-process taint checks (lines 16–26) identify instances where exceptions resulting from processes are unresolved, and these exceptions impact information flowing from processes. Exceptions are modelled as obstacles obstructing one or more system goals operationalised as the affected processes. An obstacle impacts an out-going data flow if assets associated with the obstacle intersect with information assets in the data flow. An exception is unresolved if these obstacles are not resolved by another goal, as determined by the *isObstacleObstructed* function defined in Algorithm 3. It begins by determining whether the input obstacle has been resolved by another goal. After evaluating whether the obstacle has been resolved, the check enumerates both obstacles that are or-refined and and-refined. In the case of or-refined obstacles, an obstruction on *any* of the refined obstacles is enough to consider the obstacle obstructed. Conversely, in the case of and-refined obstacles, an obstruction is present only if *all* refined obstacles are obstructed.

Algorithm 3: isObstacleObstructed check

    Data: resolvedObstacles - ran *Obstacle* $\leftrightarrow$ *Goal*, orRefinedObstacles -
           ran *Obstacle* $\leftrightarrow$ *Obstacle*, andRefinedObstacles - ran *Obstacle* $\leftrightarrow$ *Obstacle*
    Input : o - the obstacle name
    Output: isObstructed - indicates if obstacle o is obstructed

```
1  Function isObstacleObstructed(o) is
2  │   ros ← resolvedObstacles o;
3  │   if ros ≠ ∅ then
4  │   │   isObstructed ← false;
5  │   else
6  │   │   obs ← orRefinedObstacles o;
7  │   │   while oro ← obs do
8  │   │   │   isObstructed ← isObstacleObstructed oro;
9  │   │   │   if isObstructed = true then
10 │   │   │   │   break;
11 │   │   │   end
12 │   │   end
13 │   │   obs ← andRefinedObstacles o;
14 │   │   while aro ← obs do
15 │   │   │   isObstructed ← isObstacleObstructed aro;
16 │   │   │   if isObstructed = false then
17 │   │   │   │   break;
18 │   │   │   end
19 │   │   end
20 │   end
21 │   return isObstructed;
22 end
```

3.3   Implementation

We have demonstrated the feasibility of our approach by implementing it in CAIRIS release 2.3.3. CAIRIS (Computer-Aided Integration of Requirements and Information Security) is an open-source software platform for eliciting, specifying and validating secure and usable system specifications [6] developed as an exemplar for IRIS tool-support.

CAIRIS models, once imported into the platform, are implemented as relational databases. Graphical models in CAIRIS are automatically generated using a pipeline process, where a declarative model of graph edges is generated by CAIRIS; this is processed and annotated by graphviz [5] before being subsequently rendered as SVG. SQL stored procedures implement a suite of security and privacy model validation checks. Algorithms 1–3 were implemented as SQL stored procedures; these are executed during a normal model-validation check. No changes were made to pre-existing visual models and the IRIS meta-model.

4   Pilot Study: Modifying Telemetry Outstation Software

We used our approach to identify process taint in a partial specification of a software repository for industrial control software. While based on a hypothetical water treatment company, this anonymised specification is drawn from a more complete specification model created for a UK water treatment company. The CAIRIS model[1] of this partial specification consists of 1 attacker, 1 role, 1 persona, 1 task, 1 use case, 28 goals, 17 obstacles, 58 goal and obstacle associations, 11 assets, 11 asset associations, and 7 data flows. Creation of the model is not the subject of this paper, but further details of how the broader model was created are provided in [9].

The specification captures the system goals and complementary model elements associated with modifying software running on telemetry outstations. Such outstations provide the means for remotely monitoring and controlling physical infrastructure such as water pumps. Malicious tampering of such outstations contributed to the well publicised Maroochy Water Breach [18].

Table 1. Dataflows and assets

Dataflow	Assets
job	Job
software (to Sandbox)	Telemetry Software File
software (from Sandbox)	Telemetry Software File
updated software	Telemetry Software File
current software	Telemetry Software File
alarm	Alarm
update	Software Change

Table 2. Dataflow sequences and results of pre-process and post-process taint checks

Id	Sequence	Pre-Proc.	Post-Proc.
1	⟨job, alarm⟩	✗	✗
2	⟨job, update⟩	✗	✓
3	⟨job,updated software, current software ⟩	✗	✓
4	⟨job,software, software⟩	✗	✓
5	⟨current software⟩	✓	✓

Our pilot study considers the impact of human error by an overworked technician focusing on the intricate task of updating software on telemetry outstations

---

[1] Available from https://doi.org/10.5281/zenodo.3872071.

(Outstation update). This task puts in context the use case Modify Telemetry Software as shown in Fig. 2 (top), which is carried out by an instrument technician persona (Barry). Details of how the persona and tasks were constructed are described in more detail in [8]. The task model provided the context necessary to model the DFD generated by CAIRIS in Fig. 2 (bottom). Table 1 specifies the assets carried in each data flow.

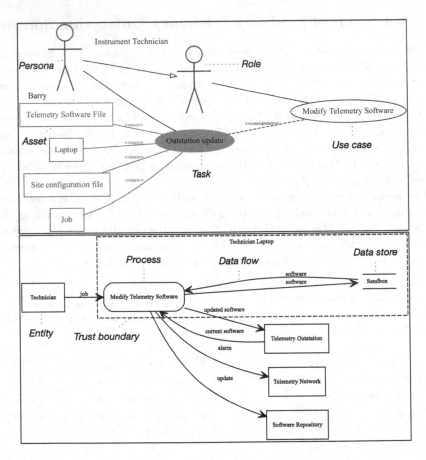

Fig. 2. Usability model (top) and DFD (bottom) of Modify Telemetry Software generated by CAIRIS

Not shown in the visible models is an attacker (Unintentional Barry). This attacker's motivation and resources are specified as 'Productivity' and 'Low Resources/Personnel and Time' to reflect non-malicious intent and a busy schedule. The task model also indicates the assets that Barry directly or indirectly interacts with in completing this task. The relationship between these and other assets associated with the specification are shown in Fig. 3 (right).

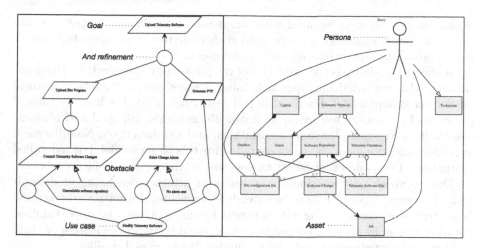

Fig. 3. Complementary KAOS goal model (left) and UML class diagram-based asset (right) model generated by CAIRIS

On performing a model validation check, five unique sequences of data flows were generated as shown in Table 2. The check indicates pre-process taint associated with sequences 1, 2, 3, and 4 resulting from the flow between the technician and the process. This was due to the *job* flow carrying alarm information associated with the task and the potential for error. The task narrative describes how Barry needs to raise an alarm to validate the setup is correct; the alert draws attention to the implications of not safeguarding this information asset.

The model validation check also indicates post-process taint associated with Sequence 1; this outgoing process flow carries alarm information. An exception is associated with the second step of the process, where the system sends a change alarm. As a cut of the goal model in Fig. 3 (left) shows, the associated obstacle remains unresolved and, although not visible, the obstacle is concerned with the alarm asset carried in *job*.

5   Discussion and Conclusion

This short paper showed how, by putting DFDs in context, we can identify process taint without changing any DFD semantics. CAIRIS demonstrates the feasibility of our approach, but it could be adapted to any inter-operable combination of tools. Solutions for resolving the problems are not prescribed besides changing the attacker model and tasks, or resolving exceptions. However, by indicating otherwise invisible problems, our approach sheds light on why problems exists, and how a system or its context of use might need to change to address them. This approach is contingent on specifications containing the concepts in Fig. 1 that might be created before, during, or after DFD creation. Small or poorly resourced teams may lack the resources to maintain such models given the user research investment required. However, this approach does allow human factor experts to become more engaged with threat modelling. We are currently working with system engineering teams with such expertise to evaluate the impact this approach has on increasing such engagement.

A threat to validity is the small size of the pilot study specification. However, we have also evaluated our approach using a more complex military medical evaluation system model described in [11] consisting of 10 attackers, 14 roles, 9 personas, 12 tasks, 29 use cases, 46 goals, 25 obstacles, 167 goal and obstacle associations, 82 assets, 388 asset associations, and 134 data flows. No differences in model validation performance were noted for this larger model, but a detailed evaluation of this and other larger models will be the subject of future work.

Our approach only considers non-malicious attackers engaging in difficult tasks. However, Algorithm 2 can be extended to consider alternative attacker and task attributes corresponding with different means, motives, and opportunities. For example, an inside attacker might be motivated by improved esteem or thrill seeking, and participate in tasks with differing levels of goal conflict.

Acknowledgements. This paper resulted from discussions at Dagstuhl Seminar 19231: Empirical Evaluation of Secure Development Processes.

References

1. Antignac, T., Scandariato, R., Schneider, G.: Privacy compliance via model transformations. In: Proceedings of the 2018 IEEE European Symposium on Security and Privacy Workshops, pp. 120–126, April 2018
2. Coles, J., Faily, S., Ki-Aries, D.: Tool-supporting data protection impact assessments with CAIRIS. In: Proceedings of the 5th International Workshop on Evolving Security & Privacy Requirements Engineering, pp. 21–27 (2018)
3. Cooper, A., Reimann, R., Cronin, D., Noessel, C.: About Face: The Essentials of Interaction Design. John Wiley & Sons, Hoboken (2014)
4. Denning, D.E.: A lattice model of secure information flow. Commun. ACM **19**(5), 236–243 (1976)
5. Ellson, J., Gansner, E., Koutsofios, L., North, S.C., Woodhull, G.: Graphviz—open source graph drawing tools. In: Mutzel, P., Jünger, M., Leipert, S. (eds.) GD 2001. LNCS, vol. 2265, pp. 483–484. Springer, Heidelberg (2002). https://doi.org/10.1007/3-540-45848-4_57
6. Faily, S.: CAIRIS web site. https://cairis.org (April 2018)
7. Faily, S.: Designing Usable and Secure Software with IRIS and CAIRIS. Springer, Cham (2018). https://doi.org/10.1007/978-3-319-75493-2
8. Faily, S., Fléchais, I.: Barry is not the weakest link: eliciting secure system requirements with personas. In: Proceedings of the 24th BCS Interaction Specialist Group Conference, pp. 124–132. BCS 2010, British Computer Society (2010)
9. Faily, S., Fléchais, I.: Towards tool-support for usable secure requirements engineering with CAIRIS. Int. J. Secure Softw. Eng. **1**(3), 56–70 (2010)
10. Jones, A., Ashenden, D.: Risk Management for Computer Security: Protecting your Network and Information Assets. Elsevier, Oxford (2005)
11. Ki-Aries, D., Faily, S., Dogan, H., Williams, C.: Assessing system of systems security risk and requirements with OASoSIS. In: Proceedings of the 5th International Workshop on Evolving Security & Privacy Requirements Engineering, pp. 14–20 (2018)

12. van Lamsweerde, A.: Requirements Engineering: from system goals to UML models to software specifications. John Wiley & Sons (2009)
13. Van der Linden, M.A.: Testing Code Security. Auerbach Pub, Boca Raton (2007)
14. Matulevičius, R.: Secure system development. Fundamentals of Secure System Modelling, pp. 199–207. Springer, Cham (2017). https://doi.org/10.1007/978-3-319-61717-6_12
15. Shostack, A.: Threat Modeling: Designing for Security. John Wiley & Sons, Indianapolis (2014)
16. Simon, H.A.: Rational decision making in business organizations. Am. Econ. Rev. **69**(4), 493–513 (1979)
17. Sion, L., Yskout, K., Van Landuyt, D., van den Berghe, A., Joosen, W.: Security threat modeling: are data flow diagrams enough? In: Proceedings of IEEE/ACM 42nd International Conference on Software Engineering Workshops (ICSEW 2020). IEEE (2020). to Appear
18. Slay, J., Miller, M.: Lessons learned from the maroochy water breach. In: Goetz, E., Shenoi, S. (eds.) ICCIP 2007. IIFIP, vol. 253, pp. 73–82. Springer, Boston, MA (2008). https://doi.org/10.1007/978-0-387-75462-8_6
19. Tuma, K., Scandariato, R., Balliu, M.: Flaws in flows: unveiling design flaws via information flow analysis. In: Proceedings of the 2019 IEEE International Conference on Software Architecture (ICSA), pp. 191–200 (2019)
20. Tuma, K., Kalikli, G., Scandariato, R.: Threat analysis of software systems: a systematic literature review. J. Syst. Softw. **144**, 275–294 (2018)
21. Tuma, K., Scandariato, R., Widman, M., Sandberg, C.: Towards security threats that matter. In: Katsikas, S.K., Cuppens, F., Cuppens, N., Lambrinoudakis, C., Kalloniatis, C., Mylopoulos, J., Antón, A., Gritzalis, S. (eds.) Cyber-ICPS/SECPRE -2017. LNCS, vol. 10683, pp. 47–62. Springer, Cham (2018). https://doi.org/10.1007/978-3-319-72817-9_4
22. Woodcock, J., Davies, J.: Using Z: Specification, Refinement, and Proof. Prentice Hall (1996)
23. Yin, H., Song, D., Egele, M., Kruegel, C., Kirda, E.: Panorama: capturing system-wide information flow for malware detection and analysis. In: Proceedings of the 14th ACM Conference on Computer and Communications Security, pp. 116–127. Association for Computing Machinery (2007)
24. Yourdon, E., Constantine, L.L.: Structured design: Fundamentals of a Discipline of Computer Program and Systems Design. Prentice Hall, USA (1979)

Author Index

Printed in the United States
By Bookmasters